LOUISIANA VOYAGES

LOUISIANA

VOYAGES

The Travel Writings of Catharine Cole

Martha R. Field

Selected and edited by

Joan B. McLaughlin and Jack McLaughlin

University Press of Mississippi / Jackson

www.upress.state.ms.us

The University Press of Mississippi is a member of the
Association of American University Presses.

The frontispiece photograph of Martha R. Field (Catharine Cole) is used
courtesy of Catherine Field Bacon. The map of Louisiana parishes is from
the U.S. Census Bureau's 2000 census.

First edition 2006
⊗
Library of Congress Cataloging-in-Publication Data
Field, Martha Reinhard Smallwood, 1855–1898.
    Louisiana voyages: the travel writings of Catharine Cole / selected and
edited by Joan B. McLaughlin and Jack McLaughlin.— 1st ed.
        p. cm.
    Includes bibliographical references (p.   ) and index.
    ISBN 1-57806-825-8 (cloth : alk. paper) — ISBN 1-57806-826-6 (pbk. : alk. paper)
        1. Field, Martha Reinhard Smallwood, 1855–1898—Homes and haunts—Louisiana.
    2. Louisiana—Description and travel. I. McLaughlin, Joan B. II. McLaughlin, Jack,
    1926– III. Title.

        PS1669.F25A6   2006
        818.409—dc22   2005014824

British Library Cataloging-in-Publication Data available

THIS BOOK IS DEDICATED
TO OUR LOUISIANA FAMILY

"There are some sluggish minds who think going away only means traveling far in search of new green pastures. But the world is never old or stale or too familiar. Everything the eye looks upon is, at that Columbus moment, new and unique."

—Catharine Cole

CONTENTS

INTRODUCTION

Martha R. Field was virtually unknown as a writer in her own lifetime, because most of her literary output was written under the pseudonym Catharine Cole for the New Orleans *Daily Picayune*. She was a member of a small sisterhood in the last two decades of the nineteenth-century South—a working woman journalist. Although she was known throughout Louisiana, and the South, for her column, "Catharine Cole's Letter," which appeared every Sunday in the *Picayune*, she was also a daily staff reporter for the newspaper.

In paging through the files of the *Picayune* it is impossible to identify her general reporting because the newspaper normally used bylines only in its Sunday feature section where the Catharine Cole column appeared. It is possible to make guesses, however, because for many years she wrote most of the stories in the newspaper of interest to women, and because her literary style is so uniquely imagistic, particularly when she is writing about the Louisiana landscape. This is a typical example of the elegance of her prose, from a June 19, 1892, column: "A pretty cabin stood by the roadside, with tall rows of red hollyhocks on tip-toe, to look out on the world with their straw-colored eyes, dear, old-fashioned perfumeless old maids. A trail of smoke, like a long-necked heron, was perched for flight over the adobe chimney."

Because much of her travel writing is about rural Louisiana, her most luxuriant descriptive passages are of nature—the cane and rice country, bayous, swamps, pine forests, and the Gulf Coast. But she also turns her poetic eye on great plantation houses and workers' cabins, on colonels and sharecroppers—white, black, and Creole.

Field brought to her Louisiana wanderings an extensive experience in European travel. It is not unusual for her to find comparisons between an abandoned parish church and the ruined abbeys of England, between the canals of Venice and Louisiana's bayous, between an elegant plantation house and the great mansions of the continent, between a Creole gumbo and the cuisine of Paris. She is a cosmopolitan traveler, who carries with her tins of foie gras, but is comfortable sharing a steaming cup of coffee and a slice of bread, and drippings of local gossip, with a backcountry housewife.

Many of the travel articles included here were written during a punishing series of trips through the state in 1891–92. During that time she logged 1,800 miles, visiting most of the then fifty-nine parishes of Louisiana. Her mode of transportation was whatever it took to get her there. This was often adventuresome, uncomfortable, tiring, and even dangerous—particularly for a woman traveling alone. She navigated over Gulf waters on small, open, sailing luggers, on bayous in a pirogue, which she described as "that airiest, delicatest, spirit-level of a boat," and once traveled for two days in a swamp boat. She was stuck in a buggy in the mud of an overflowed stream for four hours until she was rescued, and had to walk nine miles out of a swamp when her buggy virtually disintegrated from traveling too fast over a ploughed cotton field.

She typically traveled by train or steamboat to a jumping-off town, then rented a buggy and a pair of horses at a local livery stable. The buggy came with a black driver, often a teenager—in one case he was only ten years old. Her travel schedule was usually measured in thirty-five-mile-a-day lengths, although the contingencies of late starts, bad weather, impassable roads, or getting lost sometimes found her after nightfall with no shelter in sight. In such cases, she stopped at the nearest farmhouse and asked for a bed. She was seldom refused.

Although she frequently admitted to being frightened breathless by snakes, alligators, and what lay beneath the ebony ooze of the cypress swamp she was wading through, she repeatedly showed remarkable courage in dealing with the hazards of her travels. She was constantly lost in unmapped forests, prairies, or rural backroads, some no more than animal paths. At times, she found herself at a place with no paths at all. Once, like Hansel and Gretel, she tore up pages of a novel and littered pieces behind the buggy to be able to find her way back from a trackless dry swamp.

Another time, she was ferried across a bayou in an antique flatboat with spooked, kicking horses threatening to sink buggy, boatman, and passengers. She sloshed through violent rainstorms that drenched her to the bone, was nearly struck by lightning, and was forced to help her young driver repair their broken-down buggy with cut persimmon-tree saplings.

Through all of the mishaps and frights of a woman traveling alone with a boy driver through a primitive countryside, she is revealed in her writings as a confident, durable traveler willing to go anywhere at virtually any time in order to explore new, unvisited sections of Louisiana. So extensive were her travels through the state that a *Picayune* editor made the extravagant boast that "Catharine Cole knows more about Louisiana and its actual condition and real resources than any other person in the world," confident that no one would challenge him.

The purpose of Field's travel writing was normally not to encourage her readers to *visit* the sights she described, but to have them *move* there. She was in effect a real estate saleswoman. Unlike modern travel writers who depict remote, romantic, and picturesque places as desirable destinations for pleasure, she had her tours through the state repeatedly hammer out a single message: Louisiana is a land of opportunity—come live here! It is true that when she writes about the Gulf or River parishes, the vacation destinations of New Orleanians, she shifts her viewpoint to recreation—fishing, boating, bathing, exploring exotic wildlife and landscapes. On balance, however, her travel writing has an agenda—population growth.

This agenda does not detract from her passion for travel, especially the joy of preparing to visit a new place by reading other travel writers and poring over maps. She repeatedly declares that she knows "of no greater pleasure than planning for a trip away. To read up for a journey, to inform yourself of the country you hope to visit, is to double your pleasure."

In all of her writing she is a champion of women, and condemns men's mistreatment of them, particularly men with money and power. She was, however, a Southern woman with traditional Southern beliefs. She was born before the Civil War, and remained an unreconstructed Confederate sympathizer. She visited the home of Jefferson Davis, and admired the antebellum years of plantation aristocracy and devoted house slaves. In this, she followed the policy of the *Picayune*, which stated editorially that the white race was superior "by culture and experience." The *Picayune* was a firm supporter of the passage of Jim Crow laws in the 1890s.

Parts of Catharine Cole's columns are jarring to a modern sensibility; she casually uses racial and ethnic epithets—they were obviously perfectly acceptable to a *Picayune* that prided itself on being a family newspaper—and wrote conversations in dialect, white and black, a practice common before the turn of the century. (She had a particularly good ear for the nuances of all classes of speech.)

Although she was not a suffragette, she was an admirer of Susan B. Anthony and other suffrage leaders, and relentlessly promoted women's charities, women's religious and health care institutions, and women's equality. In one article, she defended the publication of Ibsen's play *A Doll's House* against the criticism that it was a "wicked book, and not fit for a woman to read."

In language that might have been written by her contemporary Kate Chopin, she wrote that some day men "will be compelled to adopt a common standard of virtue for the race. You will be obliged to recognize our souls, to respect our existence and admit that morality is more deeply rooted than in sex, and that our natures must burst the bonds and limitations with which you would confine us in doll's houses."

Her brother-in-law, Bernard Shields, wrote that to Catharine Cole "New Orleans owes its Training School for Nurses, its Woman's Exchange, and its kindergartens." The advancement of women in Louisiana, he declared, "is due in no small degree to the work of Catharine Cole." Shields described her physically as "a rather slightly-built woman with light brown hair, grayish eyes, topping a large nose and mouth, a soft, pleasant voice, and an unassuming, quiet demeanor."

Martha Field, or Mattie, as she was known to family and friends, was born in Lexington, Missouri, in 1855, the daughter of a newspaperman, W. M. Smallwood. In the 1860s the family moved to New Orleans where Smallwood took a job with the *New Orleans Times*. His daughter was a precocious writer and worked for a time at the *New Orleans Republican* before moving to California to pursue a journalistic career at the *San Francisco Chronicle*. There she married Charles W. Field, a stockbroker, and gave birth in 1876 to a girl, Flora (known throughout her life as Flo). Soon after, her husband died and she became a young widowed mother, forced to support herself. (During her career as a journalist, like so many modern women, she had to balance the demands of work and single motherhood.)

She returned to New Orleans, moved in with her parents—her mother's maiden name was Emma Reinhard—and worked with her father at the *Times*. It was there that she first adopted the pen name Catharine Cole.

(Most women journalists at this time used pseudonyms, for it was not considered respectable for a woman to work for a newspaper. Also, their husbands, who felt demeaned by having a working wife, did not wish to have their surnames published.) In 1881, Mrs. E. J. Nicholson, owner of the *Picayune* and a well-known poet writing under the pseudonym Pearl Rivers, hired Field as a full-time reporter. She was the first woman to hold a staff position on the newspaper.

Mrs. Nicholson nurtured her career by sending her several times to Europe for a working Grand Tour. She wrote a weekly column for the *Picayune*, "Catharine Cole's Letter," and here, she gave free reign to her imagination. She wrote short sketches on personalities and literary topics, philosophic essays, fictional stories, subjects of particular interest to women, and travel pieces. She also edited and wrote an unsigned weekly column, "Women's World and Work," mostly a collection of news items about New Orleans women.

The *Picayune* was not only a daily; it also published a weekly mail edition which summarized the week's events for farmers, lumbermen, and fishermen in the remote sections of the state. Through this medium, Catharine Cole's name became known to virtually every literate adult in Louisiana. Her columns were clipped, passed around, and pasted in scrapbooks.

Cole's columns were published not only in the *Picayune* but in many other newspapers. Since 1792, publishers had been permitted by federal law to exchange copies of their papers with other newspapers postage-free. Publishers throughout the nation traded dozens of newspapers with each other and then copied and freely published stories, editorials, and columns from these "exchanges." In this way, Catharine Cole's column was published widely, particularly in the South, extending her reputation well beyond Louisiana.

When, in 1892, she began a three-month horse-and-buggy progression through the parishes of Louisiana, detailing the riches and beauties of the remotest regions of the state, Catharine Cole was greeted everywhere she went as a celebrity writer. This opened doors for her into both grand and modest homes and encouraged public officials, plantation owners, farmers and laborers to speak to her freely of their lives and work.

Her reports from the interior of the state were unabashedly promotional. She saw Louisiana's untapped natural resources as an opportunity for industrious farmers, merchants, and businessmen to enjoy a future unmatched by any other state in the union. (This was before the oil boom changed the direction of economic development in Louisiana.) She beat her drum repeatedly for "immigration"—the state was underpopulated, land was cheap, opportunity was within any hard-working family's grasp. At times, her columns had the optimistic boosterism of today's chamber of commerce literature, but it was tempered by a willingness to find fault with those who exploited the land and its people—particularly wealthy Northerners—and by her unerring eye, not only for the beauties of the state, but for its ugliness, filth, and poverty.

Her reputation in the state, in the entire South, and throughout the nation, was greatly enhanced by her coverage of the Chicago World's Fair, the Columbian Exposition of 1893. She stayed in Chicago for six months and filed a total of sixty-five stories, covering virtually every exhibit at the fair. It was one of the few descriptions of the exposition from a woman's point of view. She also spent several months in Washington, D.C., and filed a series of brilliant character sketches of political figures.

Soon after she completed her writing tours of Louisiana she unexpectedly left the *Picayune* in February 1894 for its rival, the *Times-Democrat*. Her first Catharine Cole column for the *Times-Democrat* appeared unannounced two weeks later. The reason for her leaving the *Picayune* was reportedly a clash of wills between Field and the newspaper's publisher, Eliza Nicholson, the most important woman owner-publisher in the nation. Field was weak and sick; she was developing a tremor in her hand, and was showing signs of the long illness that eventually took her life. Nicholson proposed sending the paper's religion editor, Marie Points, on a travel trip in Field's place.

According to John S. Kendall, a longtime *Picayune* staff member, Field resented what she considered to be a newcomer being groomed to take her place. After a heated exchange with Nicholson, Field resigned and was immediately hired by the *Times-Democrat*, which no doubt considered itself fortunate to obtain its rival's prize columnist. (Nicholson and Field later mended their differences, and at Nicholson's death in 1896, Field published an affectionate tribute to her former employer.)

At the *Times-Democrat*, poor health soon led her to Europe to take a "water cure" from one of the most celebrated naturopaths on the continent, Sebastian Kneipp, a Bavarian priest. In June 1894, before she left for Europe, the *Times-Democrat* held a series of "Catharine Cole testimonials" to raise money to help pay for her travels. (Typically, when she reached Bavaria she filed a detailed story on the Kniepp cure.)

She traveled throughout Europe, and during this and another subsequent European trip for her health she wrote a regular series of travel pieces. She was never again to journey through Louisiana to write about the state, however, for her deteriorating health did not permit her to take the physically taxing trips that had made her reputation. Therefore, only one of the articles in this collection is from the *Times-Democrat*, the paper she worked for during the final four years of her life.

She was eventually diagnosed with "paralysis agitans," apparently Parkinson's disease, and spent her final years being cared for by her daughter, Flo. During the last four months of her life she was bedridden at a Chicago sanitarium. She nevertheless continued to write columns from Chicago until three months before her death, dictating them to Flo.

She died in Chicago on December 19, 1898, at the age of forty-three. Her body was returned to New Orleans, and after a funeral attended by city officials, literary friends, and the newsroom staffs of the *Picayune* and *Times-Democrat*, she was interred in a tomb on the Louisiana soil she celebrated so eloquently.

A year before her death, several admirers helped gather, edit, and publish a collection of her fictional stories and nonfictional sketches. *Catharine Cole's Book* was published in 1897; it apparently represented the writings Field wanted to be remembered by. None of her travel articles are included, possibly because she considered them to be journalistic rather than "literary" writing, the kind that belonged between book covers.

This collection of her travel writings introduces another Catharine Cole. Her tours through the backcountry of Louisiana give us a series of historical snapshots unlike any offered during this period. The state is seen through the perspective of a richly-talented woman writer, and this renders her descriptions unique. These travel sketches are not only of historical value, however. They also serve to introduce a Southern woman author who deserves to be recognized not only as a journalist but as a literary figure of eloquence and power.

Her writing had a number of stylistic influences. She was a great admirer of Emerson, and her philosophic and moralistic essays are brushed with Emersonian hues. The style of her fiction and travel writing belongs to the nineteenth-century Southern, sentimental tradition of George Washington Cable, whose accounts of New Orleans Creoles seem to have influenced her. But it also invites comparison with the more feminist fiction of Kate Chopin, and perhaps more directly with the lush, overblown nature descriptions of Lafcadio Hearn, who was also influenced by local colorists such as Cable. Hearn began writing for the *Times-Democrat* in 1881, the same year Field joined the *Picayune*.

Although both writers were working reporters, the excesses of Hearn's style are modified in Field by a journalistic discipline often missing in Hearn. She may write ecstatically of the beauties of the Cherokee roses winding around a cane-mill entrance, but she also notes the barrels of sugar produced, the number of workers employed, and the profits extracted. As a matter of course, one of the first stops she makes on visiting a new town is the parish clerk's office, to gather agricultural, commercial, and economic statistics for the region.

It is this combination of a poet's eye with a reporter's spade that gives the travel accounts of Martha Field their lasting value. It is our hope that by gathering her ephemeral newspaper sketches into a permanent collection modern readers may discover a writer to be enjoyed and admired.

EDITORIAL NOTE

The Louisiana parishes included in this selection represent fewer than half of those Martha Field visited and wrote about during her travels through the state over more than a decade. Deciding which of her columns to include was a challenge that was made somewhat easier by the fact that some were less interesting to a modern reader than others. However, interest alone was not the sole standard for selection. The historical, cultural, and social importance of places and personalities was equally relevant, as was the quality of fine writing.

In deciding which parishes to include we have been led by Martha Field's own travel agenda. Some of her travel pieces are mostly objective descriptions of places that might have been written without her ever having visited them. These often contain statistics about population, the number of acres being farmed, agricultural products planted, the cash value of crops produced, and the number of banks, retail stores, schools and churches in each town. These facts and figures represent Catharine Cole the journalist; they are designed to promote immigration to Louisiana, one of the main reasons the newspaper sent her on her expeditions around the state. Such details are of specialized interest and are less likely to be included when they are not balanced by subjective reporting.

Field seizes her readers' attention most directly when she invites them into the emotional buggy ride of her trips, particularly when she faces danger, hardship, fatigue, clouds of mosquitoes, sunburn, rain drenchings—even a close call from a lightning bolt. These columns, enhanced by her poetic appreciation of the beauties of Louisiana's landscape, and by what she considers the goodness of its people, are the parts of her travel writing that we embraced and included. On the other hand, some of her references to race, although typical for the time, as well as being the official policy of her newspaper, may be offensive to modern readers and have been excluded.

Few of these pieces are printed in their entirety; most are edited to make space for a greater variety of places visited—and to avoid repetition. A writer who publishes a column a week for many years is bound to repeat herself, and Martha Field was no exception. She revisited some of the parishes, and her exquisite, word-painted descriptions of a state that was almost totally rural and agricultural were of necessity at times repetitive. While traveling through Sabine Parish she commented, "I think I shall have to be writing a vast deal about the pine forests and the sky. It seems I have seen almost nothing else." Describing mile after mile of pine forests in northern Louisiana taxed the imagination of even as richly endowed an imaginative writer as Martha Field.

For the historical and genealogical record, we have attempted to include as many names as possible of the men and women she met on her travels.

Many of her meetings were with political, business, and agricultural leaders, either statewide or local, or with clergymen and educators. If they were important enough in their day to be recorded in contemporary documents, information about them is included in the notes. Unfortunately, many of the people she met were mentioned only by their last names, and many were farmers, workers, or housewives, who left no footprint on the historical record. If they appear in anecdotes or personal interactions with Field they are included; if they are among names merely listed, they are sometimes left out. Because women were so rarely mentioned in newspaper accounts of this period, an attempt has been made to include their names when Field meets them.

At the end of the introductory paragraphs for each parish, the date the article appeared is given. Readers who wish to examine the complete article can consult the microfilm edition of the *Daily Picayune* or *Times-Democrat* for that date. (Our chapter titles are not the same as the headlines used by the newspaper editors.) Those who wish to read a selection of travel articles not included here, or to peruse more complete copies of some of those that are included, can visit our Web site: www.catharinecole.com.

It should be pointed out that this is the first time that many of Field's travel columns have received a close, professional editing. When she was on the road, her columns were mailed in to the newspaper, so she never had an opportunity to proofread her own pieces. Therefore, typographical errors and misspellings were common. Her copy, normally handwritten in pencil on square pads of foolscap used by all news writers at the *Picayune*, was handset by compositors who, by her own admission, took liberties with her lines. "Unable to read my copy," she wrote, they "set up what they thought I ought to have said."

In an attempt to produce clearer, more accurate copy, the typewriter was introduced to the *Picayune* newsroom shortly before Field left for the *Times-Democrat*. Field complained in print of her difficulties in attempting to master it. "I wonder," she wrote, "shall I ever learn to think on a typewriter or to compose on one?" The answer to this question was probably no, because soon after she started working at the *Times-Democrat* she developed a persistent hand tremor, and subsequently dictated her articles to her daughter, Flo, who then typed them. Still, her dictated copy was as graceful, imaginative, and insightful as when she was composing it with the stub of a pencil in a rude country hotel room.

LOUISIANA VOYAGES

Louisiana
Parishes

GRAND ISLE

In the fall of 1892, after summer vacationers had returned to New Orleans, Martha Field took a boating excursion across Barataria Bay to Grand Isle. The waters around the island then, as now, were a fishing paradise, and she demonstrates that among her numerous interests was a passion for catching, and savoring, fish. Her visit to the Malay and Chinese fishing communities of Barataria records an exotic, delicately-balanced way of life in southern Louisiana that was soon to be destroyed by wind and water. Her description of Grand Isle and the following account of Cheniere Caminada invite a comparison with Kate Chopin's fictional account of a visit to the islands in her novel, *The Awakening* (1899).

Both women have an eye for the colorful details of a primitive way of life, but Field's journalistic instinct leads her to report much more extensively on the unique history of a people who are as much a part of the sea as John Millington Synge's Aran Islanders. Unlike the Aran Island fishermen with their stoic fatalism, however, the men and women of Grand Isle and Cheniere Caminada enjoy eating, drinking, and dancing as much as any modern Cajun. (This article was originally published in the *Picayune* September 25, 1892, but was republished October 5, 1893, four days after the devastating hurricane of 1893 struck the islands.)

A t the very foot of the state, interposed between its terra firma and the pale green waters of this shallower side of the Gulf of Mexico, are a multitudinous cluster of lonely-lying islands. No name has been given to this strange, remote bouquet of reeds and rushes, of scented willows and wind-torn oaks, and they seem, save to a very few adventuresome holiday tourists and their own small colonies of simple fishing folk, to be in truth a group of lost islands. They are wrapped, as sea fern in amber, in the faint fogs of romance, while sullenly darkening over their irresolute outlines are stormy legends of tempest and ruin, of pirate bands and ill-gotten treasures whose burial place has never been recovered.

Almost the entire coastline of Louisiana is a network of water courses. The sparkling waters of bayou and bay slipping southward over the sands seem to have washed the unstable land away, and as it dribbles off in sea marsh and shell bank, the water, cutting like silver sickles, formed in the course of time this long array of queerly-shaped islands, of which at once so much and so little is known. Each one, whether large or small, whether inhabited or untenanted, has its own marginal note of reeds and canebrake or tall marsh lilies, and as the long leaves and pliant bamboos bend in the constant winds the islands seem to waver and float, pulling restlessly at the slight tether that detain them in this sea of milky green absinthe.

As one travels Gulf-ward on the small affair of a boat that makes semi-weekly trips in the interest of the fishing trade, the country has a strangely overflowed look. As far as eye can reach, it is nothing but gray green rushes and pale green willows, with here and there oak trees like other green islands, and about all the cloudy green waters. Here and there above the sedges can be seen the three-cornered sails, stained red with tan bark, of some fisherman's lugger.[1]

It is like some felucca on the green Adriatic or purple Maggiore, and as it comes into nearer view, loses nothing of its foreign charm. The red sail casts a shadow over the boat's blue hulk, and in the stern, sitting at a high-rigged, clumsy rudder, will be seen the Malay fisherman or a bronzed, French oysterman from the Cheniere Caminada. Piled high in the boat are the big, bell-shaped baskets of bamboo filled with shrimp or crabs or fish, covered with Spanish moss, and tied down with sharp ribbons of latania.[2] Presently the man lifts a huge, pink-tinged shell to his mouth and blows the lonesome, dirge-like music of the conch. It has a cry like that of the sea in a storm. I can fancy that ages ago, when the boats that flitted these bayous carried black flags, that Jean Lafitte and his men signaled each other on these ivory and rose-stained shells.[3]

Years ago, when our country was young, the green islands of the Barataria were the hunting grounds of that picturesque brigand of the Gulf, Lafitte.[4] Every old inhabitant has his or her favorite legend of that dashing gentleman. Every young writer, imagining a fictitious value to these legends, writes them up in prose or poem, and to this day, with witch hazel and divining rod, the treasure hunters are searching lost bayous, and dig, dig, dig as if all the world were dead and waiting graves.

A year since, one of these treasure hunters from Massachusetts came to the islands and began a systematic search. He dug so persistently and deeply that finally the people on one island interfered—their island was being dug away. All the year round men in luggers can be seen stealing their way into the sinuous water courses that thread each island, there to go at it with pickax and spade, digging for that well-buried treasure of the pirates of the Barataria.

Sailing through this green country of sea marsh is as lonesome as if it were in mid-ocean. Here and there the red sail of a lugger, the sallow roof of a lonely hut, thatched with rushes and latania, or the huddled gray gables of a Chinese camp of lake dwellers tell us that life is here in these remote places; but for the most part, a tern swimming on gray wing above the sandy reaches, a grosbeck in flight over the broad-leaved lily beds, a tarpon leaping in all his silvered splendor and fury from out the water—these are the greatest diversions, the only signs of life.

Yet this is one of the most important places in the state. It is the greatest game and fishing country in the South, and from these islands is done an immense trade with China. The New Orleans markets get here their supplies of fish, crabs, oysters and shrimps, and it only needs enterprise expended in securing quick transportation to make those islands the hunting resort of those effete New York millionaires who go to Florida in the winter time and willingly spend $1,500 for the sake of catching one tarpon, the beautiful silverfish that sportsmen say is the gamest in the sea.

The fisheries of Louisiana are one of the chief, most picturesque and remunerative industries. Hundreds of people and fleets of boats are engaged, and on the islands of the Barataria country, where the foreign-speaking peasant folk have set up their simple homes, all life is set by the rising and falling of the tides: in the small shops are seines, on the sandy shores are rusty anchors, and tethered together in the bay are oyster boats. The very prayers to the sweet, white Lady of Lourdes in one of the island churches are for seines heavy with fish and for safe returns from the winter camps.

In their island homes—and some of these islands are no larger than a ship at sea—the women during the winter days sit ceaselessly at their simple looms knitting the famous Barataria seines, which are among the largest in the world. At night, by their huge fireplaces, where the wreckage cast up from the sea burns—old prows and decks of teak maybe—the women, like human spiders, coil about their fingers the cone-shaped cast nets in which the shrimps are to be caught.

The term fisheries implies all the various industries of the people who live in the salt sea-marshes. It means the hunting of alligator hides, the killing and curing of terns, gulls and white egrets that are sent to Paris. Last year one of these island huntsmen sold to a New Orleans merchant 1,600 alligator hides. Tons of catfish are shipped weekly to the western markets, where they are sold as tenderloin of trout. On the coast are large turtle pens, where diamond-backed terrapin are being raised by the thousand by men who believe there is a fortune in turtle farming. Grosbeck and duck are shot by the covey. It is not unusual during the winter for the little traffic-boat that carries the semi-weekly mail to these hunting grounds to include in her return-load 1,200 brace of birds. Even deer are sent up from the islands.

The other day, near the old, abandoned Fort Livingston, I saw a fleet of seventeen oyster boats anchored in a straight line across the bay.[5] A school of porpoise were tumbling about the boats' bright blue prows; their reefed, red sails trailed on the cordage. At the bow of each, a dark silhouette in blue homespun blouse set in the bluer scroll of the September sky, a fisherman leaned on his oyster tongs, at each lunge fetching up big clusters of shells, until his boat was piled high like some grimy grotto.

The effect of those boats drawn up with level noses like a pontoon was charming. Behind their bare poles rose the steep, green hill and fierce, red, brick bulwark of the flagless fort, whose only enemy is the ineffectual sea. On the sandy point behind, skimming the water like the snout of a swordfish, stood the lighthouse, a slim needle of shining white; ahead, the soft sky loomed. The porpoise rolled in the waves like the black wheels of Neptune's chariot, and closer and closer to the luggers crept the stealthy fin of a waiting shark.

In this country of islands is also a bit of China—as foreign and far off, as truly Chinese, as if really on the other side of the world.[6] Here, between the green of the rushes and the blue of the sky, the vivid flag of the oriental emperor whips in the wind, and here, in huddled colonies, living like lake-dwellers, in rush-thatched huts built over the gray lagoons, the yellow-skinned coolies ply their trade of shrimp drying, worshipping their joss, and eating their rice with sharp-pointed sticks of ivory and ebony. We stopped at a camp on my way to Grand Isle and I fairly thrilled at the sight of the celestial flag, and at the little wizened, joss-like men in bamboo hats. It seemed like China—less the wide Pacific—and I thought of cups of chai and spears of narcissus bloom, and faint, firefly, sacrificial rockets.[7]

There are a half-dozen or more of these camps. Their trade in dried fish and shrimps is enormous. Each camp, it is said, ships $20,000 worth of dried fish a year to China. Their specialty is shrimp. When the season is over the men go off in luggers or red-sailed pirogues and hunt otter, coon, wildcat and other fine-furred animals. The camp will consist of a large, level, clean platform, built over the water at the edge of an island. It is flanked by narrow foot bridges and along these are cheap board shanties, or else the more picturesque Malay huts, which are hatched, roofs and sides with the latania.

In one of these, lined prettily with the long poles of our native bamboo, a pleasant rustling of the dead, yellow palm tree is heard all the time. Chinese and Malays live mingled together. At one camp the native boss has his wife. Both are pure coolies, and the woman, clad in blue trousers and a long sort of nightshirt, smiled sweetly, as a woman can who has no teeth. She got out of a hammock, and let me hold a little ivory-colored image carved in flesh, and which, by dint of signs, I gathered was two months old, a girl named Teboutka.

The method of shrimp-drying is apparently simple enough. It is said, however, the Chinese have a secret formula. Perhaps it could be resolved down into simple doses of saltpeter. At any rate, the shrimp are boiled in salt water, rinsed in another salt water bath, in which is presumably the saltpeter, and are then spread on the big platform to dry. When dry, they are salmon-red, and as hard as bullets. They are then raked up and put into white canvas bags. The shells are threshed off, either by walking on the bags or by beating them on a board. The shrimps are then turned into loose-meshed baskets and winnowed of their broken shells, packed into barrels, and are ready for shipment. A barrel is worth from $60 to $70. At some of the camps the heathens have become Christianized by the Catholic influences of the Caminada folk, but at most camps will be seen the paper-paneled altar, the familiar bearded deities, painted on cloth of gold, and the cheap and simple paraphernalia of heathen worship. These stores have a fine black tea directly imported to them, and when visiting the camps it is the correct thing to buy tiny packages of it, bound in bamboo.

Chief among the islands of the Barataria country are Grand Isle, Last Island, Cheniere Caminada, the Timbalier, Little and Big Caillou, and Grand Terre. Intermingled with these are half a hundred others, only locally named. Some belong to the state, some to the government, some to foreign princes and millionaires, and many to the people who live on them. There is Cheniere Caminada, for instance, or Grand Isle. Scarcely a foot of ground can be bought for love or money on either of these islands, and the natives, loving their lands, for ages used to a free, wild life, utterly simple and untouched by contact with the world, bitterly resent the advent of strangers. One might offer a thousand dollars a foot for land on Grand Isle, yet fail to buy a rod.

These islands, lying with a southeasterly trend off the coasts of Terrebonne, Jefferson and Plaquemines parishes, are of a curiously varied formation. All are narrow, fish-shaped ledges of land—some mere sandy barrens; some are piled beaches of broken seashell or reefs of polyp; others almost hilly and set on firm sub-soils of clay. On some, only rushes, sedges, and sage brush will grow; on others the perfumed thickets of glossy-leaved bay rushes or wax myrtle are lairs for prairie hens and wild goats. On a few are dense forests of oak, the stubble of old plantations and pleasant orchards of lime and lemon and orange.

By reason of its tragic history, Last Island is the most famous of the group. Before the war it was a fashionable summer resort, and there was a fine hotel. It has always been a puzzle to me why Last Island was selected for such a purpose, for it is manifestly the lowest, sandiest and most insecure. It is merely a shark-shaped body of shifting sand, lying almost level with the seas on which it floats like a yellow, faded, lily pad. No tree will grow there, only rank bushes and weeds, and gulls breed by the million on its hot sands.

During August of 1856, a great storm swept the land and a whole hotel full of gay summer visitors perished.[8] It is said the people were dancing when the storm came up, and by-and-by the salt water washed into the ballroom. An hour later the house on the sands fell; the waves curled over the island and carried back with them the people who had not known danger when they saw it. Yet, in the center of Last Island is a hut that survived the storm, and the cattle that took refuge there that night on sharp ridges of sand were all saved.

But truly enough, in natural advantages, in situation, surf, climate, accessibility, forests, soil and immunity from dangerous storms, Grand Isle is, as the French would say, the bouquet of all the group. It has every qualification for an ideal winter resort, and is now one of the healthiest summer watering places in the world. Marvelous cures of nervous prostration, paralysis, anemia, rheumatism and malaria have been made here. Only this month a gentleman severely paralyzed was taken to the island on a stretcher. He was carried to the beach and given surf baths. At the end of a week he could sit up, and at the end of three weeks he walked on board the boat and left the island a well man.

Grand Isle, lying northeast by southwest, is a stretch of beautiful, sandy land, symmetrically oblong in shape and about ten miles long and one mile wide. On the Gulf side a superb beach, as smooth and hard as asphalt, forms a drive from one end of the island to the other. One must look on the map to see that this island is a sort of footnote to the parish of Jefferson; that it faces the Gulf of Mexico, and that between it and the mainland is that Cheniere Caminada that was once the resort of Lafitte and his pirates. It is 100 miles from New Orleans, and if it belonged to any other state in the union would become a great holiday and health resort. A little enterprise could easily bring a railroad within less than a dozen miles of its piers.[9]

Nature intended it for an ideal health resort and a camping ground for all manner of sportsmen. It has a beach and surf-bathing absolutely unequaled for safety and comfort. A ten-year-old child may go out alone into the surf a distance of five hundred yards. There is no undertow whatever, and the water is so warm that a surf bath, even in December or January, is a wholesome luxury. Dr. J. J. Diet, a distinguished physician of New Orleans, was for many years a permanent resident of Grand Isle, and now has there a charming summer home—"Chateau Brise de Mer." He is an authority on its climate, and says the highest temperature is never more than 80 degrees, the lowest not less than 40, and the average temperature is about 74 degrees.

The early fall and winter climate is charming. When I was there—last week—I had the island almost to myself; that is, with the exception of my genial hosts, Captain and Mrs. Lowden, and the islanders, but I wondered how the summer visitors could leave so lovely a summer land just when it had slipped into its golden garb of autumn, when the sunshine was softest, the sea breeze saltiest, the fishing at its best, and a surf bath was worth a whole course in athletics and hygiene. In the Bay and Gulf waters the tarpon are as plentiful as off the Florida Coast. In the bayous sheepshead, and redfish, croakers, black mullet and trout furnish inexhaustible sport. One day's fishing last week landed us nearly twenty dozen fish from eight lines. Every evening when the surf was not too high the seine drawn in the Gulf yielded its quota of fish, shrimp, crabs and turtle.

At the west end, Grand Isle is less than a mile from the isle, Cheniere. Here is a wild waste of sand barren, once a rich sugar plantation. The indented shore clasps a little blue bay. The dismantled wrecks of some old, dead oaks fling their bare arms to the sky; the winds have blown all their branches landward. Across the narrow pass the island village of Cheniere Caminada lifts its comb of roof and gray gable and soft-colored adobe chimneys from out the clumps and clouds of the chinaberry tree. Along the shores in the water shallows the fishermen have hung their long seines to dry.

At the other end of the island a slender fingertip of sand points at old Fort Livingston. Here the salty sedges are coarse and hollow enough to make pipes for Pan. They are salt-nipped and gray, as if a Maine frost in November has aged them. All day long the prairie hens croak in these coverts and the big shrimp can be heard nipping and leaping.

Grand Isle is made on a sub-soil of clay; unlike Last Island, it can never be washed away. Towards the center, the land mounds up like a whale's back, and there are dense forests of oak—all leaning land-ward, and looking at a distance—their outer branches gray from the sharp salt winds, like a long, low line of curiously-stunted, steep hills, all shot with scales of mica. Under these oaks are the orange groves, the cauliflower farms and blackberry patches of Grand Isle. Here the orange trees are never killed by the frost; the very first cauliflowers to reach the northern markets come from this little island, and here blackberries ripen a full month before they do in the city.

Along the bay side or island shore the islanders have their homes, set down among the orange groves. Their luggers and seines are before their doors. They may go to the beach to pick up driftwood, or with a cart at early morning to gather manure for their cauliflower beds. They get their living along the bay, and, naturally, their houses front that way. At the west end of the island is Kranz's Hotel, an old, popular, well-known resort, built like a plantation quarters, in a series of cottages along a grassy street.[10] At one end a ballroom, at the other a dining hall. It reminds one of the community in the Blithedale Romance.[11] It is out of sight of the surf and the sea; but three times a day a tram car runs down to the beach where the bathhouses are. In the center of the island, rising above the clustered oaks, are the gray dormer windows of a huge unfinished hotel that ought to be made one of the crowded winter resorts of the Gulf Coast.

Half a mile further on, admirably situated—an ideal hotel with all front rooms—only a couple of blocks away from the beach, is the Ocean Club Hotel.[12] It was another castle in the air of a number of enterprising Southern men who see there is money in Grand Isle, but who have not yet entirely solved the problem. The problem is easy: it is quick and easy transportation. Then, a tennis court, a billiard-room, a ten-pin alley, a reading room, plenty of sailboats to hire, will probably attract a class of people who don't want the earth for $50 a month, and who will have a refined discrimination in appreciating the charms of this lonesome, far-off ledge of land, that, to use the vernacular, has in it the making of a southern Mount Desert.[13]

A great many people who go to such a prosaic place as Grand Isle really never realize its infinite resources. They never chased a yellow sand crab, that eerie ghost of a real sea crab, to its lair under the sea drift of ship timbers and forest trees. They never broke up barnacled beer bottles in the hopes of finding that letter from the sea that never comes. They never made a collection of the quaint, carved images done in driftwood by the waves, nor joyed over finding lucky sea beans, or mildly tortured a jellyfish in the interest of amateur science.

To wander out of sight of the big hotel, to go barefooted and paddle lonesomely, in a sort of semi-barbaric luxury, across the dunes near the lighthouse on the Grand Terre; to go for a day's visit to the fishing village of Cheniere; to make a day's trip to one of the Chinese camps, or better, go in a well-stocked lugger to Bayou Bruleau, where the fishing is enough to make Izaak Walton's ashes resolve back into flesh again.[14] To stand waist deep in the sea and let the surf pummel you, to drift over the afternoon seas in a catboat with a sail like that on some old Dutch gallot, to hear everywhere on heel and pier and shore, the sleepy slump, slump of the waves, to trace out the quaint inscriptions in the old graveyards under the orange orchards, to hear talk of oysters and fish and shells, to learn how the wind blows, and to know by the feel of things when the fishing is good is to become, in fact, an islander. Thus it is, to get an ideal joy from a trip to that footnote of the state—that green sapphire floating on a sea of melted emerald, Grand Isle in the Gulf of Mexico.

One sunny Sunday morning, a week ago, I went walking across the island. The surf was tumbling in with a mighty roar. The waves came up like great conches, only all sea-green. The wiry island cattle nibbled at the wiry, salty rushes. The delicate friendly little sandpipers stood in the salt water shallows waiting to be shot. Pierre's gun banged forth. Two of the little creatures fell. The others clustered curiously around the fallen birds. I wondered how he had the heart to load again and fire at them.

Off across the island a tall figure was bent in the graceful poise of a shrimp gatherer. The net spread like a cobweb in his hands, an edge of his bullet-weighted fringe was in his teeth. I could almost hear the whiz, whiz as it fell across the water, and came dripping back, shrimp laden. The shrimp fisher was Laurent, a Colored man, upon whom rests one of those strange taboos that make this island history so picturesque. He lives a fisherman's life in a little cottage, when he is not after red fish in the Gulf. The other day he brought me a little flowered plate from Last Island. He dug it out of the sand, a relic of the storm of '56. I dare say he had been digging after that will-o'-the-wisp, the gold of Lafitte.

I walked on, knee-deep in the tawny grasses; the sand crabs retired in favor of the locusts; the seaweed died over the roots of the moss-hung oaks. The orange orchards stretched in level lines until far away the green branches knit in a deep tangle of perspective. The trees bent under the glossy green globes of fruit. Here and there the long branches lay laden on the grass. The trees were cropped low, as fruit trees are in Italy. On one tree clustered 3,000 oranges, yet nearly all might have been gathered standing on the ground. A delicate perfume emitted from the wax myrtle hedges along the dim path.

A girl—an amber-skinned, sloe-eyed islander—came along. She was barefooted and black-robed, with a face like a Marachel Neil rose. She held her olive-hued arms, deep stained with the gold of the sun and the blood of her race, full pressed against her bosom. They formed a shelf

on which piled high were ripe, red pomegranates. Their pungent perfume came to me, sucked out by the sunshine. I asked her an idle question, just to have that note of music in her soft, French elisions that was
needed to make this orchard picture perfect.

The trees gave way to the blue, green dullness of a cauliflower farm. It
looked like a toy forest out of a Christmas-stocking Noah's ark. Under
the oaks in box frames the young plants were taking root. At my feet were
a thousand rows of broad-leaved plants. On the seaside of each a shelter-
ing bush of bay leaves kept off the scorching salt of the sea breezes. An old
islander went under the trees, in his arms a load of grass, and at his heels
followed his calves, like tame cats. Across salt pools left by some high tide,
besides the whistling banks of rushes, I followed a shell path until I came
to an old hand-made brick and adobe house, put up when Lafitte was
young. It was built by a Rigaud, and is yet owned by one.[15] On the walls
hang a superb series of line engravings of pictures, made by the elder Le
Brun.[16] The owner thinks they are paintings. Fig trees grow on the red,
lichened, mellow walls; a bramble of vines in a thorny thicket creeps
about the huge brick cistern. Old Mme. Rigaud showed me a water line
marked by the high tide of 1832, a foot above the gray tiles on the hearth.
Fancy the happiness of getting to a place where events are dated from the
high tide of 1832, from anything rather than the war.

One day, nay, many days, we went sailing. Captain Lowden, a gallant
ex-sea captain and the kindest and gentlest of gentlemen and best of
hosts, his charming family, and two or three others composed the crew
and passengers of our lugger. One day it was across the bay to Grand
Terre, to the desolate grandeur of the picturesque fort built long ago by
Beauregard.[17] It is approached by a steep hill, and there are drawbridges
across the moat. Inside it is a hollow square, and tall, steep flights of
marble steps lead up the ruined ramparts where old hulks of cannon
stamped "1821" lay rusting in the salty grasses. Far below, the sea booms
on the beach or spends its sprays on the salt-crusted walls.

Lizards sun themselves in the silent corridors, and elderberries ripen
on the bushes that have grown into huge trees on the steep, artificial hills
of the quadrangle. A little gray and gold snake lay coiled like a lady's
bangle at the entrance to one of the stone-walled cells. Blackbirds and
redbreasts kept the only lookout. In the big barracks, once filled with
soldiers and cannon, the keeper of the Grand Terre lighthouse stables

his Alderney cows. The steep drawbridge, broken and old, hangs across the moat. It is picturesque enough to set a sentimental young lady off into raptures of delight over its medieval look. It is knee deep in filth, where tumble-bugs busily roll their balls.

Or we went to the Bayou Bruleau for a day's fishing. At the dim, chanticleer hour we crept sleepy-eyed from our rooms to the nipping air of the gallery, where Lena, the best of Hebes, because her urn held only coffee, poured us cups of the transparent, black liquid.[18] The gray mule would be hitched to the big tram car, the lunch-baskets, bait-box and fish lines piled on. The coffee pot and frying pan and bag of corn meal to roll the fish in were not forgotten, and then we set forth. The landing place for the Ocean Club Hotel is reached by a tramway. At the pier we found the lugger and then we easily set sail for Bayou Bruleau.

What fun it was that sail, perhaps with a head wind and a strong tide dead set against us. How deftly we learned to trim ship with the ballast of our bodies when we had to change sail, beating down the wind. What narrow bayous we scoured with the cast net, always for more bait. Did you ever, fellow-fisher, feel that you really had bait enough? Did you ever willingly give one small worm or one fat shrimp away? To stand in the sun for hours, slowly broiling and puffing, like those wonderful fried potatoes you get in France, catching fish as fast as you can pull in your line; to hear the line whip through the water, cutting your red palms, and finally, to pull up a beastly sea cat; to land, after a gamey flurry, a red fish big enough for "steaks"; to pull in black mullets or trout, as full of color as dying dolphins, all of this is bliss to a fisherman's soul.

And finally we return to an abandoned oyster factory, where the boys cleaned the leaping fish, and the captain, prince of chefs, fried them in a big Dutch oven after he had dipped them in salt, pepper and cornmeal. We sat at an old table on the shady porch, the uncaught fish splashing in the water at our feet, the reed birds calling in the grasses. With a croaker on my plate that half an hour before had been on my line, I would not have exchanged places with Mrs. Grover Cleveland.

After all, was ever a narcotic like a sea breeze? Was ever a specific for "nerves" so good as fishing, when bait is plenty and the fish bite well? Was ever any tonic so strengthening as a fish dinner cooked and eaten al fresco? Has any other city than New Orleans so incomparable an adjacent island as Grand Isle?

CHENIERE CAMINADA

This description of Cheniere Caminada is particularly poignant because Martha Field's one-day visit, exactly a year before the hurricane of October 1, 1893 struck without warning, is one of the last accounts of the island before winds and storm surge washed away all but a few of its houses. Cheniere Caminada was buried beneath eight feet of water, and more than eight hundred islanders were crushed or drowned. Many of those Field met on her visit lost their lives. The island was partially submerged and never recovered from the storm.

Kate Chopin, in her novel, *The Awakening* (1899), describes some of the same scenes reported by Catharine Cole. (*Picayune*, October 2, 1892)

Gentle Reader—somehow, I feel disposed to begin this story of a week's outing with a sort of personal appeal to a personal reader— that gentle reader whose suffrages have been sought by all sorts and conditions of writers.

In the days of Addison and Steele, and Lamb, of Thackeray, Leigh Hunt, and Miss Mitford and Shelley, how often was the patience and the interest of the gentle reader delicately and timorously invoked![1] What did not those brighter writers, who were as modest as their worth was real, who never set themselves up on any pedestal of superiority, or were self-elected as the final arbiters of fate, and the Last Judgment of others of their craft, imply when they dedicated all the electric fluids of their ink bottles to the ubiquitous person, that protean compound of patience, grace, toleration, sprightliness and curiosity—the gentle reader.

In my last week's letter, which you, gentle reader, may be polite enough to remember had to do with the orange orchards and barrens of Grand Isle, I mentioned, incidentally, that one of the charming summer homes on the island belonging to Dr. Diet, was named Chateau Brise de Mer. It should have been written Villa Brise de Mer, and I might have gone on to say, for the benefit of that remarkable majority of our people who have neglected a rare opportunity to know French, that in English this would mean Sea Breeze Villa.

I have been asked to give names to many homes, in response to a pretty growing custom, and it is something pleasant for me to remember that according to a loving article of Catholic faith, the naming of Sea Breeze Villa was attended by the picturesque ceremony of blessing the new house. At an appointed hour Father Grimaux, the faithful and well-beloved priest of the Barataria country, appeared in the dining room of the Sea Breeze Villa in his official vestments of lawn and lace.[2] On the table before him stood a little white bowlful of holy water and a bunch of the fragrant wax myrtle.

The eldest daughter of the house held a lighted candle, and friends and the family were gathered about. The proper prayers were said and the priest, dipping the myrtle spray into the holy water, dashed it into the four corners of the room, making with the green sprig the sign of the cross in the air. Then, preceded by the child carrying the lighted candle, and followed by all the family, the priest visited each room, the yard and stable, blessing each and all in the same sweet formula. The candle was then put away, and someone stuck the myrtle branch in the ground to grow. That myrtle bush, by the way, is particularly handsome, and the vanilla fragrance of its long green leaves is lasting and most delicious. The bushes are studded all over with tiny green pellets. These are covered with a regular wax, and in the old days the islanders used to gather the berries and boil them in huge pots, where the wax unloosed and floated on the water. Of this they made their candles.

It is pleasant to fancy that in the old days of the Baratarian privateers the gentlemen of the black flag may have counted their gold and sat over their flagons of rare Lachryma Christi, illuminated by the mild radiances of myrtle wax candles.[3]

Father Grimaux lives on the Cheniere Caminada, and the little, dark-browed, sturdy Breton priest seemed to have no realization that his is a lonesome life. He has become a pure islander. For his promenade there is only a stroll among the drift on the shore. His horse is a red lateen sail, his best chariot a delicately balanced pirogue. In this way he accomplishes all his goings and comings. Not long ago, his grace, Archbishop Janssens, was the guest of Father Grimaux, and with him made the tour of all the islands.[4] It was perhaps the first time so high a dignitary had ever sought a way to the hearts of the Barataria islanders. It was a great event. In fact, the cross of the Christian faith has not been too long hung in the air admonishingly over the heads of the Barataria fisher folk. It is true the faith was there, but they had neither church nor priest. For a long time only civil marriage ceremonies were performed, and a pretty story is told of a young couple, hearing the old justice was dying, hurried to his home to have said over them the simple formula that legalized and purified their union. He was too far gone, but a young clerk repeated the words for him.

In time, a priest from France, of noble family, the Baron d'Espinose, asked permission to found a church on Cheniere Caminada, and did so. He built a high, narrow Gothic edifice, midway on the island, and dedicated it to "Our Lady of Lourdes."[5]

The islanders loved their priest and took joy in their church, but full of an autocratic, insular conceit common to all real islanders—the English, for instance—they wanted to observe some of the ritual their own way. This obstinacy and sense of superiority is to me naïve and charming, all the more so that in time it wore away, and the church observances are now as correct as in any cathedral. But the good priest sickened, and just as permission came for him to give up and go home to that *douce de pays de France*, he died, and then Father Grimaux came to take his place.

While Grand Isle is the best known because of its holiday resort features, the long, low, narrow island of Cheniere, directly behind it is the most populous of any of the islands on the Louisiana coast. Here live 1,300 souls. These Baratarians are a proud, purely French people, with not one taint in their fine French blood, tracing their lineage back to worthy families of France. They are islanders in a strong, picturesque sense, and no place in America presents so perfect and provincial a picture of a simple Acadian people, getting their living from nets thrown into the sea. There are old women living on the island who were born, raised there, will die there without having been further from home than Grand Terre or Grand Isle.

Cheniere Caminada means a roadway through oaks, or a traveled oak road.[6] Years ago, the island was a long oak forest, but this has all been cut away to make room for the orchards and homes of the islanders. The island has a distinct front and back door. On the front, facing the Gulf, whose waters are just beyond Grand Isle, a mile away, all the houses are built. They are a long row of little gray, pleasant homes, set close together, for space is precious, and before each is a grassy yard, where zinnias and marigolds grow and orange trees pelt their splitting globes of fruit into the long grass. In the corner of nearly every yard will be a shed, where luggers are lying bottom up, out of the sun, or where a new boat is being beautifully built. The shore winds form little rough capes and bays, and here are shells and wreckage; old hulks of rotten boats, and ballast of rocks are knobbed over with barnacles and mollusks. The fences are made of drift wood stuck into the ground just as it floated ashore. It's a curious barrier, like huge branches of a gray and blackened coral. Here and there are pools of salt tide water set thick with sharp pipe rushes, and fiddlers, holding their long yellow and blue elbows around their Nile green bodies, sidle off lazily as one comes up.

In the bayous are luggers, schooners and pirogues pulling at their anchors. The pirogues look like that bit of foot gear known as a Creole slipper. The names on some of the boats are suggestive. Here is Jack Kilrain, John L. Sullivan, Buffalo Bill, *Il Destino*, and *Nativita di Caminada*. There is a smell of tar and paint in the air and the fishermen are busy getting ready to sail off to the winter fishing grounds.

They will go as Indians on a warpath, leaving the camps and women in charge of the few old men who are too old to fish. Many of them will not come back again until next spring. When they get a load of fish they will sail with it to New Orleans and then return to their fishing ground. Everything whispers of the sea. At one house the cistern is a huge, rusty buoy, lying on its side, with a hole cut, through which the water is dipped. The island is silent, with a sleepy, grassy, sort of churchyard quiet.

There are nine grocery stores, and in each one are seines and cast-nets, sails and oil coats among the chief articles for barter. On the counters are strange, foreign-looking flagons of wine. Sometimes on the façade of these shops there will be, by the way of ornamentation, a portion of the old, weather-beaten figurehead from some ship. On one was a huge hand, grotesque and gigantic. Attached to each store is a ballroom. During the idle season, when the men are at home and the boats lie housed and sail-less, the chief amusement is a ball on Saturday night.

The ball will be free, but the giver of it will sell drinks, gumbo and coffee, or perhaps even that Acadian luxury, boiled mullet.

This is truly a delicacy, and I have known of New Orleans gourmands, when visiting Grand Isle, to make a bee line for that hospitable board that was sure to be graced by this dish—called in the vernacular *meuil bouille.* The mullet and putto boil in a little water seasoned with onion, pepper, salt and bay leaves.[7] The secret of success is with a knife to remove that long black string that runs down a mullet's spine. Eaten with lemon juice, nothing in the fish way could be more delicate. I saw a sign up of an approaching ball. It ran thus: "Mons. ____, desiring to pass the time of his stay on the Cheniere Caminada agreeably, to its inhabitants and in sympathy with them, offers them the compliment of a ball on Saturday night. Admission, including a supper with red wine, 25 cents." Speaking of signs, out at the clean, bare, turf-less little graveyard, there is a sign on the gate which reads: "He who is in want of a grave must come to me," and then follows the name of the sexton.

Once in the days before there was a church and a priest, the justice of the peace or judge, whichever he was called, buried the dead as well as married the living. The cemetery was a jungle of myrtle bushes and indigo, and at one funeral the mourners had to divide and hunt the grave that had been dug, so high were the weeds. And so the justice, when the prayers had been read and the poor clay housed away in its coat of oak and cell of earth, made a little lecture on the disgraceful condition of the island graveyard. Next morning, before daylight, men, women and children were at work among the graves. They took out weeds and all the grass, sanded the land and kept it so clean that now scarce a spear or blade of green grows above the island graves of those who go down to the sea in ships.

I went into the quiet church of Our Lady of Lourdes. Father Grimaux himself has just painted it all over in a cheerful yellow and brown. Up in the choir loft is a sweet-tongued organ, but no one on the island can play it. Sometimes in the summer a visitor will add its music to the sumptuous beauty of the mass. There are no acolytes, and a faithful woman or two performs the duties of attendants on the priest. By the door are two bowls; in each is a large sponge, kept wet with holy water. A dried old islander entering the church as we did, pressed her talons to the sponge and then offered her wet fingers for my sharing. It is a pretty custom, and I took the trace of water at her hands. The last time it had been so offered to me was in the grandest, most beautiful church in Paris—the Madelaine.

The day I went to the island landing in a lugger from Grand Isle, we tried to find time to visit all the houses, and if any were omitted it was an unintentional rudeness. Each married woman is locally known by her husband's first name, and so it was we came to call on Mme. Clement and Mme. Emile, and Mme. Jean and Mme. Pierre. Never again do I expect to see such exquisite refinement of cleanliness. Everything had on it this polish of soap and water. The huge, old French beds in the rooms were draped with immaculate, if coarse, linen, and the floors were sand-scrubbed or painted with brick dust. The fireplaces were enormous, and on each high and narrow shelf were trophies of the sea—conches, coral and carved things from far away countries. On the table I found a book. Its name was *Histoires des Pirates*. I could not help smiling over the eternal fitness of things. Surely, no volume in print could be so aesthetically appropriate to the home of Gambi—the haunt of Jean Lafitte—as the three-volumed book entitled, *The History of the Pirates*.[8]

Each family bakes its own bread and has out among its orange trees a home-made adobe oven, like a modern tomb, set on pegs up in the air. The oven is first filled with a fire of driftwood that burns fiercely for several hours. Then it is drawn out, all but a lot of red coals, which are banked just inside the door. The huge round loaves of bread, each one nearly as large as a water bucket, are put on a paddle and slipped into the oven, the coals banked before them. When the loaves go golden brown and crusty on top, the coals are withdrawn and the bread left to bake itself. Nothing could be better. I wish I had a hot, crusty chunk of that bread from Mme. Clement's oven at this minute, to dip in a cupful of her black coffee.

In every house we were offered, and, of course, politely accepted, the hospitality of a cup of coffee. Being women, this was followed by an invitation to take powder. The best rice powder, that incomparable Parisian *Advocat*, is to be found in each house, and madam passes you the powder puff gravely and as a matter of course, as if it were a ceremony on no account to be omitted.

It has not been so long since old Gambi, the dashing, handsome confrere of Lafitte, died on the island. The house in which he lived, one of the best on the island, and in which he, Lafitte, Youx and Beluche had many a gambling game at cards, planned many a dashing excursion, is now barred and abandoned.[9] It is not so long since a gold-hilted sword that had hung in his buccaneer days at Lafitte's side, was dug out of the yard of the Gambi house, and was sold to a New Orleans gentleman for $300. Gambi's family still live on the island, and possess many curious treasures of the dashing founders of the Caminada village.

Lafitte, as is well known, was not always a pirate. He and his brother had a blacksmith shop at the corner of St. Philip and Bourbon streets. They became the agents or commission merchants of the pirate lugger-men who came up from the islands of the Gulf. He openly sold their precious wines and silks, and ivory and herbs and jewels in the streets, but the blood was in him, and when the century was young his "long, low, raking schooner," as a pirate's schooner is always described, seldom crept furtively away from Point a la Garde without the private chief, the corsair of the Gulf, pacing its deck. Point a la Garde is much farther inland than the Cheniere. Here is an old haunted house. No one can live in it because something like hail pelts down on the broken roof all night long. On the ancient oak trees on the point, the name Lafitte is cut deep into the bark. It must have been put there nearly a century since.

On the Grand Terre are ruins of Lafitte's home, the crumbling bricks of a rude fortress, behind which, treasures were hidden and the pirates defended themselves. Not long ago, three men in a lugger were stealing for weeks in and out among these islands. They had a faded, ragged, old bit of a map and were hunting a certain lost bayou, where a dying sailor had told them Lafitte's treasures would be found. I believed implicitly until one of them said they should certainly know the bayou when they found it because a red snake lived in the shells by a bank.

It was sunset when we sailed away in a big lugger from Cheniere Caminada. All around, the water lay like a liquid of dissolved mother-of-pearl. The varied sky hung behind the island like a painter's palette. The island, boat-shaped, rush-bound, floated in a deepening mist. The long row of pale gray houses, gray from lack of paint and with age, seemed to resolve into a dull cloud. A cluster of women stood on a spidery pier, their blue gowns whipping in the wind. They shaded their eyes, and one waved a red neckerchief after a lugger whose red sail laid over until it almost skimmed the water. They were fishermen's wives watching their men go off to the winter camps. As we sailed on from sight or sound of the old, quaint pirate village I could still see that bit of blue of the women who must weep, blurring the soft gray coast line of the Caminada.

Just below Canal Street, on the river, there is a wharf known as lugger-landing. Here you may see the red-sailed, felucca-like boats from the Barataria, and some day even buy redfish, or shrimp, or that white pelican that Audubon used to hunt on the Grand Terre, from the olive-skinned captain of *Nativita di Caminada*.

POINTE COUPEE PARISH

In this article, Catharine Cole describes how she sailed from New Orleans to Pointe Coupee Parish by steamboat, then set out—on a whim, she tells us—to explore the False River countryside by horse and buggy. Her adventures start in an uncomfortable room in an antique hotel, and continue in an antique carriage with Creole ponies too tiny for the task and an antique driver who speaks only in consonants. Everywhere she goes—and this happens frequently in her travels—she is piqued to find that she is mistaken for a saleswoman, or a patent-medicine showwoman. (One housewife contradicted her husband, in front of Cole, saying that no, she was not a showwoman. "She's too plain to be a showwoman"—a comment that Cole, with self-deprecating humor, reported.)

At New Roads, the parish seat, she enters into a small piece of old France, and writes of it lovingly, with charm and beauty. (*Picayune*, November 22, 1891)

Almost midway in the center of the state, cut into fantastic shape by the twists of the river, there is a parish that is like a shield, with one side gold and the other silver. It is here that the cotton and the sugar cane meet, and often the wind lifts the long snowy banners from the one field and loops them, frayed and feather-light, on the purple scepters of the other. It is here the smokes of the cotton gin and sugar mill marry in the sky. And it is here the grand plantation home stands beside, but dares not encroach upon, the modest domain of the simple French peasant farmer, whose father's father's father had these woolly and cane-struck acres in a grant from a foreign king.

Possibly there is less land for sale in the rich and smiling water-clasped parish of Pointe Coupee than anywhere else in the state. It is so, because bred in the bone of the people is that intense, old-world love of land, that duty to it and loyalty to it that the average American has not at all, and which keeps these homesteads secure from the octopus grasp of any syndicate.

The very name Pointe Coupee is more French than any other. It is a bit of the vernacular, not a namesake.[1] Before the war its wealth was of the richest, its social life the most brilliant. It was called the "suburb of New Orleans." Julien Poydras, who was rich as he was good, had his home here on the banks of the river, and in the parish he was but one of many distinguished in an opulent world by wealth.[2] In those days that are not our days, it seemed that everything grew in Pointe Coupee, and often a steamboat would lie all day at a landing taking on fruit—oranges, grapes, apples and peaches. Most of the apples and peaches came from a boat-shaped bit of land lying between the Mississippi and the locked-in waters of an old channel, now called False River, and which island is known as False River Island. It is on the island today that one may find a most exquisitely primitive and charming race of people, who speak no English, go not away from their homes, and live today just as their ancestors did a hundred years ago—with all their graces of gentleness and courtesy, and all their virtues of cleanliness, hospitality and honesty.

The parish, one of the smallest in the state, has an area of 575 square miles, with a population of 30,000. Within a radius of five miles of New Roads—the old church town of Sainte Marie and the parish seat—5,000 persons are located.

The average value of farm land in Pointe Coupee is $17 per acre. Timberland, of which there are 308,855 acres, is fifty cents an acre. There are at present 52,340 acres of open land. Last year, 46,255 acres of land were cultivated. On 3,225 acres of land were raised 4,964 barrels of molasses and 3,076 hogsheads of sugar; on 27,000 acres were made 12,325 bales of cotton, most of it planted after the overflow; on 12,000 acres were raised 138,522 bushels of corn, and on 50 acres, 2,475 bushels of potatoes.[3] The parish has a river front of sixty miles. When secure from overflow, the crops are not excelled anywhere in the state.

This parish has a Poydras school in each ward and an average public school session of five months a year. It owns no schoolhouses, pays no rent for them, and teachers or pupils must provide the schoolhouse and fuel to keep it warm. So much for statistics.

About ten days ago, I had the, to me, beautiful idea of a long outing in some of our country lands, and to travel as the wind blew, or like Mr. Peter White of Mother Goose fame, to follow my nose.[4] Naturally, with such eccentric inclinations, I was sure to get away from boats and railroads. To ride cross-country in a one-horse shay—to stop either whenever or wherever I could—seemed to me on that Sabbath-like sunny afternoon just the most delightful thing in the world. I don't suppose any explorer ever prepared for the tropics or the arctic with more anticipation than I did for that cross-country trip. It seemed then that really anything might happen. The boat might blow up; the one-horse shay be overturned in a bayou; I could be waylaid and robbed, or lost in a swamp. In fact, adventures were piled rosy red in the dawn of that outing.

But nothing of the sort really ever happens. Had I not planned such things on every trip I ever took? Is not one of my multitudinous castles in Spain a hospital of horrors, of battles, murder and almost sudden death? In fact, I must admit that things are generally as uneventful as one of Mr. Howells' novels.[5] Truly, the unexpected always happens to me, in a queer, prosaic way.

It never occurred to me until really under way that I was sure to be mistaken for a drummer. Not even the measles of steamship and foreign hotel labels erupted on my big leather bag could prevent it from looking like a sample case. Now, after a long acquaintance, scraped on the roads of life, I am prepared to say drummers are the kindest, most polite and pleasant of men. I never saw one who was not a credit to his brotherhood, and there is no longer room on the road for that man who abuses the use of liquors, or trades in coarseness and impertinence.

But somehow, being a woman, I did not want to be mistaken for a drummer. The other day, when a traveler very politely undertook to carry my heavy bag, I, to disabuse his mind of any impressions, said: "I'm afraid you will find it very heavy, for really, it is full of books." I picked books, because for some indeterminate reason we are all vain about liking to read, and each of us talks about it as if it made us a very superior person indeed. But in this instance it served me right, for at once I was set down as that forlornest of little wage-workers and breadwinners, a woman book agent.

It was dark night when the good steamboat *Laura Lee* pushed her nose in at the bank of Hermitage, and Captain Sullivan helped me climb the steep bank, giving me over, like an express parcel, to a pleasant-voiced gentleman called Monsieur Trudeau, but who, to me, was simply a protesting shape, outlined against the violet ink of a moonless night.

Somehow, we got through a long warehouse, piled with barrels and smelling of new molasses, and out into the open. How still it was, how dewy and how dark. Black, cone-shaped shadows, like an African kraal, dotted a pool of glimmering yellow. The first, I think, must have been clumps of Cherokee roses, the second was the road. We stepped into its soft cushions of dust and, muffled and noiseless, went on through the night to the hotel. The air smelled sweet, and across from some far somewhere, there came the grinding music of a sugar mill. We stumbled on; it was like walking snow-shod in that quicksand of dust. A gate let us into a dungeon of trees, and across the invisible steps we found ourselves in a dim, wide corridor. Some French voices were talking in the distance. I waited in the hall while Monsieur Trudeau went to investigate. I think I felt like little Ellen in *Wide, Wide, World*, when she stood in the chill entry, fumbling for the latch that was to let her into her Aunt Fortune's life.[6] By and by my kind friend came back. He looked big and lion-maned in the half light of the deserted hall. "Yes, there was a room," in a tone showing he had had difficulty.

It was a big room, of the regulation United States cheerlessness, with two big beds in it. I went to the window. The soft black night, smelling of cane juice came pushing in. Some bees, great golden things, were flying about the lamp—I think they were trying to be moths. Alas! Idleness is not the only snare; even a bee may singe its wings.

It is very unpleasant to sleep alone in a room that has two beds in it. Try it, and see if you do not finally fall asleep, mentally trying to occupy both and with a creepy feeling that your ghost or your doppelganger lies yonder, listening stealthily to your every manifestation of self.

That little, impertinent night watchman, an alarm clock, cackled out that it was six o'clock. A big black old auntie, whom I sleepily thought a bat-like evolution of the night, handed me a cup of coffee and a sugar bowl. "You doan take sugar? Migod, migod!" She got to the door: "You sho' you doan tak sugar?" and then went out.

I put out the lamp. Really that empty bed had made me as scary as a country colt, and now I was ashamed of it. Two bees, little shriveled wisps of golden leaf, lay dead on the table. Ah, that light, that light! Must it always singe until put out?

The broken shutters went flying wide at a touch—they leaned that way; and there came pushing in a rare white fog, flopping into the dismal room and laying curious, long, white curls of vapor and filmy veils on the mirror and about the lamp. All out of doors was one white mystery. This battered, once fine old house, with its defaced frescoed walls and high lintels, was like a skeleton wrapped in cerements, or the vaporous garments of a ghost.

At the door stood a huge chariot of a dead-and-gone fashion, and gray with age. Old as it was, I somehow felt that to ride in it would make me feel more stately and dignified than was compatible with my plan of campaign. Two wiry little horses, so slightly caparisoned they positively looked indecently naked, stood remotely in the traces. I thought, with a flutter of anticipation, how easy it would be for them to kick out. The bag was stowed away and we started, being, as it were, sucked into that white woolly sea that merged the morning world into its shapelessness and invisibility. Was there ever such a fog! I stretched out my arms—the very fingertips seemed blurred.

Calamity Pop sat up in front as silent as a dumb waiter.[7] Now and then he rattled the reins over the bones of the ponies. I had asked him his name, receiving in reply a muttered combination of chiefly consonants, and "Calamity Pop" seemed a good, reliable mouthful, even if he never had been, nor could be, "the king of Canoodle Dum."

The ponies shuffled on through the dust, sending it up so that it fell back on the road like heavy drops of rain. As we moved along, the fog peeled away like a thin silver skin, leaving bare the beautiful False River country. We were bound from Hermitage to New Roads—twenty-four miles inland—lying just at the back of the crescent moon-curve that is made by the False River. Once the river went inland by New Roads, and Bienville let his men cut a canal across the land from what is now Hermitage to what is now Waterloo, a distance of three miles. The moment the canal was cut the river took to it, leaving that long new moon of dead water, abandoned like a child in the heart of the forest. This was diked and became False River—a silver arch of water clasping the island and its quaint and kindly folk. Here the first houses were handmade, without nails. Even the splintery shingles were fastened on the long roofs with pegs, and the heavy beams, set like a broken crucifix across the walls, were filled in with a soft, colored plaster of mud, that polishes in the sun and wind until it shines like putty.

One day later on, I went into one of the oldest of these island homes. Walls and ceiling were as immaculately white as a convent—severe folds of white cotton hung across doors and windows—the floor, polished with many scrubbings of sand, shone and was as hard as cement. On the mantle shelf were set a row of rare old teacups and a flowered water jug that went to my heart. On the wall was a china doll dressed in a calico gown, with a rosary and crown. It was there as an emblem of the Virgin, and above it hung two faded palms, that in case of a storm might be laid in the fireplace. What an air of dull and tireless monotony hung in the house. The self-same duties, the little round of patient work. On Sundays, mass on the little gray and gold island church where the beautiful altar—all forests of silver sticks and red roses, with stars shining—is faintly veiled, and made more sweet by the incense rising over all.

And after mass, patiently waiting on the green while a little service is said over a little white coffin that looks like a long lily fading on the great black catafalque. And then a visit to Father Berthet's, a cup of *café noir* on his porch, among the rose geraniums. Was ever a good priest so loved, I wonder? For years the island doctor, and always priest, he is knit into the fabric of life of that quiet, unchanging neighborhood. Not long since, the little priest set out for France on a sad errand. All the people of the parish assembled in the public hall at New Roads to write for him their testimonial of regard. Jew and gentile, Protestant and Catholic, and materialist, too, signed the paper. It was as an unfading rose, gathered in the home garden they gave to the good father. When they told me of it, somehow the simple, direct loyalty, untarnished by any corrosion of selfish interest, went to the heart like a poem.

The sun swung overhead like a disc of gold on which the earth had breathed and blurred. The cane quivered with its own heavy height, the cotton flaunted its tiny flags of truce. Off on the river the great silver-frosted green lily leaves were set like plates of Sevre for a dinner party. We slipped by old plantation houses, retiring from publicity behind rows of huge pecan trees. Beside each gate post stood a tower of brick with a curious conical roof. These monuments of dull red and gray and lichen patches are pigeon cotes. From generation unto generation there is always the whir of wings on the air and dove cries in the ear as the pigeons tumble and whirl and circle about their cotes.

The pecan trees of False River are famous. There are trees there whose nuts sell for thirty dollars a barrel. It is understood on every plantation that the nuts are the perquisites of the daughters of the house.

Ever so many times we passed buggies and other chariots, laden with the hob-nailed trunks of drummers. There are thirty stores between New Roads and Hermitage, so no wonder the drummers are thick on the road. Caravans of carts, loaded with cotton or sugar, or molasses, passed us by, on their way to Cook's Landing, the nearest shipping point, five miles away. Mr. Seibert, a planter, who lives, with his accomplished family, in an old Creole plantation home—that pleasant, high house, whose stone porches are like cloisters, and which has no hall, but a long row of front rooms (I have seen such a house one hundred feet long)— told me that the first carts in Pointe Coupee were made without any iron. As a lot of them went along the country road, their shrill, sour creaking could be heard two miles away.

New Roads, the parish seat of Pointe Coupee, is an old French settlement. Before the war there was no one in it who could speak English, and for a long time it really had no name save that of the church, Sainte Marie. It sets out in a long row of big and little houses along the sloping shoe of False River, just as the villages on the Lake Coast are made.[8] The old church of Sainte Marie is at one end, the big red courthouse with its deep-set porch at the other, and thus between the law and the prophets the town thrives. There are two newspapers, the *Democrat* and *Banner*; there are two hotels, six or eight large stores, and three physicians, of whom one is Dr. R. M. Caruth, a distinguished graduate of the Baltimore Medical College. And among the well-known citizens is Colonel Claiborne, as straight as an arrow, despite his eighty years, as gallant as every old-school gentleman invariably is, and a staunch and brave old Democrat.[9] The Poydras Academy, open free to all children of the parish, is a new, beautiful schoolhouse, having Prof. W. C. Caruth as principal, and now educating one hundred boys and girls.[10] The new grave of Julien Poydras, with its pretty monument, is often snowed under by flowers. It stands in the school-yard and someone has taught the children the beauty of roses of regret and gratitude that do not often find their way to the graves of those long dead. There are no telegraphs nor telephones at New Roads. The daily mail comes overland on the haunches of a pony; life is the more serene for this. It seemed that day I spent in the old red courthouse, gallantly assisted by the officers of the parish, that there was no later literature than the voluminous Spanish and French archives that lined the high, white walls. With what flourishes and ceremonials had this and that one occupied three large pages in particularizing his pious creed, in order to will away a cow and a saddle on the fourth! With what patient elaboration had some long-ago scribe illumined the books in which the law required a facsimile of each other's brand for cattle! Like line engravings were the maps of the river and bayous, and nothing was ever better in a way of India ink than the plan of New Roads, drawn up ages ago, when some good woman gave the land for a town that should grow like children about the wooden skirts of Sainte Marie.

It was dark and moonless, and I stood happy in the peaceful solitude on the porch of the little French hotel. A Jac. Rose below held up as a hostage to the night a cluster of incomparable cinnamon-scented buds.[11] I could hear from off "the island" opposite to me the buzzing of a harmonicon, and the pretty melody of a concertina. Nearer, a woman was rocking her baby to sleep, pounding the floor with the forefeet of her chair to the rhythm of *"A Paris, a Paris."* [12]

It was election night in the far-off great city. It was opera night at home. Something rushed by me like a black lightning flash. I think it was a belated pigeon hurrying back to one of those red tower-like cotes. An old soldier had been talking to me, telling me about the war—why the elections of all the world couldn't switch him off from that battle of Manassas! I wonder if *Rigoletto* was as sweet that night as a thin, grandmother's treble quavering out: *"A Paris, a Paris."*

Between me and the water there loomed a great cross—tall and black and heavy as the one once carried to the height of Calvary. It stood on the green before the church just as I have seen one like it in far-off Brittany, or in the olive hills of Tuscany. Its shadow leaned out and fell across the still waters, where stars seemed to enamel all its length. It almost reached the island across the waterway. Somehow from no part of the village was that cross or its soft admonishing shadow invisible.

THE LEVEES OF
POINTE COUPEE

Levees are the Dutch dikes of Louisiana; without them much of the state would be marshland, and New Orleans would be another Atlantis. At the town of Waterloo in Pointe Coupee Parish, Martha Field observes the cultural price of levee-building: lives are disrupted when farms and towns on the river side of a new levee are doomed. The only way to repair damage from a crevasse—a breach in the levee—was to abandon the buildings and crops that had been inundated, and build another levee along the banks of the new riverbed. Field describes the precise engineering and maintenance of nineteenth-century levees, which differed in construction from modern levees built after the great flood of 1927, and learns that the levee's worst enemy is that delight of Louisiana cuisine, the crawfish. (*Picayune*, November 29, 1891)

There came a day when Calamity Pop and I drove away from New Roads and came on to Waterloo. After awhile, the willows spread their green curtain betwixt us and the silvery pools of False River. I looked back to give that goodbye-forever glance, without which one cannot part from even the least regarded place.

It was wash day, and all along in the shallow of the river, women were standing, their petticoats, looped up just as a Claddagh fishwife loops her gown.[1] Each stood before a bit of a beach set in the water, and on it lay the sopping linen, which she deftly beat with a wooden paddle. The soft, muffled patting came across the water, knit in with a bar of song, a laugh or a bit of homely gossip. A man and woman stood by the fence. She wore a blue gown and a red kerchief turbaned on her black head. She lifted from her shoulder a basket of cotton, and poured it all frothing like new milk into the bag he held. He put his hand on her shoulder, and they stood idly leaning on the gray rail fence. The sky was blue overhead, and the smell of the willows sweetened the sunshine that fell on them.

Slowly, Calamity Pop pushed our old horse over the road that leads over the levee to Waterloo. The levee is being raised, and when it is finished it will be a high, steep, inaccessible wall, shutting out the fated town from all the world. How will the people who live there get out, I wonder, or will they all move away to safer homes? A few years hence, when Waterloo was condemned and the present levee put up, most of the people moved half a mile down stream and set up a new town behind this levee, which they called Cook's Landing. But this proved another Waterloo. In the new distribution of levees in Pointe Coupee thousands of acres have been thrown out, the little town of Cook's Landing along with the rest.

We traveled along a road sown deep in a pall of cottonwood leaves, that lay in russet heaps everywhere. A little church at the right had been lifted high in the air on slender trestles. It perched there like a white stork. How still it was! Not the silence of nature, but the forlorn silence that man leaves behind him when his life is moved away, or misfortune stays his enterprises. A brown, unpainted cabin, with two rooms, stood by this road. It was the public school, and there came from it a rushing noise, like so many sparrows chattering in a mulberry tree. We crept along the edge of the river, squeezing in between it and a great warehouse, whose bricks shook in their sockets like dead leaves on a tree. At any moment the bank might cave in on us.

Calamity Pop carried my bag up to the porch of the little house where the semi-occasional traveler is lodged. We rattled and pummeled, but got no answer. The wind off the river whined like a sick puppy under the shrunken doors. A neighbor went to the edge of her cotton field and called something in French—I think she said, "Someone is at your door." A moment later it opened and I was left sitting on a chair in the gray little room where now I am writing this.

The operation of levee building is a curious, intricate and scientific piece of work. It is work moreover that is never done. I should guess from all I've been told on this trip that in dangerous places the life of a first-class levee is about seven years. In less honest times levees were badly made, filled up with any sort of debris, and often broke at the first wave of high water. Today, however, the people would very speedily mob any levee builder who trifled with their lives and property. The most difficult and dangerous levees are those built on sandy soils—the sandy earth will not hold. This is specially true of such levees as Morganza, in the upper part of Pointe Coupee.[2] Riding along it the other day I saw holes, rain-washed, in the soft sides, big enough to hold the body of a man. The river is found to rise higher than it used to, and all along its waters old levees are being raised, or new ones built further inland, away from the sweep of the current. In low water times the menace is from caving banks. The other day in Pointe Coupee, a bank caved in from being relieved of the pressure of the water, taking with it a warehouse in full operation. In fact, that river is capable of all sorts of deviltries, from the unexpected to the anticipated, probable and impossible.

In the early days of the state, grants of land were given in alluvial districts on condition that the owners keep the levees along their land in repair. It was easy work then, with free labor, and the levees were splendidly built. After a time, as property changed hands, the law became inoperative, the parish assumed the levee building, and then the state. It is now estimated that since the war the state has expended the enormous sum of $30 million for levee building alone. The congressional appropriations for levee building are always designated as "for the improvement of navigation"—without this aid the planters of the state would have a hard time.

A new, fine levee put across the river front of Pointe Coupee is called Grand Levee.[3] It is in some places thirty feet high, with a base of one hundred feet.

After the levee has been surveyed and staked off, the builders come with their army of men and mules. Camp is spread in an adjoining field, a rude board stable set up, and usually a store opened in a tent. Generally the workers are Negroes, and the domestic work, cooking, etc., is done by a few of the wives who follow the camp. The levee tools consist of spades, hoes, rakes, plows, patent earth scrapers and carts combined. Also, axes, scythes and dynamite. The ground along the route is cleared, the Cherokee rose hedges that are in the way are cut off, burned close to the ground and the roots grubbed out. If trees are in the way they are cut down and the roots blown out with dynamite. Then the land, as wide as the base of the levee is to be, is plowed. You can't build a new levee onto hard land; it will all wash away. The dirt won't "marry," the levee men call it. If a levee is to be made higher the old top must first be plowed.

After the plowing, a ditch about four feet wide and as many deep, or more, is dug along the center of the levee line; then the work of filling begins. Outside the works, on the condemned side, men and mules are plowing up the land. Then the earth scoops, curious sugar scoop-shaped iron shovels swung on wheels and drawn by two or three mules, go over the plowed land and scrape up a cart-full of earth. This is driven to the levee and dumped, as an overseer directs. Other men are at work leveling the soil and sloping it with geometrical precision. When this levee is built it will be absolutely symmetrical and as smooth as a bed for flowers. The final work is to sod it all over with tufts of wire grass, and no weeds of any sort are ever allowed to grow upon it, but every year are patiently pulled out by the roots.[4]

If the new levee is behind an old one, the old one must be cut before high water times. The worst crevasses are caused by an old levee breaking and sending the water pounding with terrific force against the new embankment. No levee is safe until the grass is well grown upon it.

During high water the planter watches for the signs of the crayfish. It may almost be said that if there were no crayfish there would be no crevasses. So soon as he finds a soft, wet place in the levee, or where the water comes through clear, if only a drop at a time, he knows a channel is cutting from the river that will burst the stoutest levee if not stopped. So a hole is dug hastily over the crayfish hole and when the level is reached a tall, square watertight wooden box pipe is sunk over it, standing upright, and round it the levee is piled again with a little special embankment of its own. In this pipe the water running through the crayfish hole rises to its level and no damage is done.

All along the levees these queer-looking box tubes are planted in the green banks. Unless one knew, one could never guess they had a use.

Accompanied by the beautiful Mrs. Dr. Tircuit, wife of a prominent physician of Pointe Coupee, we made the tour along Grand Levee, passing the builders' camp—getting out of the way of the dynamiters— stumbling over the plowed lands and inspecting the entire process.

And now, night and the shadows have taken Waterloo. It is easy to fancy we have all long since died in this quiet, outlawed village. Tomorrow, Calamity Pop—that is, a third volume of him—and I set forth for Williamsport, thirty-five miles away.

AVOYELLES PARISH

None of Martha Field's travel articles demonstrates her determination and courage more than this one. The description of a ferry ride across the Atchafalaya River aboard an unstable flatboat with frightened, out-of-control horses threatening to sink one and all is treated with humorous detachment, but the danger was real. The tranquil town of Marksville is anticlimactic after the hazards of getting there.

Catharine Cole was not unique among nineteenth-century newspaper-women in pursuing stories that involved personal risk. Notably, in the highly competitive New York newspaper market, the *New York World's* Elizabeth Cochrane became famous as Nellie Bly, a "stunt girl" reporter who specialized in investigative stories involving risk, deception, and disguise. Her most notorious feat, publicized and acclaimed throughout the nation, was traveling alone by ship, train, coach, and rickshaw around the world in seventy-two days in 1890. This, and a competing globe-circling trip by Elizabeth Bisland, a former *New Orleans Times-Democrat* reporter, may have influenced the *Picayune* in launching Cole on her 1,800-mile horse-and-buggy journey through Louisiana in 1891–92, defying the image of what was the proper mode of travel for a well-bred Southern lady.

In an article on June 1, 1893, extolling Catharine Cole's "good work for Louisiana," the *Picayune* compared women who were sent on "time races around the world," traveling luxuriously in "Pullman cars and in first-class steamers," with Catharine Cole's journeys by "buggy, canoe, and lugger." This has enabled her, the newspaper boasted, to "penetrate almost every nook and corner of the state," giving the liveliest account of the state's "people, schools, towns and social aspect that has yet been printed." (*Picayune*, December 6, 1891)

Seven o'clock in the morning and the rain coming down like the proverbial "cats and dogs." What a pleasant plashing music it made on the gray window panes and how noisily it sputtered in the tin gutter-pipe that ran down the corner of the house. It was a huge room in a cheery old house and a huge fire roared in the big fireplace. Now and then a drop or two of rain came down the wrong way and sizzled on the big oak backlog. Out on the porch a long red row of geraniums shivered feebly in the wind. Surely somebody would take them in by and by. Out of doors it was one gray blur, as if one had breathed on a mirror, and under the naked trees the dead, russety leaves lay sodden and sad, as if at least they had yielded to the time of the year.

This was Williamsport, a little village up in the extreme northern corner of Pointe Coupee Parish. Across the way were several stores and beyond an arm of the river, up which great boats can only come in high water. I could see from where I stood a silver wedge of water that seemed like a bit of mother of pearl enamel let into the brown and gray tangle of field and forest and road. Everywhere were great trees, in clusters, avenues, and singly set about the big yard. Just beyond, in a beautiful level park, stood the Episcopal Church, one of the prettiest in the state. Behind trailed the church yard, broken into billows, where the dead lie secure from the rain. I could see through the trees the white crosses and tall columns shining luminous and rain-polished. Nearer was the pretty rectory, and I knew what a charming family it sheltered. This Episcopal Church and the rectory are the result of woman's work. The ladies of the church gave entertainments and built this beautiful home for their rector's family. They put the neat fence about the grounds and they kept it all in such excellent repair that their record is the pride of all the women in the parish. There are some very sadly-reflected Episcopal Churches in the state; little churches whose broken walls seem to cry "come help me or I fall." Somehow I fancy it would do their parishioners good to know what a handful of women have accomplished in four years in Pointe Coupee.

The rain poured on and I stood by the window watching my driver tie up his horses' tails, tighten the covers all around the big carriage, and otherwise prepare for the forty-five-mile drive before us. A vagrant line of somebody's poetry kept looping its phrase and thought in with my idling fancies. It was:

> "View the drizzly day
> And watch the self-same cowslips blow."

After all, could anything be better than that? Do we not know, oh tired workers, wearily pushing on with that pack of hounds, with want, greed, selfishness, ever at our heels, that the poet has the best of it! To know the same roses year in and out, to have the history of generations of birds in the same sweet hedges, to watch the graveyard grow and be all unafraid of the quiet spot that shall be ours some day, is not that better than a front seat on the platform?

How cozy it was, tucked away under a big red blanket in the dark of the closed-in carriage, with the rain fusillading on the leather roof, and the big horses slopping through the mud or plashing breast high through the coulees; only one may know who has traveled cross country in this fashion.

The road led on past plantations with a bayou hiding behind its banks at our right, on through the gray forests where all life seemed in a state of suspension. The long moss trailed to the dead leaves in the hollows, threading its tendrils over the haw trees beaded with scarlet and subduing their joyous wintry color. Now and then we passed a roadside cabin—a forlorn little cabin with a mule browsing on the porch posts, or a hen scratching in the cotton piled against the window. Two or three sticks of wood lay in the yard, never any more, and sometimes a man or woman shaking with the cold, would be feebly trying to chop off a stick or two. If the Negroes only knew how to economize, if only there was someone to teach them how easy life can be made in the South, they would soon be the richest, most prosperous and powerful set of people in the country.

I said as much to Steve, my intelligent Colored driver. He laughed—Steve is a city man: he has a metropolitan contempt for the cornfield Negro. "That is so, madam," said Steve.

In wet weather, the Atchafalaya is able to furnish one with about as disagreeable a quarter of an hour as one can wish. The rain was over when we got to its steep bank, but the sky hung down like a sponge soaked full of water, and off at the horizon the piled gray clouds seemed to fairly spill their moisture on the wintry fields. There was a flatboat, just large enough to hold the team, two steep banks, a world of mud—and Atchafalaya mud is something unique. It was too steep for me to remain in the carriage, so out I came. The banks were piled with willow mattresses loaded down with huge rocks to keep them from caving in low water. The yellow river slipped slowly by, braided into waves by the wind. Across, beyond the steep banks, was Avoyelles Parish; in the distance the cotton fields looked like drifts of snow piled against the sulky sky. It wasn't a beautiful view, but I stood still, unable to get away, caught in the fastness of that Atchafalaya mud. In all probability I should be standing there yet had not a polite citizen come along and pulled me out.

We were an hour crossing that wretched river; Steve holding on like mad to his frightened horses; I dodging the wheels and trying to listen sensibly to the directions of the big Dutch oarsman, about what I was to do if the horses pushed us in the river. It seemed to me that I might as well prepare for the worst. The flatboat was rocking like a cradle. One of the horses screamed. I did not mind that much, for I screamed myself, and then I could see his white eyeball glaring. Now, if there is anything on earth, or on the Atchafalaya, that absolutely disturbs my equanimity, in fact makes a driveling idiot of me, it is the white eyeball of a horse glaring as that horse's eyeball glared. I said, almost involuntarily, an abject, cowardly kind of prayer, and wished I hadn't my best black dress on. Steve called back at me not to be frightened, "dat hoss was only foolin'," under the excitement of the moment dropping back into a vernacular that is apparently the object of his life to emancipate himself from, but, as at that moment Steve was in the air, both feet off the boat, swinging to the "hoss" bridle, his assurances were not particularly comforting.

But, of course, nothing happened. Half an hour later my driver, dead bent, was driving me up the black Avoyelles bank, and saying, "I thought we was gone that time, for shore."

I said nothing at all. I even had not the spirit to boast over the danger I had passed, as convalescents always do. Steve was a man, and I was a woman. In times of danger a man always will insult a woman's intelligence by telling her nothing is the matter, and when the danger is over, be he black, white, red, or yellow, he can't for the life of him help crowing over his own prowess.

And now we were well on our way into the rich heart of beautiful Avoyelles. In my note-book I find vague words that mentally make for me a wonder mosaic of color, woven leaves flying in the wind like a flock of sparrows, of red berries and purple grapes, of long fleeces of Spanish moss, of a gray cloud that thinned away until, bending down, almost it seemed, to the black branches of the denuded trees, there pressed the soft and humid beauty of the rain-washed sky. Once in the woods we saw some children drawing a large wagon, piled high with branches for the fire. They had harnessed themselves to the pole, and dashed by us, barefooted and bareheaded little sprites of cheerfulness making home even of the forest.

It was late afternoon when the horses lifted their muddy feet over the last rod of bluff land and struck the dry, hard road of the prairie. Here and there a peaceful spire was set into the sky, or a smoky cluster of roofs showed a tiny village off in the distance. Comfortable little farms were scattered over the flat land. Everywhere were signs of prosperity and easy life.

The influence of this prairie is invigorating. On its broad face the native grasses give rich food to cattle. Its soil is the best in the state for the culture of certain fruits. It fairly invites the plow, the seed, and its promises of a harvest are always faithfully fulfilled. Over to the west the Red River is not four miles away from Marksville. Between it and the town is a broad band of woodland. Nearer are the curious clusters of Indian mounds, whose mysterious purpose is an undiscovered secret, and beside the mounds is a long, low levee or embankment built inland by the Indians, and of which even less is known than of the mounds.[1] Still skirting the forest there is an Indian settlement, but theirs is a lost tribe; not even its name is left them as a tradition.

In the town of Marksville one can strike the keynote for the parish. It is a thrifty, neat, well-appearing little place, having about one thousand inhabitants, supporting two newspapers, several hotels and many stores. It has no ragged, old or "picturesquely poor" features. In the center is the courthouse and public square, and around this quadrangle the town has arranged itself, with business houses confronting the square. A neat Catholic Church stands nearby, and pleasant, hospitable residences form the outer margin in all directions. Social life in Marksville is refined and cultivated; a piano is in every house, and an accomplished musician will be its owner. There are many other flower gardens, only less elaborate than the famous rose garden of Mrs. Joffrion.

The quaintly picturesque gabled country house of ex-Senator Joffrion stands in the loveliest rose garden in all the country.[2] Every wind that stirs scatters a fairy flock of rose petals, and these banks of bloom perfume the air with a vespers service all their own. In this garden the mistress of it has one thousand varieties of roses. It is indeed a wonder garden. One day I had from it a welcome written in its roses. There was a rose for every day in the year; white roses and others that were old pearl pink—soprano roses they seemed to me—and salmon roses and rich pink ones that if they could sing would surely have mezzo voices, with finally the perfumed Jacs, American Beauties and Marachel Niels, whose voices, if roses were prima donnas, would be contralto.

At the edge of the town Mr. J. L. Normand, a nurseryman of national reputation, demonstrates in superb fashion the fact that Avoyelles represents an unequaled combination of fertile soil, cheap lands and delightful climate. The condition of Mr. Normand's fruit farm should convince the most indifferent that Louisiana, not California, should be the fruit market for the East and North. Peaches, pears, plums, pomegranates, oranges, grapes, guavas, and figs are all in this orchard, not as exotics but as hardy, growing trees, from which each year fruit is shipped to the city markets.

One day in mid-November I sat by the fire in my room at a Marksville hotel. Beside me on a table lay the immigration document for all Avoyelles. It was compounded of a golden heap of fruit, sugarcane, nuts, cotton, corn and rice, and beside it stood that basket of royal roses, one for every day in the year.

Somebody had asked me what I should say of Avoyelles, and it seemed to me, looking at that little harvest of half a day's outing, that all the story was told—that no sponsor was needed—the parish spoke for herself.

ST. JAMES PARISH

In this visit to the "Golden Coast" of St. James Parish, Catharine Cole is once again confronted with heroic efforts to preserve parish levees from the high-water threat of the Mississippi River. She recounts stories of the curative powers of the "mad-stone" she is shown at Vacherie, and visits the plantation home of one of the legendary figures of St. James Parish, Valcour Aime. Field captures the pathos of Aime's old black caretaker when he relates his plan to purchase the plantation by winning the Louisiana lottery.

When she describes the decaying plantation house and gardens of Aime, the sugar Croesus of St. James Parish, Field wades into the tropes of English Romanticism, with its melancholy musings on lost grandeur, lost wealth, lost youth. She mines this vein of writing with ease, comfort, and obvious pleasure. (*Picayune*, June 12, 1892)

Once, in days that are dead beyond recall, the country between New Orleans and Donaldsonville went by the opulent name of "The Golden Coast."

To this day, it is an old, familiar phrase that if murmured over many a desk's dead wood in the stony-hearted town, recalls to the worker bending there spice-scented memories of an incomparable land. It was a princely land, and those whom ill fortune has forced to leave it must needs look back with longing on its powerful river, so tranquilly and forcefully moving between the green dikes of stately homes. They were like castles in a new Spain—each one inspired by a remembrance of the Parthenon or Temple of Diana, on sunny old courts, all tapestried with vines and alleys, all one pink blur of myrtles and oleander. Or of brown belfries under the shadow and protection of the cross; or of far green fields where corn and cane, tobacco and yams, make this, with their riches, indeed a Golden Coast.

St. James parish has always been the home of aristocrats. Its traditions are all of splendor, brilliancy and wealth, and of a refined and pleasant society, excellent educational institutions, superb homes, grand families wearing with honor brave and distinguished names. To this day it is famous for its marvelous crops, its perique tobacco, once only made for the king of France, and made nowhere else in the world but in this parish, for its Jefferson College and Convent of the Sacred Heart, and for its beautiful old plantation homes. It is the land of magnificent mansions, those grand old Doric-columned dwellings, great square edifices like the Parthenon, with porches like cloisters rising one above the other, three and four tiers high on all four sides, and topped by a roof studded with blinking dormer windows, like old faded eyes looking calmly out on an outlived world.

Seen from the river, brimming to its banks and giving back its own mirrored idea of sky and cloud, or oak alley and church, and convent and home—how beautiful it is, this parish of St. James. The brown and rutty road winds on endlessly far below the dike. Queer gray hooded carts pass over it. Bread carts, piled high with the sweet, wholesome, real French bread that is made as in the *douce pays de France* with a leaven of flour and water alone, rumble by, the vender in his cool, professional blue blouse, stopping at every home to hand out gnarled loaves, like twists of an old orange tree.

Off, under the trees, like an old mother hen, the sweet parish church spreads her red skirts, and the baker, when he passes that sanctuary, tips his hat. It is an old world courtesy that thrives well in this parish of the Golden Coast.

It seemed to me, that sunny, summer morning when I stood on the narrow rim of the levee, the level river touching with its frothy tongues the hem of my gown, or occasionally splashing over in long curling waves a trough of water into the roads, that never was a country place more fair, more artistic, more enticing. For two days I had been domiciled in a big, cheerful house under great oak trees that stand on the corner of the Jefferson College grounds. It was the feast of Pentecost and a holiday for the hundred gallant and manly young lads to whom this old, famous hall is Alma Mater.

In the great park they were all at play, a black-skirted priest tossing a ball like a boy—one of them in love, spirit and influence. A splendid peacock sat in the sun on the high, white wall, his train of Juno eyes trailing over the mossy stones, his strident cry woven in with the halloo of young voices; the whistled concert from the oak trees, where birds were teaching their young; the mellow winding of a horn.

The long, white, college building with its forest of columns might for an eye-flash have passed for a side view of the great church of the *Madelaine* in Paris. That day, flags floated from it everywhere, the yellow and white papal flag flanked by our national flags, and these in turn by others. From the building an avenue of trees extends out for nearly half a mile, over what in dry weather is known as College Point batture.[1] Now it is an avenue through the water lovelier than Venice, because such trees may not be had in Venice. As I stood timorously balanced on the levee I could hear the faint, far-off tinkling of iron on an anvil. I knew well the little crowded junk shop, blacksmith shop, curiosity shop, all in one, that stands behind the college. Had I not loafed there and tried a halting talk in French with old Frère Jean Marie, the gray-headed old eighty-year-old brother who planted the avenues of trees and lovingly named it Avenue Père Napier in honor of a gentle brother whom no one in the college can speak of with dry eyes.

The tankle of the iron sounded musically. If one could only make a picture of Frère Jean bending at his bellows, a little bushy, gray man, burrowing in a jungle of rusty metal, with old clocks, old pipes and barrel hoops, lancets, staves, locks, keys, hinges piled everywhere. The only beautiful thing there was the patient work, and high on the stone chimney above the blinking eyes of fire, in a cheap wooden frame, the tender face of old Frère Jean's divine mother.

Jefferson College is well known to be one of the finest educational institutions for young men in the South.[2] It is in charge of the Marist Fathers, an order distinguished for their scholarly attainments. The present president of the college is Rev. Father James Blenk, a man of ripe culture and a most lovable and winning personality.[3] The college is admirably equipped, the library and physic room being all that could be desired. At present there are a hundred students, and this year seven will graduate. The manly sports are wholesomely cultivated, and under the excellent care of Mr. Homer Dupay, the college band is one of the best in the state, and the boy's choir for the college chapel is equal to one of the best in any English cathedral.

This beautiful chapel, with fine oak-raftered ceiling, a handsome altar and a very fine copy of Murillo's *Annunciation*, is one of the most perfect pieces of Gothic architecture in the country. It is lovely inside and out. The chapel was the gift of a rich planter many years ago, Valcour Aime, who named it Felicity after one of his daughters.[4] Only the other day it was further enriched by the gift from Mrs. Captain Joe Brown of Algiers of a fine jewel-studded missal holder, and of a handsome altar cloth of Mexican work, from Miss LeBourgeois of Mount Airy plantation.

It is indeed a parish to be proud of, St. James, with its fine old traditions, its grand old houses, its superb crops, its king's tobacco, and its present plucky and patriotic citizens. Why, by the sheer strength of their broad backs the men of the coast kept out a crevasse the other day. The river is level to the brim with water. A falling leaf would almost seem to send drops splashing down into the road. Several crevasses have occurred and have been closed by the planters. This is the first time crevasses have ever been closed. When the planters do this work it is by a system too successful to be criticized. They will have nothing to do with the steam pile drivers. These jar and loosen the ground and seem to increase the damage. The boards, or cribbing as they call it, really a fence of posts and lumber, are driven in by big mallets wielded by stout arms. These are braced on the land side and then filled in with sacks of earth.

In the Tessier crevasse, successfully closed last week, 150,000 sacks of earth were dumped. At the Hope crevasse a few days ago, on the right bank of the river, when the boards were pounded in, the men got down in the water and set their backs against the boards and kept out the river by sheer physical force until the wooden braces could be set. The boards bent in landward with a curve, under the mighty force of the baffled river. If only one man had given out all would have been drowned and three parishes ruined, but no one gave out; the crevasse was closed and it was closed by these men—black, white, rich, poor, high, low, laborers, professional—of this Golden Coast.

Just after the Tessier crevasse, and while all the men available were at work there, an ugly break occurred in the river bank just above. No men were to be had; the Italian watchers lost their heads, and a dreadful fate might have been in store for the planters, but the plucky and accomplished daughter of Mr. Trudeau gathered up the Colored women out of the quarters, led the way to the levee, and for an hour, until the men came, kept them bravely busy filling and piling sacks.

It is perilous times along the levee. Watchmen patrol the levees day and night. At night, armed with lanterns and rifles, they are on the lookout for crawfish holes and levee cutters. These last come to cut the levees in order to save their own domains. The firing of a gun is the signal of a break. Then the guards rush away crying "Crevasse! Crevasse!" The plantation's bell rings out its alarm. The people rush out pell-mell and the valiant fight begins. The other night the gallant Marist Fathers of Jefferson College worked at an incipient crevasse on their levee until four in the morning. It was a picturesque spectacle to see those black-gowned shapes, in broad-brimmed hats, spading in the half moonlight, their soft robes beating in the wind as they strenuously worked to save the parish from a crevasse.

Next to its fairy-tale accounts of sugar yields, the fabulous rice crops and the yellow yams that grow so freely here, the great produce of St. James is perique, that famous tobacco that tries the nerves of the most nicotine-hardened smoker, that but few persons are brave enough to smoke pure.[5] Perique, the cornerstone of how many castles in Spain! Perique, the Pegasus on which many a poet has attained Olympus. Perique, the solace of the lonely, the wife of the widower, the song of the musician, the lost chord of the singer. It is at Grand Pointe the best and most is made. Nothing is quainter than a carat of perique all rope-twisted and looking like a section of weather-beaten Atlantic cable. It has been said that perique is a secret of applied flavor handed down by word of mouth from generation unto generation of Creole tobacco farmers. But this is not so. It is only "perique" in St. James: the same seed, the same methods, applied elsewhere produce an inferior tobacco. The method of culture and drying is extremely crude, but the result is like incense in a temple. No wonder that in those old days "dead beyond recall," perique was saved for the royal pipes of France.

There are fine plantation homes in St. James, whose names and whose beauties should pass into history. Among these are Belmont, the property of Mr. LeBourgeois, set in a grove of magnolia trees, a house fit for a temple, that originally cost $60,000, whose superb fluted columns were the work of the original owner, and which today is a treasure house of art, of statuary, of books.[6] Another place on the river that is of note, famed for having the most beautiful grounds of any place in St. James is Union Plantation, the property of Mme. E. A. Jacobshagen, an accomplished and charming woman who, while chatelaine of a lovely home, is nonetheless capable manager of her fine plantation.

Between Union and Belmont, on the left bank of the river, lies Convent Town with its horde of stores, its many sweet homes, its parish church and presbytery and convent and college.[7] Convent Town is one of the most important commercial centers on the river front, the only town on the left bank between New Orleans and Baton Rouge.

On the opposite bank is the magnificent old homestead of the Choppin family, like Belmont, one of the few estates of the Golden Coast in the hands of its original family. Home Place is now occupied by young Dr. Choppin, and his brilliant wife.[8] It is a three-story-and-a-half-high building with galleries twenty feet broad all around. The stately apartments, as if planned to lodge a king, are fitted with old oak and rosewood with priceless furniture and antique portraits, and all these are graced by the dainty devices of modern luxury, directed by a refined and cultivated taste. It is enough to turn a Vermonter into a New Yorker, green with envy, to penetrate such homes as the artistic and sumptuous Union plantation or the Home Place.

"How would you like to see a mad stone," said the courteous owner of Home Place, as we sat, a large party, at breakfast in the great dining room the other morning. It was ten o'clock; the men at table looked tired. Planters, guests, professionals had been up all night watching the levee. Half an hour later found us in a big carriage, drawn as is the ideal country carriage, by two strong mules, and on our way to Vacherie.

Vacherie is down on the maps; it means a cow place. It is sugar land, half prairie, half cleared swamp that lies fifteen miles west of the river and flanked by cypress forest and a most beautiful lake, Lake des Allemands, whose practical outlet to the Gulf is via Barataria Bay. In Vacherie the original settlers were German, but now only a trace of the Teuton survives in names, whose owners are picturesquely Gallicized. In Vacherie dwell, in simple homes built by their forefathers, about 2,000 souls. They are prosperous, peaceful and simple. Nothing could be sweeter or cleaner than the home life of the Vacherie folks. Their doors are wreathed in grape vines; fig trees fill their flower gardens with shade. One little church and one quiet priest offset their temporal natures. On the dun adobe walls of their homes peaches of fabulous size and flavor ripen in the sun, and in their fields the cane grows as nowhere else. Lake des Allemands, with its little semi-occasional steamboat beating its way up from the city, is at their pasture bar. On our way we met a peddler. His cart was a cara-van, such as one sees in England. It was drawn by two mules, and looked like a Noah's ark. It held seven hundred dollars' worth of goods, the owner said. "But the New Orleans exposition killed our trade," said the peddler.[9] "Before that, everyone bought of us. They all visited the city, and since then nothing will do but they must deal directly with the city men."

It is the king of Vacherie who owns the mad stone. Mr. Joseph Webre—the largest landed proprietor in Vacherie—is known by all his neighbors as the king of Vacherie. His fields are the broadest, his home the richest, his cattle the sleekest, his crops the finest.

The mad stone is a small bit of a brittle, friable, shining stone with a remarkable and lovely polish, a beautiful purple, brown, and gray in color. It was given to Mr. Webre's father more than thirty-five years ago by an Indian chief. Mr. Webre had befriended the Indian, and as he was bidding him goodbye he drew the stone from his breast and said: "It is all I have, but while you have this you need never fear the bite or sting of any animal, bird or fish."

It has been tested a hundred times. Last year, a man, horribly bitten by a mad dog and already affected with lockjaw, was cured by this stone. Another man, said by physicians to be literally dying from rattlesnake bite, swollen to a great size and vomiting, was cured in half an hour. The stone is put on the wound, it sticks there and after a time falls off, like a leech sucked full. It is put in water to cleanse it, but the water is never discolored and no stain or liquid ever comes from the stone. Only the other day a man badly poisoned by the sting of a catfish was cured by applying the mad stone to the wound.

Who in Louisiana is there who has not in some faint and legendary way heard of that splendid spendthrift, that prince among gentlemen, that gentleman among princes, that American Monte Christo with the heart of a Don Quixote and the purse of a Fortunatus—Valcour Aime?

Along the aristocratic right bank of the river you will be shown plantation after plantation—all had belonged to Valcour Aime. This one he gave stocked with slaves to one daughter; the next worth $500,000 to another daughter; a third, equally fine, was a bagatelle of a gift.

As we drove slowly along the hot, sun-washed levee road my historian stirred all my pulses with stories of that gallant, generous, chivalric Valcour Aime.

They fairly drank gold in those days, said he. In the old days at the grand home they entertained princes from France, and the best people from everywhere.[10] It is said that once, when a particularly distinguished guest had been entertained, as they left the table slaves came in and, lifting the corners of the cloth, tilted on to the marble floor all the priceless service of rose-cut crystal and Sevres. It had served royalty and was never to be used again.

"And then they say that once when the beloved son went abroad he spent $25,000 in six weeks, and that Valcour Aime wrote him it was not enough, he should spend like a gentleman and give like the son of a Valcour Aime!"

It was a member of this family who once gave a dinner party for gentlemen in New Orleans and put on the mantel shelf $20 bills rolled into cigar lighters. At least that is one of the traditions of St. James. Oh yes; at any rate, that family drank gold, as one may say.

Just beside us, in a bend in the beautiful river, there appeared at the right of the road the red crumbled remains of an old brick wall. Over it had been spiked the iron bars and iron columns of a fence. Far away, peering out like a timid stranger through a green tangle of bramble and bloom, its old porches washed in sunshine, its multitudes of windows grayly blinking in the midsummer noon's glare, stood, or rather huddled, the stately, solitary half-ruined home of Valcour Aime.

All above the tangled garden grew vines luxuriantly, as if in haste to knit a tapestry of secrecy and awe over the old home that never again shall have such a master.

Just inside the stone fences, half hidden by the trailing moss fingers of green time, there was a marble slab, on which was cut 1844. It slept half sunken in the earth like an old, needless tombstone above forgotten dead. Oh, Valcour Aime, Valcour Aime: what ghosts of your splendid past troop down these palm-planted alleys, listening to the hope-less dirges of frog and mockingbird all set to that inevitable sad refrain,

Life and Thought have gone away,
Side by Side. [11]

In a cool stone house with brick columns and a broad roof and long rooms all in a row, true Creole fashion, lives old Andrien, the last rem-nant of the grandeur of Valcour Aime.

As we lifted the latch and came past the ruined conservatories, where once were orchards of fabulous value, a present for an empress' table, where trumpet vines held aloft their scarlet cornets about the capitals of the yellow and red stained marble columns, as if ready to bleat out a funeral march, old Andrien, a stout-knit, sad-faced Negro, like a statue done in onyx and framed with beard, came out to meet us.

His hat was off, his greeting was courtly enough for a king. He stood on the stone courtyard where tangled vines adventured, a protest from the past vainly asserted against the present. The old man led the way across the cool gray flags of the deep porch. The house was a large square house, with two deep wings on each side, forming, with the broad balconies that spread everywhere, a noble courtyard. It looked down upon by three tiers of porches and the wide glass folding doors of the great dining hall, with its black and white marble floors and wide man-tel shelf of hand-wrought iron.

Andrien led the way to the dining hall. "It is fifty-one years I have been living here," said he. "We did not finish the house until 1844, but my old master and me lived here and built up the place. This room was the din-ing hall. When we had company, all the slaves were sent into the court-yard here to dance 'Bamboula' and the great ladies and gentlemen came out and tossed money to them.[12] In this room my master's only son died. He had the yellow fever, and from the beginning there was no hope for him. After he die, my old marse he pray, pray all de time. Every day he go to the grotto in the garden, and in that, a cave where all was dark, he put the crucifix, and there he pray, pray for all the sins of the world."

"My marster very good. He give us everything. He send three times a year cart-loads of food and clothes along the road on both sides the river for the poor. No one too sick or too sorry or too poor for my marster. He live to make smile come into somebody's face. Oh, sure, my marster he is in heaven this day. And, as for me, well, I more slave now than then."

We climbed the broad stairs running up through the porches, and old Andrien led us into the big salon. "All this once very grand," said the old man, "but everything gone away now. Then, the new marster come— Marster Porche Miles—and when Dom Pedro come to New Orleans they furnish up the place and put in these leather chairs and beds for dat emperor.[13] He come, he walk through, he look like he think of my old, old marster, and then, he go away."

Out on the broad porch we stood in the wind whipping on from the opal-tinted river. A sleepy crooning seemed to sigh up from the old, deserted garden, made of leaves rubbing in the wind, of insects dropping, of birds calling. Through the tangled coverts I could see a blackbird pluming himself, a green lizard slipping like an emerald shuttle, a butterfly poised above the white vale of a Holy Ghost lily.

"Hit cos' my master eighty-five thousand dol," said Andrien, strangely lapsing into a dialect. "Once we have eighteen gard'ners for dat, now only me. You see the lak' was full of a long, black boat, with silver prow. You see the red stone wall, whar de myrtle climb and de palm tree lay its shadow? That the isle St. Helena, once a fort, and on it the statue of Napoleon.[14] The gentlemen go on the fort, then, bime-by, the ladies come in the silver-prowed boat and bombard the fort with oranges.

"Oh! Those gentlemens surrender easy! Yonder the banana grove, there was the pineapple house, near the big camphor tree, and there the cactus house. It break my heart to see the vines, like cobwebs, the gloom, the rain. I did think to buy it back. For long time I buy every month a lottery ticket, but when I spend eight dollars my hope give out. Never again will the home of Valcour Aime, my dear old marster, be fit for him."

Slowly we drove away, and a bend in the road hid from us, from me forever, the deserted home of Valcour Aime, with its faithful, loving servitor, whose memories are fond and sweet, but who has no hope of ever buying back and making beautiful the grand old museum and its garden of dead delights.

NATCHITOCHES PARISH

Martha Field's account of her visit to Natchitoches (NAK-a-tish) Parish is typical of the pure joy of travel expressed in so many of her columns. It is also one of her most direct endorsements of progressive education, in particular the education of women. As a self-educated working mother, she obviously identifies with the "young widow lady" with three children who is educating herself. She expresses an ideal for women that goes beyond the traditional role of dutiful wife and mother.

Here, and throughout her writing, she shows undisguised contempt for upper-class women who do no useful work—the "parlor ladies," with their "card-case in hand and simpering silken phrases on the lips." Her vision for women goes well beyond the Victorian standard. She openly admires the young women students at Louisiana State Normal School, preparing themselves to become professional teachers with the power to revolutionize the educational system in Louisiana.

Not only is she a champion of women's education, but as usual, she promotes the idea of progress in all its forms. (*Picayune*, October 2, October 28, 1888)

E arly one morning of last week I was seated in a Pullman sleeping car of the Texas and Pacific Railroad, rolling away over fragrant willow copses. I said to myself that I was in search of new green pastures in which to browse; as if ever there were any that grew old.

To be traveling in a Pullman car is not the time for reading. How can anyone care to be buried in black letters when all the world is rushing by and when there's plenty of lusty life aquiver and jostling at one's shoulder. I lean back in my corner and look out of doors—or rather down the sides of the cars at the picture gallery that is of more than Mr. Pullman's providing. It is a beautiful coach all peacock-blue velvet and cherry wood, and with a mighty polite porter, because he divines that when I leave I am going to tip him for nothing at all. But the prettiest part is that it is a sort of long, narrow salon lined with four-and-twenty pictures of field and forest and farm, of cattle grazing and of cabin homes. Can any book be better than this?

Just out of doors the cane glitters like green, frosted silver. The brown, plowed fields have that rich productive look of being good for many successive crops. The haze of autumn, tremulous, translucent, violet, palpitates on the forest and dims the deep perspective of the country road. The cotton fields, drenched with their snow, are like old corn fields in Minnesota when the young year's sun shines warm enough to half melt out the snow.

Negroes—men, women and children—distinguished for their free, fine carriage, were at work everywhere plowing, picking cotton, cutting cane and loading it into carts. In the car there were not many passengers; one nosing in a novel like a pig after truffles; another sleeping and waking at stops to ask what place is this, not waiting awake to be answered; and a young slip of a girl, at the slate-pencil age, voraciously buying things of the sharp train boy. Oh, he could see through her, so to speak, and knew what easy prey she would be for his bananas and trashy literature, his chewing gum and grapes.

Donaldsonville, Plaquemine, East Baton Rouge and twenty minutes for dinner. The day wore on and the pictures framed in the wooden carvings of the car windows began to change, something richer and mellower seemed to come into them; the glow of the red leaves, the joyous beauty of yellow. There came down a sizzling rain that went like a wet sponge over my picture gallery. The sky grayed like the face of one tasting a mortal pain, and just as I was to turn to a book, since the car was all but emptied now, we slowed up at a station called Prudhomme and I and my traps were transferred to the coach of the Natchitoches Railroad, and I was on my way to that quaint and charming town that is so old its very church belfries are bearded with mosses and grass.

The very last sight of my gallery of landscapes had been a hill studded all over with huge gray rocks, and as the train bumped along in the dark I felt pretty sure of my ground and that it was hilly and uneven and covered with great forest trees. And then after a time the train stopped and all the passengers got out and I stepped off into the ever-to-be happily remembered town of Natchitoches.

Towns have an unmistakable social or unsocial, cultured or uncultured atmosphere. There are places in Louisiana that have a murky, musty social atmosphere; they are dead tenements in which nothing that loves sunshine and is truly wholesome can live. And there are other places in which the stranger has a sense of being made at home, whose inhabitants are so many goodly utterers of "welcome." The bristling, living spirit of true hospitality fills the air; it is abroad in the streets and shines from the doorways. Nowhere is it more supreme, so regnant, so diffuse as in this ancient city of the Red River country.

It is the gentle genie of the hills and sits on the bluffs above the dried up Cane River, that feebly tries to flow past the mellow mansions and wonderful old Spanish houses that go to make up a town which boasts of being existent away back yonder in 1600-and-something-or-other.

Natchitoches, in the parish of the same name, is distant from New Orleans a little more than 300 miles. It fronts on Cane River and is distant from the main line of the Texas and Pacific Road about eleven miles, with which, however, it is connected by the Natchitoches Road. It is situated in the heart of a country that is inexpressibly lovely with hills and rolling uplands. About the town on the sleeping hills are forests of beech, spreading their green shelving boughs amongst the pines, the sweet gums and long trellises of hawthorn. The grass is thick and so plentiful that even the deepest forests are green-carpeted.

Here and there a red or golden brown trail shows where an iron spring runs away down the hills. I think Cane River must be the crookedest river in the world. It changes its route every hundred yards. It is a wimpling stream of blue water that bubbles up ceaselessly from a million springs. It is generally low enough for boys to wade across, but sometimes it rises high in its tall banks and then it floats such big boats as the *Jesse K. Bell*. Before the war it was always navigable. It has curious banks—this river that was a great river before the war—high yellow bluffs topped with green grass and beneath these, sloping down with a most gentle yielding, terrace after terrace, green and plushy, until the edge slips into the river.

To see how charming a place the town is one must cross the river and look at it with its proper perspective. It lies along the bluff and up the hillside, and like any other peaceful town, shows its peaceful spires above the encampments of great trees. They are cottonwood trees and they keep up a silver singing all the while like fountains playing in marble basins. The twin towers of the cathedral, not unlike those of Notre Dame, glow darkly red above the trees, and nearby is the steep roof and the exquisitely beautiful belfry, with its red stone slender columns and its grass-bearded crown, of the Episcopal church.

The town rambles as every picturesque place ought to do. The streets are narrow, showing the old European force of habit strong on its founders, and the houses are fortresses of masonry, built to last forever and a day. There are wonderful old red brick edifices, standing jamb on the street and built Spanish-wise with the threshold level with the street. The lower story will be surmounted by a broad balcony or porch and even this may have a brick pavement worn into shallows by the tread of feet that have been dust these fifty years. Occasionally, a broken board shows that the original house is of adobe and has been recently planked over.

The prestige of being the cathedral town of the state and of being one of our great educational centers belongs to Natchitoches. It is the home of distinguished men. Judge David Pierson, one of the most elegant and scholarly men on the bench, and a man of universal popularity in his state, has his beautiful home here.[1] Colonel William Jack, equally known and honored, and a man of brilliant conversational powers, Ex-Attorney General Cunningham, and Mr. Daniel Scarborough, a young lawyer of note, and his intellectual wife, are among those who make the place their home.[2]

President Thomas D. Boyd of the Louisiana State Normal School is a newcomer whose good influences will speedily be felt in intellectual circles.[3] In addition to the great Normal School, the Convent of the Sisters of Providence, just established, and a large public school, there are several other private schools.[4] The churches are Catholic, Episcopal, Methodist, and Baptist; all are flourishing.

The society is of the best, and nowhere in the South can be found a more elegant and cultured people. Among the ladies are musicians of a high order, notably Mrs. Prudhomme, Mrs. Brazeale and Mrs. Edward Phillips; and fine concerts are given with comparatively more frequency than they occur in New Orleans. The Shakespeare Club, of which Mrs. Phillips is president, is an organization of note. It is composed of both men and women, and possibly the best Shakespearean scholars in the state are to be found in Natchitoches as members of this delightful club.

The literary taste runs high; even the children have it, and conduct amongst themselves a literary club that would do credit to older and wiser heads.

It is not possible for any other town in the state to wrest from this place the laurels that are here. It is and must remain the beautiful old cathedral town, and the home of a normal school that bids fair to become in the course of a very few years one of the great woman's colleges of the country. A fine town, a refined society, progression and prosperity are certain to attend upon such a school, and in the near future Natchitoches will find its Normal School to be an element of success not second to its rich country, its farming resources, and its cheap lands.

Just at the edge of town on a high hill that overlooks the old churches, the tangled graveyards, the sweet rose gardens and the blue ribbon of rivers, there stands the Normal School, a state institution of which we may all well be proud. It is a fine, mellow old mansion with deep porches and huge columns, a grand old building not unlike our City Hall. It is old and shaky in some of the joints, but perhaps some day in an excess of virtue some legislature may give the money to repair and beautify it. It has now been in operation for about four years, and it is one of our ventures into advanced methods that has paid well so far. There are no cobwebs of old customs that ought to be honored in the breach; no old methods prevail simply because of a fondness for the grandfather's way.

This school is up to the latest notch in educational matters and barring the fact that it is too economically equipped for its great work of training teachers, it might to all intents and purposes exist in the progressive educational center of the country. The method used is that known as the Quincy method, the same used in the famous Cook County Normal School of Dr. Francis W. Parker near Chicago, and in Boston, Indianapolis and elsewhere.[5] The spirit of the method, the moral of it, seems to be: teach the child to think, then give him something to think about.

Teaching is not done here by plummet and line but by sheer force of brain. Each pupil may go to any source or books she pleases for her facts. She must make them hers understandingly and write out her reasoning and her information in tablets. She studies like a scholar, not as a parrot. In the geography room, for instance, a pupil molds a state, a country, a continent in sand or clay so perfectly that water poured upon it will fall at once into its riverbeds, its lakes and ocean basins. Or she will paint it on a linen canvas, with its grain belts, its races, its products, studying these, one after another. Life at this normal school is one big WHY? The practice classes for the Normal pupils compose a primary and intermediate grade and these are filled by half a hundred or more pupils of both sexes.

When a class is to be taught the Normal pupils go into the room, notebooks in hand, and the children are taught one lessen by one young lady, another by a second, and so on. The Normal pupils then criticize each other's method, and their comments are umpired by their own teachers. The best teacher is she who arouses the liveliest interest in her pupil, who asks them the most thoughtful questions and elicits the most thoughtful replies. There is no dreary teaching of the alphabet, no blue-back spellers. Children in the practice classes by the Quincy method are put at once at reading and script writing.

There are more than one hundred pupils in the school and about forty are young ladies who attend the Normal classes. When they have graduated and have become teachers in our state schools they will go far to revolutionize the cause of education, provided they use their method with the modifications that time, circumstances and individuals may suggest or demand. The Quincy method as it exists in this school is worthy of close study, and a teacher cannot do better than to pay a visit to Natchitoches and personally inspect it.

The faculty of the school includes the president—Prof. Boyd, formerly of the Louisiana State University at Baton Rouge—Prof. Smith and the Misses Carter, Oswald, Ezernac, Phillips, Washington, and Hughes. These young ladies with the exception of Miss Carter, who is a graduate of the Nashville Normal School, are all graduates of the Natchitoches school and go in the summer to Indianapolis or Chicago for a course in normal training. They have imbibed the spirit and the philosophy of education and are real teachers, not simply persons warranted to teach pupils in a given time. These young ladies—handsome, elegant women of the world in that broad beautiful sense of a liberal spirit and wisdom—are Louisiana girls of whom the state must be proud.

Among the pupils of the normal class is a young widow lady, who has three little children in the primary department. There is something fine and inspiring in the thought of that gracious young mother going to school every day with her own little ones, full of patience and ambition, setting herself at the task of educating herself above the petty incidents and occasions of life, growing round in a mental way, fair and comforting at all times. If a woman is rightly educated this is what will have been accomplished in her—no more. She will simply be a better and truer proportion.

The normal pupils and young lady teachers live delightfully in that fine old mansion that was once a convent and a barracks and is now a teachers' training school. They have a sort of mess, as soldiers and university students do, and the teachers act as housekeepers in turn. I suspect they are all pretty well managed by the dusky queen, who certainly knows more about delicious cookery than I do about normal training. It costs each about eleven dollars a month to live there; the schooling, of course, is free. I spent a delightful day in the old college, and my winsome and gentle young hostess gave me surely enough rosemary for remembrance and pansies for thought.[6]

A school so admirably founded as Louisiana State Normal ought not to languish for funds. It should be the showplace, the model school for the entire South, and with a little state aid, and a hearty interest on the part of the people, it can readily fulfill the fair promise it now makes.

The other day I went a-visiting in Natchitoches—not a fashionable call, with card- case in hand and simpering, silken phrases on the lips, but a comfortable all-day visit. When luncheon was over the bonnie mistress, sweet Lady Alice, and I put on our bonnets and seemed to step into the Natchitoches of years ago. We paced the old winding streets with charmed feet and looked into the great brick houses with charmed eyes, and stole pearl-pink roses from the garden fences because it seemed they were the roses of a century ago.

Over these terraced streets, like a tiny Edinburgh, once grew huge plantations of indigo. Once under the yellow adobe walls of the Spanish man's castle, grew the broad-leaved Natchitoches tobacco. Once the old trail winding over the hills and far away was dried with the dust of trading caravans from Mexico, and once these stately brick houses were banks in which bullion of fabulous value was stored. They will point out to you, to this day, the very house in which at one time so much bullion was stacked that the heavy floor gave way and all the precious hoard, like Humpty Dumpty on the wall, came tumbling down.

We traveled down the hill towards the level of the great bluffs that half frown, half smile down upon the innocent ambling of the blue Cane River. There on a corner stands a huge brick house, big and solid as the home and shop of an ancient Antwerp merchant. It is a landmark and cost half a century ago the price of half-a-dozen plantations. It is fine enough to have been the home of that mysterious Spanish countess whose ruined grave is in the gruesome old cemetery at the edge of town, whose bones have been dust for 161 years. God rest her soul!

Well, well, everything and everybody save the winsome young woman at my side seems to be a landmark, even the wonderful and delightful old doctor, who talks always in the third person plural, and was never known to take a money fee. Even from the odd, old fellow hobbling by, his stunted foot dragging. It was years ago, perhaps so long since that it was in the days when Love was a little boy, that this old grizzle was young and playing hide and seek in the gruesome graveyard. A centipede crawled over his foot, and the mere touch left him maimed. Oh, what will the town do when such landmarks crumble out of it?

There on a corner stands the soft-hued cathedral with its twin towers. It is a charming church, that cathedral, with its huge brick arches and walls of brick stained a soft yellow like faded parchment, and the door-way is of great square brick tiles worn into shallow cups by the tread of thousands of feet. Up in the chancel are two graves and over the altar, with its winged worshipping angels is a fine copy of the historic Madonna.

We go across the way to the bishop's palace and, entering by a garden gate, find ourselves in a garden of zinnias and bachelors' buttons and yellow marigolds and snap dragons, with cabbage roses like sweet old maids blooming patiently and hopefully, and pretty tufts of periwinkles blinking their blue eyes at the feet of the iron cross. And tall trees, and jasmine branches cast a quivering garment of leafy shadow down on the white Madonna in her shrine—so sweet, so white, so gentle she seems the Madonna of sad hearts, the mother of the hopeless, who find hope at her feet.

And then there comes across the porches of the palace—a spic-and-span mansard-roofed "palace," indeed—a gentleman, a kindly-faced man with hair like spun glass and eyes brown and bright as a squirrel's, and cheeks like apple blossoms. He has the kindest smile and the kindest manner, and he calls us "my children," for it is Monsignor, the Bishop of Natchitoches.[7]

We visit awhile in his home and then are away under the fall cedars to the fine Episcopal church across the way.[8] Fine outside, but oh so poor, so shabby, so sadly in need of everything within. What would one not give for a divining rod to lead one to gold and thus be able to make this mellow edifice lovely to the eye and worthy of its uses.

In the long-gone trading times when it took three months to make the journey to New Orleans, and Natchitoches was the trading point with San Antonio, the traders with their donkey loads of bullion were often set upon by robbers, and when about to be overcome they would bury their gold and silver. There were terrible robbers in those days. A leader, or chief leader, was a woman—a fierce, rapacious creature, a blood-lapper, a murderess. She once murdered a man near this town by driving a spindle through his head from ear to ear. She too, they say, is buried in that tangled old graveyard on the hill at the edge of town.[9] We went out there the other afternoon.

What odd graves are in that burying ground! Queer little stone and stucco houses, with a front porch and side windows erected over the mounds of earth, or spidery iron crosses, such as are seen only in the oldest gardens of this sort. Vines clamber everywhere and trees of great girth have grown out of the graves, forcing apart the stone-house tombs or monuments. Here and there we trace a date all the way back in 1700-and-something-or-other, and we pick our way about fearsomely, for there are centipedes, and we cannot forget the old fellow hobbling on his stunted foot. The mere touch of some things wicked and evil may maim or stunt or harm one for life.

Even before the time of Natchitoches there was, not far from here, a village, the last before the traders plunged into the wilds of the vast tract of Mexico. It was called Adyas, or "Adios," a village of adobe houses and Spanish inhabitants.[10] It was a pretty name for a town, and the translation, "the jumping off place," takes all the poetry out of it. There are no traces of Adios left any more save that mysterious clearing that Nature never forgives nor re-clothes when once man has usurped her forest of cedar and oak and pine by his forest of mortar and brick and hewn timber.

Another time we went into the land office and looked over the curious maps and the grants and patents issued so long ago. There is a great deal of good land in this part of the state, and it is waiting for settlers from other parts of the world. Here for the price of $18 a thrifty farmer may possess one hundred acres of good land in a country where a total failure of crops was never known, where starvation cannot be, nor deaths from cold or famine, or heat or drought.

And then we went to the courthouse, and were shown military orders musty with age, court notes and records, and bills of sale, or whatever they may be called, dated away back yonder in 1725 and 1750. What a jolly lot they must have been a century and a half ago, for many of the receipts, written in French or Spanish, were done upon the backs of old, thin, faded playing cards. And there was the signature of St. Denys.[11] When you go to New Orleans you must inquire for Père Antoine; when you go to Quebec you must speak of Leon Jacques Cartier, and when you go to Natchitoches you must reverently pretend to know all about St. Denys. We looked at his signature, and we read over some of those records and orders, eaten into fragments by the literal, actual book-worm, and then we came away from the old courtrooms, and had nothing more to do with landmarks at all.

And still another day we turned our backs on the old town and went with a crowd of citizens and citizenesses to follow the blue windings of the Cane River. The broad country road kept close to the edge of the yellow bluffs, and, looking over them, we could see the green hillsides falling in terraces to the water and lined on every ledge with stately cottonwood and water oaks. The water, bubbling up in springs, was blue as Lake Lucerne, and the white geese dappled its blue in the far-off bends like reflections of clouds. Beyond the bluffs the cotton fields were like snow fields. They were so white that even under the blue sky and the yellow sunshine the landscape took on a wintry feel.

We went by old adobe houses, sinking down behind their shade trees and rose thickets, and after a time we stopped to rest beside a country church, pretty and old, and decked out with treasures on its altar. This church was built by one Metoyer, I think is the name, a Colored man, who before the war was a rich and highly-respected citizen of this parish. He lived nearby in a fine old adobe house, with rambling rooms and trimmings and chimneys of beautiful red brick.

He lives now in a brick tomb behind the church that his piety had erected, and his memory is good and sweet in the land. Judges and politicians and priests and bigwigs generally used to be the guests of old Metoyer.[12] He dined them and entertained them elegantly, but he never sat at table with them, nor differed from the customs prevalent between the two races.

It was ten o'clock when we stopped at one of the finest old houses in the South, the Prudhomme house, now owned by Judge Kilgour and used as a stock farm.[13] The avenue of pecan and cedar trees led up to the huge house and a heavy flight of brick steps enclosed in brick masonry led to the broad porches. Who could have been the genial-hearted man to plan such rooms with a fireplace filling all of one side, with folding doors opening wing after wing until when they are all folded back, lo! One has a dancing hall, a lecture-room, a concert hall fit for a king. That was the way to build houses, and such a home is worth the finest Queen Anne cottage that ever offended the peaceful fields with its gauds and gimcracks and gingerbread work.

Judge Kilgour has tested the capacity of the north Louisiana soil more intelligently than is usual with farmers who care only to raise cotton. Corn, oats, wheat grow plentifully, and off his fine fields of alfalfa he is steadily mowing a crop of fodder every three weeks.

After breakfast we bid farewell to the judge and his handsome wife and went on our way. It was a drive of sixteen miles to the plantation of Mr. Matthew Hertzog, where we were expected to dine. Mr. Hertzog is a great cotton planter, with something like 2,000 acres in cotton, and a visit to his place is a visit to an ideal Southern planter's home. For six miles we drove along the line of his estate and finally the clustered village of his house and quarters came into view and behind a long avenue of magnolia trees, still in flower in these late October days, we saw the red ruins of the stately home, "The Magnolias," burned during the war by the federal soldiers, who first locked the overseer into the building and then fired it.[14] The house with its ruined walls, its lonesome chimneys, its crawling vines, is tenanted by pigeons and bull bats. The stately columns, made of brick red and soft of hue, that cluster about the ruins in groups might satisfy Ruskin; a more picturesque ruin cannot be found of any that were made in war.

Mr. Herzog, a handsome, courtly and elegant French gentleman and his lovely and sweet-voiced wife—he like a ruddy winter apple, she like a dainty china teacup or a fragrant Picayune rose, pink and cherry—make life beautiful in the adobe house that is their home. Trained servants are everywhere, and dogs and horses and Durham cattle with droves of turkeys and Guinea fowl and pigeons, with ducks and geese innumerable, so that the place is alive with life and comfort and cheerful noise, and plenty of smiling everywhere.

It was late when we started home. Captain Caspari, president of the Natchitoches Road, suggested that we leave the carriages and return home by rail, and so when the sun went down, quenching the incomparable beauty of Cane River and the country all about—having only glimpsed the beauties of the Natchitoches country—we turned away from "The Magnolias" and traveled back to town.[15] A day later I turned my back on that old cathedral town that in so many goodly ways still seems to me to be the king, queen and all the royal family of Southern places.

LIVINGSTON PARISH: SWAMPERS

Two articles are combined in this extended trip to Livingston Parish, up the Amite River to a Blind River cypress swamp. The two pieces are revealing examples of the contrasting literary wells Martha Field drew from. Her description of the industrial pollution of the New Basin Canal in New Orleans shows her skill at muckraking as she deplores the savaging of her beloved state's landscape. This is followed by a tale told her by an old woman she met on the steamboat carrying her to the Amite River. Field is obviously sympathetic to the woman's hard life as the wife of a share-cropper, and she tells the woman's story with a Dickensian sentimentality, typical of her short fiction.

Her account of the loggers in the cypress swamp, on the other hand, reads like a modern *New Yorker* piece, with close reporting and an eye for the telling detail. Not only does this segment show Field at her journalistic best, it also demonstrates the sheer nerve and endurance of a petite, ankle-gowned woman who is rowed in a small boat forty miles into the inky-watered depths of a cypress swamp to get the story of how magnificent first-growth cypress trees are cut, trimmed, and floated downstream to civilization. This at a time when no well-bred woman, in her wildest imagination, would ever consider traveling with a pair of backwoodsmen for fourteen hours—until mid-night—through the darkness of a Louisiana swamp. How in the world, her readers must have wondered, did she relieve herself?

At one point, she asks herself what she was doing "in a dismal swamp full of horrors and shadows and cold?" but her regular readers knew that she was chasing after another backcountry Louisiana story. She had pursued such adventures in the past and would no doubt do so in the future. (*Picayune*, February 21 and 28, 1892)

It was full of suggestion and invitation—that little wisp of paper I found among the bills and dust on my desk one morning two weeks ago. It read: "The *Alice* sails from Magnolia Bridge at 3 p. m. sharp; won't you sail with her?"[1]

Out of doors it was one of those soft, flabby, gray and depressed sort of days that nature resorts to when she is low down and out of spirits. If one went away one might find sunshine. That was it! I would go in search of a sunshine land. And besides, was ever anything more alluring as a point of departure than Magnolia Bridge? Tall, dark trees, newly greening and showing pale spikes of unfolded leaves, like bayonets set to keep off the frost of evening: a worn and creaking old bridge, in whose shadows of mossy shrine children sat patiently crawfishing, while drifts of dead leaves danced like queer little Brownies over the broken boards or lodged in the iron girders of the bridge.

Oh, yes, clearly I would go away after sunshine, if only for the pretty sake of sailing from Magnolia Bridge. If there is one thing concerning myself of which I have been pleased to be modestly proud it was my ability to travel *en garcon*. The smallest of hand bags, the least assertive of rain coats and no umbrella at all has left me moderately free to enjoy outings, and has robbed highwaymen and disasters at sea of all their terrors.

Recently, however, I have added a camera to this outfit.[2] This means a big black box held by a strap, with little doors and windows that constantly flap and fall open. A pair, or rather a triple of three wooden legs that even when dissected, trussed and folded up take up as much room as a pair of crutches; a big, heavy beer bottle full of hypo, a little box of stuff called developer, a rubber cloth and a wooden rack on which to dry plates.[3] When loaded up with these things, to which must be added my personal traps, I inwardly concluded that it was useless to begin a search after sunshine, or anything else, thus handicapped. How would any one pass me who met me in the street? There would be nothing for me to do but to lie down and let them walk over me.

The *Alice*, a square, dingy, busy little boat, more useful than beautiful, had steam up when I went aboard. She was piled high with the delightful medley of freight usually sent to country folk. Machines, harrows, garden seed, rocking chairs, lamps, and demijohns were packed roof high. Blind River, Black Bayou, Catfish Bluff, Clio, Port Vincent were some of the names on the bundles.

The boat lay at the extreme end of the New Basin and a stone's throw distant was the bridge I had pictured so vainly.[4] Instead of drifting leaves was the filth and debris inseparable from a dark neighborhood: instead of boys catching crawfish, dumb beasts dirty and ungroomed, straining at their loads and straining anew at the sting of lash and croak of curse.

The New Basin! Barring the lumbermen, shipping clerks and a few others, how many of our intelligent tax-paying citizens ever see this pride of the city, this flower of governmental patronage, this official soft snap, this slimy, black, foul-smelling imposition palmed off as an enterprise. Inadvertently, a drop or two of this witches' broth fell on the skirt of my dress; the smell of it stays there like murder on Lady Macbeth's hand.

All along the edge are decayed logs, gaping under old rotting piers, like broken stumps of teeth in a vile mouth. The boats that must use this basin bump along warily; its bottom is chock full of logs which it is nobody's business to clean out. Whatever falls in the canal stays there. At the mouth of the basin the channel is scarcely wide enough for a pirogue, and the *Alice* must, with her propeller and ropes, dig her way in and out every trip. On our return trip it took us from five o'clock to half-past twelve at noon to drag over the mud and logs between St. John's Rowing Club and the scenic beauties of the Magnolia Bridge.

What an unknown land to most of us is that on the other side of New Basin. The lumber and sash mills give place to creosote and pottery works. Schooners lie in tangles sucked in by the soggy shores. The perfume of pine is struggling in the air. The dust of charcoal hangs in a black powder over the lumbering craft just in from Wolf River. All along shore are squatters—those forlorn, homeless Arabs of civilization—clinging to their poor holdings until the canal company shall say "move on" and they are crowded off into the swamp. Hundreds of Colored people live this way along the basin. They patch up a tiny shanty of floating boards, eked out perhaps by the half of a broken boat. They set going a bit of a garden and here they venture to live, tax free and rent free, eating crawfish from the basin, fruit from the forest and gathering fuel from the refuse of the mills.

How soft and peacefully gray, like a dove's wing, seemed the wide lake after the hideousness of the basin. It spread like a melted film of mother of pearl, the far-off edges soaking up into the violet of the night sky. Off in the West, a cloud turned on a lazy shank and let some rose color into the gray. Away where the land was, the cypress trees in the swamp loomed out like the ruins of a great city over which giant spiders had spun their webs. And so night came down on the *Alice*, walking away in search of a sunshine land.

In the tiny cabin reserved for ladies were two or three rocking chairs and a bright light. I sat down to read. But are the best books always printed—are the stories that touch the heart always preserved in printer's ink? There sat opposite a gentle-faced woman, whose tired eyes made one think they were the homes of unanswered prayers, and whose shoulders had the weary droop that only overwork can give. It was so friendly a face; so full of a gentle, naïve interest, that I put down my book and smiled into it. For an hour or two we talked, comparing notes. What were we but wayfarers meeting in a desert waste, glad to talk of our load and our road, to tell what flowers we had seen on the way, what stars were in the sky of our night, what hurt the burden gave.

She lived up in New River, not that it was much of a river, since in the summer time it went as dry as your hand. They lived on a cotton plantation, working on shares. The owner furnished them twenty acres of land, a cabin to live in, tools, plow, a mule, fodder for the mule, and all they had to do was to give him half the cotton they raised. They generally got about two bales to the acre. She had a cow, chickens, some pigs and a garden. The young onions and greens were mighty nice now, and the cow was making a bag, so she had nothing to complain on, except pestering over her husband's Maw.

"What's the matter?" I asked.

"Well, she's dead. Poor old lady. It was this way. My husband is Irish. When he was a lad his father, who was a soldier, was burned to death, and so my husband's Maw lost her mind for awhile. Before she came to, her kin took her three little children from her and sent them to America. They did not know their mother was living, and nearly forgot she ever had lived. Well, the time went by, the children grew up, married, separated, and the boys fit in the war.

"About forty years had gone by when my husband's sister began to worry about her family in Ireland. All those years she had had a book given her by a teacher over there, so what does she do but write to that teacher and get an answer. Then she finds out her mother is alive, old, living alone and still wearing a bit of black for the children she had lost forty years ago. They say it was a powerful work explaining to her that her babies were alive. Well, we all got up the money and sent for her to come.

"I shan't forget in a thousand years the day she got off the boat, this identical *Alice*. A little bit of an old lady, as delicate as a dogwood blossom. Her three children was there on the bank. It would have broken your heart to see them together. And somehow she had been looking to see them babies. She used to take my husband's old gray head in her wrinkled hands and whisper, 'Is this my little baby?' until she couldn't stand it, and she would go out in the bushes and cry.

"She just lived two weeks. You see, God was jest waiting for them to find each other. It had to be so."

She drew her hand across her eyes. It was a brave hand, gnarled with work, and somehow the action more than the story touched me with a consciousness of the thoroughly sympathetic nature of the woman to whom it belonged.

Could anything be lovelier than an early morning ride up the Amite River? The boat seemed to fill the brown stream and to bulge over the brown banks on the other side. Now and then a trout or a cat, or a bass turned in the water with a mighty walloping. The tall trees crowded to the banks, and after them as far as eye could reach, pressed dim, gray hordes—a phantom army of skeletons whose cerements were confederate gray. Upon the bare, spiked poles of cypress the sky hung down, caught by clouds and held like a canopy over the answering rivers. A schooner with sails trailing like broken wings was feebly trying to beat her way out to the lake.

Here and there a bit of thrifty clearing, with green grass and clean wood pile, ran down to the bank, or a pirogue shot by like a sword fish, its owner sweeping the waters as with a broom by means of a double-ended paddle. Now and again we slowed up to have the pulley ropes on one of the flatboat ferries loosed, so that we could float over, or to wait while the ferry carrying an ox-wagon load of cotton was slowly pulled across the water, on which there were shades of light as if the sunshine were somewhere not far away.

Occasionally, near the shore, we saw one of the earliest spring brides of the forest—a haw tree set forth with airy tufts of bloom. As the boat drifted by the neat, quaint colony shown on the maps as French

Settlement, I made my first effort at a picture of great oaks. And when we finally came to a halt at Port Vincent, where the hospitable home of Mr. and Mrs. Thomas Leftwich was mine for the time, I managed to catch a good light on the queer, old adobe house known to all the parish as having been built by one of Lafitte's pirates.[5] A good enough hiding place it must have been in those old days, when the high ridge of pine land on which Port Vincent stands, inserted like a green wedge in the cleft of the swamp, was one unbroken forest. Today it is the pleasant home of Messrs. Collin.

Livingston Parish, lying over in the east part of the state, is even to Louisianans almost new ground. Twice a week the *Alice* carries the mail to its chief town, Port Vincent. No railroad crossed its borders—no telephone nor telegraph wires. Its ways and its people remain practically unchanged since the war. When some of the loyal and the royal old citizens would call a ferryman over the bayou, they give a little "rebel yell." Undiscovered by speculators, unknown of new settlers, its rich lands and marvelous resources, almost at the door of New Orleans, have made no stir in the world, and attracted no interest.

The prices of land in Livingston Parish range from fifty cents an acre to five dollars. All the parish needs are more men to make homes in it, more women with dairy farms, more woodmen with axes, more plowmen to plant potatoes and easy crops that bring in more money than cotton. On the 600 square miles in the parish there are not more than 6,000 persons living.

Without any fertilization whatever the farmers count on an average crop of two bales to the acre. Last summer, on two acres of land a gentleman sold one hundred and ninety dollars worth of watermelons. Grapes, peaches and apples grow as well as in Missouri. The farmers raise all their own corn, and kill all their own meat. In fact, no one can be said to be poor in Livingston. The woods are full of game, deer, snipe, quail, rabbits and squirrel, and the bayous, that almost make a myriad of lakes of the parish, swarm with the best fish. The northern and eastern parts of the parish are pine and farming lands; the southern part is a dense cypress swamp of incalculable value, threaded here and there by small ridges of high land from which fabulous yields are secured.

Three days have gone since the *Alice* left me at Port Vincent. The rain soaks drearily down into the swamp and through the pine tree roof.

Overhead is pent with gray. Neither pirogue nor jumper would be good to get away in now.

Perhaps the greatest industry in the South is the timber trade. One of the earliest devices for making money, it is still in its infancy, and while other sections of the United States have been practically denuded of their forests, the swamps of Louisiana and Mississippi still wear their virgin trees, and not all the resources of syndicates will be sufficient to exhaust these forests for many years to come.

In some of the best advertised timber districts, as in Michigan, the average price of woodland is $27 an acre. In Louisiana, where forests are in less demand and are more plentiful, the average price scarcely reaches two dollars an acre. In many places, on questionable lands, the trees are to be had for the cutting. Squatters stake a claim and all they make is clear money.

Sail from New Orleans in whatever direction you will, you cannot get away from the sight of saw logs, shingles and oak staves. The hard, tasteless woods, such as white oak, are cut wherever found and shipped to Europe for wine barrels. They are worth to the cutter from $10 to $12 and $14 a thousand staves. They are rudely cut out by hand, with just the suspicion of a curve to them and are shipped in bulk in French and Italian ships from New Orleans.

Trees are loosely divided into saw logs and trees that will split. Any good tree that will not hand split for shingles or staves makes a good saw log. A practiced swamper can tell from the look of a tree, from its bark particularly, whether it will split or not. Swampers' lore is very curious. A swamper can tell, if you show him a log, which is the north side of it, for on that side the bark will be thicker and rougher, and, if lost in the swamp, he has only to consult the trees to find out the points of the compass.

Cypress trees are very uncertain. Many of them are hollow-hearted. A very smart swamper can tell a hollow tree from the look of its top, but others cut open one or two of the "knees," that strange brood of children that grow about the feet of all cypress trees in a swamp. If the knees are hollow the tree will be; if they are sound the tree will be sound.

Among the trees growing in value that will not split are black gum trees. Their wood, when cut and planed, shows a very tangle of grain of exquisite beauty. This wood is often mistaken for satin wood, and panels of it are used in the decoration of steamships and sleeping cars. There are illimitable forests of black gum wood in Louisiana, but the market value does not pay for getting it out, and it is practically untouched. It is more than probable that from the one parish of Calcasieu alone a billion feet of pine timber are cut each year. In Livingston Parish there is one sawmill, that of Mr. John Opdenweyre, Lone Star sawmill, that has on hand and in sight 25 million feet of logs to be sawed up, and this is the result of the last float.

The woodlands of Louisiana comprise swamp lands and pine lands. Ash, oak, hickory, etc. are cut for firewood, bringing the woodman, when delivered on the levee ready for boat or schooner only $1.50 or $2.00 a cord—of very different measure, by the way, from that of the average retail dealer in the city. In the swamp lands grow cypress, oak, gum and ash. Chiefly the trees will be cypress and white oak in the swamps, and these are of the greatest value.

It is an ill wind that blows nobody good, so high water is the profitable time for the swamper. He calls this a "float," and he counts on two floats a year—in the spring and in the fall. He always lays for a crevasse, however, and perhaps once in six or eight years a crevasse happens somewhere near enough to his swamp to float out the biggest logs whose sale will make him practically a rich man.

Unless you have visited one you have no idea what a deadly, hideous, horrible, fascinating and eerie place a Louisiana swamp is. Here for miles and miles and miles dreary trees, gray of coat and gray-bearded, stand in multitudinous array growing up out of a black liquid mush that is half mud, half water. A walk over this plunges the swamper often up to his middle in black, ill-smelling mud. Alligators make such a place a favorite haunt, and deer and other game abound here. Of the deer caught in the swamp by the way, it is really believed that in time they will become web-footed; already it is noted how much longer and how strangely web-shaped are the feet of swamp deer.

The trees grow thick—so thick that when a woodsman wants to cut them down he must first clear a path for them to fall in. Yellow jessamine vine grows here, profusely mantling the trees with its fragrant cloak of yellow stars, and the poison oak—a splendid, deadly vine—vies with the wild grape in rich foliage and swings its hardy coils from tree to tree till all the forest is caught in its green festoons.

Dagger plants grow everywhere; the stately latania opens its green fans, as if all the world were summer and all the summer Chinese. Lithe snakes wind in and out with the poison vines, and from out the black mire iris flowers unfurl their purple pennons. There are few birds in a cypress swamp. The stillness there is complete, and overhead the long, gray draperies of Spanish moss, thick as stalactites in a mammoth cave, swing slowly to and fro, like voiceless bells mourning and tolling for the dead.

Here and there through the swamps, threading it like veins in a man's body, run narrow waterways three and four feet wide, bordered with rushes, all hollow, that can be cut into pipe-stems or whistles, and with a wide, wiry grass so sharp of edge that the swampers call it cut grass. These water lanes are always full of water, a yellow-black liquid that the men call cypress tea, so stained is it with the juice of the red, growing cypress knees. These water alleys generally filtrate to some great, deep, black bayou that may wind from swamp to swamp or find an outlet in lake or river.

The first work of a swamper, whether he be a squatter or a land owner, is to build himself a hut. Boards are plentiful—towed from the nearest mill—and the shanty rapidly rises on pegs set up in the air. It is built facing the main bayou and the only way of leaving it is by boat, a pirogue, a gar, or a skiff. However, the swamper owns a pair of boots with legs that come up to his waist so when he wishes he trudges off on foot through the swamps not in the least minding floundering through the black ooze. His utensils will be an ax, a saw, a rive, a wedge and a spiked pole.

His first work in the forest is selecting and killing trees. This is winter work. He cuts a deep rim all around a tree, taking off the bark and the wood to a depth of two or three inches. Meanwhile he has determined whether the tree is a saw log or a split tree. If the latter, when the time comes, he will cut it on the spot into shingles or staves. A tree must be killed before cutting, because green, it is hard to cut down and then will be so heavy with sap that it will sink. Dead, the sap dries out and it will float for six or eight months. After that, it waterlogs and sinks.

The waters of Louisiana are chock full of sinkers. Often a man buys the sinkers in a certain district. He pays very little for them, and his contract calls for a certain number, more or less. Not long since, a swamper bought 150 sinkers, more or less, in a certain bayou. He went to work feeling with spiked poles, and by means of chains, boats and floaters he pulled out six hundred logs, none worth less than $5.00 apiece.

The next process after the trees are killed is to cut them down. In the swamp this is done in a curious way. With his ax, the swamper cuts a deep wedge in a tree. In this he inserts a stout board four or five feet long and about eight inches wide. This is inserted not close to the ground, in the skirts of the tree, as it were, but away up in the air, sometimes as high up as he can reach. On this board the swamper stands poised cutting at the tree until it is ready to fall.

When the tree is ready to fall he must have already laid a sort of rude trough of small trees in which it is to fall, otherwise it would come down with a crash and sink far out of sight in the mud of the swamp and be literally swamped forever. There is at French Settlement, in Livingston Parish, a one-armed woodman who cuts more trees than almost any other man in the parish, excelling them all in rapidity. It is a sight to see him perched on a tree scaffold wielding his ax. And as well balanced as any two-armed man in the state.

If the tree is to be a saw log, that is, sent to a saw mill, it lies trimmed and branded with the owners' initials, until a "float." East winds back up waters from the lakes into the swamps; and heavy rains sometimes cause a float, but best of all is such a crevasse as happened last year when the swampers got out logs that had been waiting for years—that is, floated them through the swamps to some bayou, where they are easily towed to a mill. One way of floating is in a boom. That is, a lot of logs are let loose and are girdled around by a series of logs all chained together. The loose logs cannot get away, and a boom is said to be the easiest way of managing logs.

If the swamper is to make shingles or staves, he does the work on the spot where the tree fell. For staves, it is cut or sawed into three feet lengths and then split and fashioned. There are little portable engines for shingle making in use in the swamp, but thousands are still hand-made, and old reliables have a firm and fixed belief that hand-made shingles will last at least five times as long as those turned out by machinery. Shingles or staves made, the swamper carries them to the nearest water lane, where he loads them on long narrow flatboats and, taking to his pirogue, tediously tows the lot out to the main bayou to wait for a schooner or boat.

In the matter of timber, Livingston, Ascension, St. James and Tangi-pahoa are the richest parishes in the state. On last Saturday the receipts at the New Basin from these parishes amounted to 310,000 feet of lumber, to say nothing of oak staves. On Wednesday the receipts were 180,000 feet of lumber. The receipts at the Old Basin are almost as large. One end of each of these parishes is superb farming land, but they trail off with their innumerable bayous into Lake Maurepas and are covered with dense, virgin swamps, that it would seem as yet scarcely know the sound of the swamper's ax.

It is difficult to realize the value of these swamp lands. If a hearty young man were given 150 acres of virgin cypress forest it would take him more than a lifetime to denude it of saleable trees. It is nothing unusual for a man to cut down a cypress tree that has in it the makings of a good, comfortable one or two-roomed house, and such a tree is worth to the swamper, at rough estimate, twenty dollars.

In the parish of Livingston alone are thousands of acres of rich swamp land. It is claimed respectively by the state, by the city of New Orleans, by the city of Baltimore and by the United States. Some 200,000 acres are in dispute. Much of this land is in the actual possession of squatters, who are getting out logs and earning a very decent living. Last year the attorney general of the state collected in the Blind River district alone $10,000 or $12,000 stumpage. One squatter paid Mr. Rogers the sum of $2,800 for stumpage at the rate of one dollar a tree. This is in place of rent or taxes, but the squatters demur, saying the land is still unidenti-fied and no person has a right as yet to claim its proceeds.

For the past fifteen years the most faithful friend the Amite River people have had has been the brave and staunch little boat, the *Alice*. How many billion feet of lumber the *Alice* has carried in that time only her owners know; but she has never failed the swamper nor the farmer, and her record is a proud one, illustrating not only the enterprise of honest and kind-hearted Mr. Alexander Muir, her owner, but the thrift, enterprise and richness of that beautiful and picturesque parish which its residents wickedly refer to as the free state of Livingston.[6]

It was one soggy Monday morning when, perched on the precarious back of that vehicle known as a jumper, I and my kind guide, philoso-pher, and friend, Hon. Levi Spiller, left the quaint and flowery little town of Port Vincent, bound for the swamp.[7] It was still raining, but having an abiding faith in the old proverb, "If it rains before seven it will be dry by eleven," I had insisted on setting forth. My baggage was reduced literally to nothing, since a jumper implies only a seat and a place to rest the feet. Very sweet and peaceful the little village looked as we drove along its grassy no-thoroughfares, all gray and green, with footnotes of daffodils explaining all the nameless streets, making banks of joyous spring blooms everywhere.

We rode off into the forests, where the gray rain soaked through the gray moss, and gray, stealthy woodpeckers dashed noiselessly through the underbrush. Redbirds were perched on haw and holly. Here and there by a fallen log a wild violet delicately uncurled its purple scarf; a faint, suggestive green blush seemed tremulous in the air. The clouds drifted airily and by eleven the old weather saw was vindicated.

It was a drive of forty miles to the edge of the great swamp, a drive over a level, lovely land, with great forests of magnolia and ash and holly, with roads winding as in a private park, and beautifully ornamented by stately clusters of mammoth latania, with brown streams threading a way to the Amite River. It was difficult to realize that there is practically no demand for this land, that emigrants do not come this way, and that its riches are unknown and unadvertised, even by speculators.

Stops were made en route at the Lone Star sawmill; at Whitehall, the home of Mr. Stephen LeBourgeois, who may be called the father of the parish; at Catfish Bluff the riverside home of Mr. and Mrs. John Cleneay, who have nobly built a church and sustain a Sunday school for the benefit of themselves and neighbors.[8] It was yet afternoon, when leaving the jumper at "the Widow Collins" I first set foot in a swamp. A weary walk of half a mile over loose boards brought us to a wide, black bayou, and the pretty boat of Mr. Arthur Cornet, of Blind River, in which we were to make the swamp trip.[9]

The black water street wound in and out among the trees. The trees spread their strange, sinuous limbs and crawling roots; each one had a weird, reptilian look; the moss trailed its gray fingers, delicately dabbing them in the water; the wind whispered in the yellow rushes, and silent blackbirds eyed us from their eyries.

Forty feet overhead, in the top of a dead cypress tree, a splendid palm grew victoriously. Time and time again, as we wandered during the next three days over that wild, silent, mysterious swamp we saw palms growing in the tops of the trees—beautiful mossy pedestals of nature, with only the quiet skies and stars to note the grace and drink in the beauty.

Blind River is the main waterway of the great swamp. Up this wide, ink-black and treacherously deep river schooners and small boats come from the city in search of logs and lumber. Hundreds of swampers make here a living, and along the river, if river it can be called, so vast and lake-like are its dread and beautiful expanses, are comfortable homes built on pegs up in the air, and from which the only means of transportation is by boat.

There are families who have lived in this swamp for forty years— women who know no other home and who sicken and sigh for it, if taken away. One swamper, an intelligent German, who has lived in Blind River almost half a century, told me that a few years since he bought a fine plantation in the hill country of the state; that they faithfully tried to live on it, and gave it up to come back to their Venice-like home, where no sounds are heard save the cries of wild birds, the falling of trees, the plunge of fish in the river, or the beat of the paddle of a passing pirogue.

A swamp house will be built five or six feet up in the air on stout pegs; occasionally there will be huge logs attached to the corners, so that in exceptionally high water the pegs can be knocked from under and the house will float. Galleries run all around and raised walks lead to the outhouses. Generally a hollow cypress tree is used as a cistern. A pipe from the roof turns water into it—it having been burned out and scooped out to make it clean. Many of the women train vines about these tree cisterns and they are lovely to look upon. In front of the house the boats are chained to a small pier. There will be flatboats, a skiff for the family, and pirogues for the master and the children.

Often the mistress of the house will have a garden. A space of swamp at the corner of the house will be tightly boarded in and then filled up with laboriously collected earth. Here she raises cabbages, onion, potatoes, lettuce and always a rare red rose or two. In the dainty and charming home of my kind hostess, Mrs. Arthur Cornet, spring chickens were fattening on the porches, and in her bit of a hanging garden beautiful flowers were beginning to blow.

Fur peddlers frequent these swamps, buying furs, and one swamper told me his sales for the season had brought him $800. The valuable furs are otter, mink and coon. These cost nothing to catch, and a fine otter skin is worth to the hunter from five to eight dollars. One young swamper had just skinned two otters—which can only be caught in a trap—as we paddled up. The fat, red carcasses still hung on a horizontal bar, and the skins, as neatly peeled off as a woman would a glove, had been fitted on to boards like stockings, and set up to dry.

Shall I ever forget that longest day's swamp ride, when we started at ten in the morning and did not get back to Mrs. Cornet's and a big fire until twelve at night; when Edouard, our brawny oarsman, pulled us forty-two miles over the dead, unyielding waters of Blind River; when we visited every hospitable swamper's home in the district and ate enough to give us the colic and drank strong coffee enough to give us the delirium tremens?

What a Grand Canal it was, black as pitch, shiny as quicksilver, winding and curling and coiling its sinuous way from nowhere to nowhere! Nothing to be seen but gray trunks of trees and gray moss with here and there a green palm, and all repeated over again in the oily mirror of the water. Twenty-one miles of this—I, working in sympathy with Edouard's arms until I must have been as wearied as he said he was not.

Once in a while a mighty crash sounded like an avalanche on the Jungfrau or a cannon battle. It was a tree falling under some swamper's ax. When the twenty-one miles were accomplished we found ourselves in the logs. The river was covered. They were chained together or tied together, and were all being slowly towed up to a track, where they should be hauled off to Lutcher and Moore's mill. A boat was at work dragging logs out of the swamp. By this machinery the swamper does not have to wait for a float. A chain is run out in the swamp, a distance of a mile being possible, the log is grappled and is pulled in a few minutes out into the bayou.

"How much farther?" I asked Mr. George, my patient and gallant pilot.

"Oh, about eighteen miles," he answered cheerfully.

It was plumb dark. The moon floated in a bowl of water and glared at us sickly and mournfully. The cypress trees looked like the ghosts of monks with their cowls drawn up over their heads. Eighteen miles! Edouard must be already dead and rowing in his death-sleep. What a River Styx, with its shoreless sides, this Blind River must be. It was cold, too, and off in the forest an owl cackled with a sound like the scraping out of an iron pot. I thought about Mr. Cornet's and the genial fire, and she bustling about so heartily.

A terrible thing, black and a million miles long, plunged up out of the black water right at my side, sending its cold breath all over me.

"Sit still," cried Mr. George.

Merciful heavens, who would sit still, floating on a bit of board over sixty feet of black oily water full of monsters.

"It was only a gar," explained Mr. George.

I wished myself at home. What woman was ever such a fool I thought weakly—when all the other women I knew were at the minute seeing Sarah Bernhardt—why should I be off in a dismal swamp full of horrors and shadows and cold?

A black lightning flash showed at one side.

"What was that?" I demanded.

"Bayou Response Pas," said Mr. George. "Once, two men went up there in their pirogues and one got lost. His mate hung around all day and night hunting him and calling him, but got no answer; so ever since the bayou's been called 'Response Pas'—no answer."

"Where does it lead?"

"Nowhere."

A faint bulb of light, a sort of will-o'-the-wisp, glowed in the distance.

"That's Dutchy's," said my guide. "He lives all alone, a sort of bad man from Bitter Creek. Nobody will let him come near their houses. There was a drunken Negro drowned there the other day. He's buried just in Dutchy's garden. He hasn't got more than three inches of soil over him. Soil's expensive here. He is the only company Dutchy has."

Stealthily we crept on, black shapes in a black boat, slipping through the black night.

"Hark," said Mr. George.

Edouard stopped the boat. The water gurgled under its prow.

"What is the matter?" I whispered.

"Listen to the crazy man," was the answer.

Filling the night there came the wild voice of a man praying, crying, preaching, all in one. In that black, dismal hour this voice of one crying in the wilderness made the very flesh creep with horror.

"He lives over there," said Mr. George, pointing into the vague black where the gaunt trees crowded like skeletons, and where owls flapped their hideous wings. "He used to be in a madhouse. But he got away and lives all alone in a shanty. He keeps that up all night, but he does not often have any other audience than gars and alligators, and an owl or two."

The next night, more dead than alive, I crawled aboard the good boat *Alice*. In the middle of the night I heard some one on deck say we were just in Lake Maurepas.

I put my head out the porthole and off in the distance could see a piled up shadow of crags and ragged peaks which I knew to be the black and evil forests of Blind River swamp. I thought of the kind hearts I had found there, of the pretty floating homes, of the hospitable welcome everywhere, and I sent back swamp-ward an airy craft of good wishes. But yonder, along the track of Blind River and across the night, sailing like a pirate ship frightened from its harbor by the tooting of the *Alice*, there floated towards the sinking moon a buzzard, giving as he went to his covert under the moss, one long drawn, dismal croak. It was the voice of the swamp crying in the night.

BAYOU LAFOURCHE
PLANTATIONS

Louisiana, Catharine Cole writes in this column, is like a "priceless bit of old Delft-ware" that lies unnoticed "until some connoisseur comes along and opens our eyes to its beauty and value." She is that connoisseur who discovers along Bayou Lafourche a richness of history, commerce, and antique Southern grandeur and describes it for her readers. Her catalog of the lands and homes along the bayou is a Burke's Peerage of Louisiana's plantation aristocracy, for much of the wealth of the state is produced by the sugar fields along this waterway.

On this trip she is accompanied by her daughter, Flo, for the kind of weekend excursion she encourages her readers to take. Acting as a typical tour guide, she points out the attractions of the bayou from the comfort of a steamboat's deck. Unlike her extended, solo buggy escapades, filled with hazard and adventure, this is civilized travel, the kind a New Orleans family might enjoy for pleasure and edification. (*Picayune*, July 3, 1892)

It has always been a source of wonder to me why so few of our people, who can afford the pleasure and luxury of a two or three days' outing do not spend time and money visiting some of the beauty spots of Louisiana.

In half a dozen pen strokes I can give itineraries of many charming journeys, chiefly by water, the ideal way of traveling at this time of the year. To how many of the *Picayune's* readers has it ever occurred to make a little outing up the river Teche, or to seek a water way to Grand Isle, via the picturesque Bayou Lafourche, dotted all along its way by lovely homes and charming little towns and villages. How many fishermen have tasted the luxury and delight of angling in the still pools of Bayou Coru, that threads its way through the forests of Assumption and Lafourche, on whose banks a famous chef has his tent, his pots and pans, where, for the inconsequential sum of half-a-dollar a day he will lodge you, and, a la English lodging house, cook divinely all the fish and game you catch or kill.

Nothing is pleasanter than a small voyage from New Orleans to Lockport and return. It will be a little jaunt into an unknown land, a series of circlings around the wide fields and forests of some of the fairest parishes in the state, your affable little craft, so to speak, knocking at the door of every grand plantation home and warehouse, stopping amiably while you pay a visit of admiration to this or that sweet church, and then, beating a patient way along shore, the mossed and shiny green wheel behind, coiling up on its broad flanges the silver rope of the river, until the June day drowses off into the June night, and the end of the tether is reached at Lockport.

If you are particularly lucky you travel during this bayou trip on the steamboat *Assumption,* with her genial Captain Dodd, her handsome clerks, her incomparable steamboat rolls at breakfast and supper, her general air of comfort and hospitality, all resulting in the wish that the round trip was half a dozen days long instead of barely two days and a half.

We shall never begin to truly succeed and prosper until we acquire a pride of state that can only be acquired by informing ourselves of our possessions. We are like the ignorant possessors of a priceless bit of old Delft-ware that we hide away in a sort of dishonor on a kitchen shelf until some connoisseur comes along and opens our eyes to its beauty and value. Did we but know it, we have the greatest state in the union. It costs less to live in Louisiana than anywhere else; the climate is milder, lands are cheaper, and not even California can produce more varied, more enormous and more remunerative crops. Everything good that California is, we are that and more too, and a sort of halo of cheapness enhances our glory, for in California the price of land is twenty times what it is in Louisiana.

Bayou Lafourche, flowing contrary-wise from the Mississippi River into the Gulf of Mexico is nature's own argument in favor of the outlet theory.[1] At this present time of unprecedented high water the bayou booming in its banks seventeen feet above the level of the fields and country roads, carries off from the river enormous volumes of water.

The current is something tremendous. It sweeps along like a millrace. To ride over its surface high up in the air looking down on the earth-world as one may look out of a fifth-story window, is indeed a curious experience.

Like a silver sickle the beautiful and historic bayou cuts its way across the rich, green country, making long, sweeping swatches, clasping in its steel-white arm cane and corn, oak grove and paddock, factory and farm, church and marsh, village and lagoon, until its liquid tip touches with narrow point the salt, blue waters of the Gulf of Mexico. Across the parishes of Ascension, Assumption, Lafourche, and Terrebonne, Bayou Lafourche slips and slides and gleams and glides until it dribbles off through the sand dunes and sea marshes into the Gulf, draining on its circuitous way a country of fabulous riches, of undisturbed prosperity, of a crowded population and a most charming aspect.

From Donaldsonville to Lockport, Bayou Lafourche is almost as populously settled as St. Charles Avenue. Not an acre goes to waste, not an arpent lies idle.[2] Great fields of corn and cane roll away three and four miles deep, and between these are the forest groves in which the plantation homes are placed; while always and ever in the air tremulous betwixt earth and sky, as if suspended from the hand of an abbess, the cross of the church marks to north and south, to east and west the points of the moral compass.

The country of the Lafourche is a superb illustration of what is possible to the whole state. Here everything is tidy, well cared for, and pretty with that soft pastoral prettiness so gentle and so restful. In the clover fields dun-colored Jerseys, and Holsteins with maps of the world worked out in black and white on their sleek bellies, stand in groups under the pecan trees.

Along the levees black mountains of coal are piled against the coming of the "grinding;" corn almost disputes the supremacy of cane, and well kept homes and neat barns attest the truth of the claim that the Lafourche frames in some of the richest and best kept plantations in the South. This country, in fact, reminds me of a bit of begun embroidery such as one sometimes sees for sale in the shops. One figure of the pattern has been worked, as a sample of what the whole will be when finished. It is an object lesson full of inspiration and information, and it spells out a great prophecy, if only we are wise enough to heed.

There is no land for sale along this bayou, nor is there any land idle—not a single field between Donaldsonville and Thibodaux. Not long since a small farm was sold at auction, fetching $1,000 a front acre, making, owing to its slight depth, an average price of $100 an acre. On the plantation, cane and corn are raised. The small farmers raise plentiful crops of potatoes, yams, onions and melons, and in every garden beside the bayou's brim grow posies of roses and lilies and jasmine, olive and japonica. In one old rose garden—at Woodlawn, the stately home of the venerable and distinguished W. W. Pugh, are the two largest sweet olive trees in the state, as large as forest magnolia trees, casting their fragrance far along the coast.[3]

In fact, nothing is more charming than these rose gardens of Lafourche. They stand at the side or behind the fine old Grecian temple of a house, and in their thorny thickets the birds build, while every idle breath of wind that blows casts down into the clover a pall of petals, all snow-white and rose-red and moon-yellow, so that the green is dappled with the floral shells. It is like that old-fashioned rose garden we read of in English novels, set apart from the wide park in the midst of which the house rises like some mountain island in an ocean of green. It will be fenced off, and adjoining will be the kitchen garden; but of one thing you may be sure, nowhere else in the world can you find such chalices of bloom as lift their pale pure lips in these gardens on the bayou; nowhere else do roses blow more sweet than the roses of Lafourche.

A vague, dark shapeless cloud melting off into the nothingness of a suffocating fog—such was the beginning of the bayou country as we made for it from the river early one morning. It was five o'clock, and as we sleepily tumbled out on deck, determined for once to have the luxury of early coffee out in the open, the *Assumption* turned her nose inland, away from the river. The mist on the river, the feel of the air, touching the brow like the breath of a whispered benediction, the perfume floating out from the tall, green vase of every willow tree spelled June in all its tenderness, opulence and sweetness.

Under the stress of a faint wind the river lurched in its banks slowly, the fog floating off of it like the breath of an elephant. A mingled haze and halo, all pearl-tinged and pink-tinted; all saffron-streaked and purple-flecked, emitted about the elongating spokes of the new sun. The big bridges at Donaldsonville swung slowly to one side, like sentinels in salute, as the boat plowed past. We seemed so high above earth, almost as if poised in air. From the pilot-house I could see the bayou country far inland. It was unwrapped, like a wonderful green tapestry rug, across which, in quaint device, like a thread of tarnished silver, was looped the liquid cord of the bayou.

Here and there some grand gateway, fine as the entrance to Luxembourg Palace, but more perceptibly time-stained, showed through the trees, or the Doric column on some ancient porch sent its white shaft into the air. One could not feel that sort of Columbus inspiration that is evoked by a new country. The air of culture and completeness was unmistakable. It was the finished bit of pastoral embroidery, the figure of rural perfection in the corner of the great work that charmed the eye and made the observer long to see the whole work on the way to completion.

On Bayou Lafourche are situated some of the most magnificent sugar plantations in the state.[4] Chief among these is the famous Belle Alliance place of Mr. James Kock. From the steamboat's dock I could look out on level rows of cane and corn, each row three miles long.[5] Belle Alliance is the model farm of the South. Its owner is progressive, kind, and philanthropic—the best friend to the working people. His quarters are the best, his machinery the most improved, his fields the finest cultivated, and the whole history of Southern plantation life might be written from the point of view afforded by the Belle Alliance, whose owner proves its appropriate name by wedding next week one of the kindest-hearted, and most accomplished young women in New Orleans.

The sugar record of Belle Alliance is six million pounds, which this year it is said will be raised to eight million pounds. The Belle Terre place of B. Lehman & Bros., of Donaldsonville, is another showplace.[6] Near it is Sweet Home, belonging to Landry Dugas, owning a fine new refinery, and also an open kettle sugar house at which is made a molasses so sweet that the fabled queen of Mother Goose melodies might clamor to exchange her mess of bread and honey for it.[7]

Locust Grove is the name of the large and lovely plantation of Mr. R. B. Ratliffe, and adjacent is the pretty home of Mr. Ernest L. Monnot—Elmfield—famous alike for its beautiful daughters and superb crops. Between Elmfield and Colonel Pugh's Woodlawn is the richest wedge of sugar land on the bayou, and here also is Madewood, perhaps the largest and finest home in the state, built sixty-five years ago by a member of the Pugh family, and now the handsome property of Mr. Llewellyn Pugh, whose sugar crop is about two million pounds.[8]

Laurel Grove is the estate of Trosclair and Robichaux. George is the charming home of Mr. Charles Matthews, and on the other side of the bayou is Palo Alto, the big plantation of Lemann and Lum; St. Elmo, belonging to Mr. Ernest Barton; Magnolia to Mr. Carroll Barton, and Elm Hall to Leon Godchaux.[9] Elm Hall is a great place. This year, $100,000 worth of improvements have been added, and here is one of the finest of the sugar refineries, buying cane from a dozen neighboring planters and doing a beneficent work among small farmers and a thrifty laboring class, who by this means will speedily become independent.

Among the young planters who have acquired wealth by the sole means of hard work and a splendid pluck is Mr. Clarence Barton, who in ten years has made a fortune of $80,000 at the sugar industry. He was a college-bred lad, educated at Sewanee, Tenn., I am told, and when he began his planter's life had no capital save a young man's best capital— brains and grit. Today, his is a fine plantation, with crops excellently culti- vated. The story of this planter's success ought to thrill the pulses of every masculine failure and ne'er-do-well from Caddo to Terrebonne.

The central sugar refinery of the Lafourche is on the plantation of Senator E. D. White; nearby are Leighton, the home of Major Legarde; Raceland, belonging to Mr. Leon Godchaux; and Bushgrove, the superb property of J. W. Libby.[10] Some idea of the value of these estates can be gained from the fact that not one of them raises less than a million pounds of sugar. The land is cultivated to its best capacity; the most improved machineries are being introduced, and blooded stock is fast crowding out the Creole pony and the Creole cow. At Napoleonville, Mr. John Foley, the manager of one of Mr. Godchaux's fine places, makes a spe- cialty of Kentucky horses and Jersey cows. His herd of Jerseys is one of the prettiest sights imaginable, and in his wife's dainty dairy is made such golden butter as ought really to revolutionize the butter industry in Louisiana.

At Enola, the beautiful and picturesque home of State Senator Perkins, are preserved many memories of Henry Clay, who, when Enola was the home of Colonel Sparks, was a frequent and honored guest. Sev- eral of the fine plantations still belong to the Pugh family. There used to be current a conundrum: "Why is Bayou Lafourche like the main aisle of a church?" And the answer was "Because there are Pughs on both sides." The grand old family distinguished for its charming women and chivalric men, has somewhat died out, but the name of Pugh is a household word, and still as in the old, rich, antebellum days, the representatives dominate by virtue of their intellect, with influences all for good.

At Woodlawn, the home of the head of the family—Colonel W. W. Pugh—plantation life, according to the old regime, exists with charming effect. One may not easily forget that many-roomed mansion, the long, dim, drawing-rooms, building like the trace of perfume the memories of past festivities, the spacious halls where hospitality seems the presiding genius, while the library with its rows on rows of priceless volumes, its rare edition of Shakespeare, its volumes of Audubon, its treasures of British dramatists, is an all but perfect realization of a gentleman's library.

The charming little town of Thibodaux, named after a gallant governor of the state, is the fitting metropolis of a district like that of Lafourche.[11] When we left the *Assumption* we followed along some very neat thoroughfares until we came to a very neat hotel, where we finally came to a halt in a particularly neat bedroom, with a bed like a rosewood sarcophagus. Right opposite was a fine big jail, where blackbirds roosted gloomily above the gray battlements. Across the way was a neat, clean town hall, and in sight the stately Corinthian proportions of a courthouse.

The best managed, the cleanest and neatest town in the state is the unhesitating verdict of any visitor to Thibodaux who knows of what he is talking. The town is laid out with the regularity of a chess board. The residences, modestly retiring from the public view, wear on their gables draperies of rose and honeysuckle vine. Mockingbirds sing in every tree. The level streets are beautifully kept and flanked by deep, clean gutters. At night they are well lighted by gasoline lamps. On every street in town is a fine brick sidewalk that would be a perfect sidewalk in London or Paris, that is warranted to last a century and that, though on some streets it has been laid for forty years, shows not even one uncertain brick.

On the side streets are clean, well-kept wooden walks, so that in the rainiest weather one may walk from one end of Thibodaux to the other, dry shod. An air of neatness, simplicity and elegance, like that observable in a refined home is supreme. First-class shops and a large bank are practical evidence of progress. To these must be added a list of several factory industries, boiler works, an ice factory, two good newspapers—the *Sentinel* and *Comet*—two fire companies, a theater, churches, including the finest Catholic Church outside New Orleans, excellent schools and a refined and cultured social life.

The town is cut in two by a canal that runs from the old Terrebonne country to the Lafourche. In the old days this was the only way the Terrebonne planters had of getting their crops to market. Now, railroads render it useless, and the canal is simply a storage of water for the fire companies. The fire companies, by the way, own a large hall which they have just beautifully and elegantly fitted up as a theater. It has 400 theater chairs on the parquet floor, a comfortable gallery, windows on both sides, and really beautiful sets of scenery.

Thibodaux has a number of clubs, lodges, and societies promoting social life and benevolence. Its hardy young Society for the Prevention of Cruelty to Animals was organized by Miss Nellie Goode.[12] At this moment the young men of Thibodaux are trying to secure an elocution teacher. There is a world of suggestion in this fact. During the summer there are many towns in the state that would gladly welcome teachers of singing, painting, music, elocution, dancing and fancy work. The chief point of interest in Thibodaux is the beautiful Catholic Church, one of the richest parishes in the state, and a structure of great beauty.[13] In the recesses of the central altar is a relic of St. Valerie exhibited on her feast day. The pictures comprising the stations of the cross are superb, and the church is further embellished by ten fine statues on the altar and under the dome. The superb pulpit is a marvel of Flemish wood-carving and gives the sweet old sanctuary a kindred look to some Belgian cathedral. In the churchyard, whose green robes trail, all clover sweet, about the red-brick edifice, is erected a superb Calvary. The marble Christ on the cross, the two Marys and the St. John are more than life-size and are particularly fine and valuable.

It was more than sundown when we came in from our idle inspection of the quiet, tidy, Frenchily neat and foreignly dull town. Not a flaw had we discovered in its management; not a quibble could we find to discuss.

Over in the jail, across from the hotel, a man's voice was heard singing, "Ah, I have sighed to rest me." It was like a page out of *Trovatore*.

"Hits a big trip down to Napoleonville," said a still, small voice and an amber moon of a face slowly uplifted above the gallery rail. "The bayou is as big as all outdoors. If we don't git a move on us, we's gwine to git dumped in the mud."

The speaker was a tobacco-colored lad of ten years or less. "All right Persimmons," said we, "daybreak is not too early for us."

Somehow, there is an important, cozy sense of responsibility about getting up early to go on a long journey by carriage that nothing can dissipate. I packed our traps over night, took a last look at the barometer and finally crept like a culprit under the gloomy roof of the rosewood sarcophagus.

ASSUMPTION PARISH: MADEWOOD MANSION

Catharine Cole discusses in this column one of the often overlooked pleasures of travel—preparing for and anticipating the trip. She goes over her maps, plans her itineraries, discusses with locals the routes, roads, weather conditions, and the best hotels, then carefully packs her bags—her "traps" she is fond of calling them. She always travels with books, and these, by her own admission, are often popular novels, or maritime adventures when she and her daughter, Flo, are off "to sea"—in this case, a sea of mud.

Her almost childlike joy in getting ready for a trip gives a clue to her motivation for choosing to write about travel. During the actual journey, she is sometimes frightened by close calls and is exhausted by the hardships of long buggy rides over terrible roads, but as she prepares for a new excursion, she is once again as excited and enthusiastic as her daughter must have been when she accompanied her mother on her first adventure away from home. (*Picayune*, July 10, 1892)

Of course, we didn't start at daybreak, nor within half a dozen hours of it, but somehow to pretend that we were going to, really added a new zest to a trip that might easily have fallen to the level of the commonplace.

The night before we sailed—a perfectly appropriate term for a journey that proved to be through seas of excellent mud—Flo and I sat up quite late talking it over and, as it were, traveling it over in the air. That is, we sat up in bed, having been driven there by flocks of small snipe, whose local name is mosquito.

The grand scale on which life used to be lived is to be estimated by the magnificent rosewood and mahogany bedsteads that are still to be found here and there in Louisiana. If the second best bedstead that Will

Shakespeare left his wife Anne was like unto one of our Creole affairs, the lady did not fare so badly after all. The grand high altar of St. Peter's Church in Rome is an exact copy of one of these big bedsteads, and they are precisely like the grand high altar, so that I have no doubt St. Peter reposes well in the heart of the greatest church edifice in the world. I have seen only one more sumptuous bed than those of the old Creole families of the South, and that was in beautiful Fontainebleau, the bed of Marie Antoinette. Its half-tester was in the shape of a crown and it had no foot-board at all, the satin brocade draperies flowing over the corners in stately grace. The average Creole bedstead is six and a half by seven feet. Often the columns supporting the roof will be elaborately carved and on the sideboards will be broad steps, cushioned, on which to kneel for prayer, and afterwards to step into the downy depths.

The unsocial quietude of the trim little town, so unlike the gay hospitality of other places, like the darkness that fell on Egypt, was thick enough to be felt. Propped up by pillows, the common enemy held at bay by the cloud-like screens of bobbinet, a crisp breeze puffing in at the lattice and fetching with it the tireless song from *Trovatore* of the unknown man in the prison over the way—I fancied his was a grim humor that made him sing everlastingly, "Ah, I have sighed to rest me"—we planned our coming journey.[1] The small sea box must be packed tight, as if that would lessen its weight, and proper volumes left out to read on the way.

These naturally were books of adventure, to accentuate the flavor of what was before us. On those blissful occasions when we go to sea our reading consists of the most tempestuous and realistic of Clark Russell's stories.[2] *The Wreck of the Grosvenor* and *The Lady Maud*, for instance. To lie in one's berth during a gale and read *The Wreck of the Grosvenor* is simply money in one's pocket in the way of a frightful enjoyment.

We spread out a map and studied it. Now, a good map is an adjunct of travel not to be neglected. It enables you to see where you are. The map I carry is the topographical one of Lockett, lately reissued by the State Board of Immigration.[3] It looks like a plan of a crazy quilt—but a better array of the valuable character of our land could not be made. My own map is by this time pretty well ornamented with private marks. Most of these refer to the relative comforts or discomforts of hotels. I may say that there is a hotel in New Iberia, another in Opelousas and a third in Abbeville where the cooking is as good as one may get in Paris.

Our map showed that we were to travel up a gentle northwesterly incline to reach Napoleonville, and that the road ran beside the bayou's banks through rich alluvial lands, the best in the state, and mainly across the sugar parishes of Lafourche and Assumption.

It was ten o'clock in the morning when we drove slowly across the fine bridge at Thibodaux and struck into the country road. Just opposite the town is the pretty home-place and successful dairy farm of Hon. Taylor Beattie.[4] As we crescented along the pale green half-moons of cane fields that margin the bayou a fearful, sulfurous string of blasphemy blued the air about the front seat, where our small, yellow Persimmons was slapping the reins over his ponies.

"What on earth is the matter?" said I.

"Well, Madam, you see that blank, blank, blank of a gray will rat on the hoss."

This was equally Greek, but by and by we found out that to "rat" means to shab off your own work onto somebody else's shoulders to impose upon, and that the gray mare was an adept at ratting.

It was very pleasant rumbling along that level, country road, on one side the broad pale fields, on the other the high, green, earth wall that kept out the water. The road was not so even, either, for here and there great pits had been dug to provide earth to strengthen or build levees. These ditches of course were filled with water, and often left the roadway so perilously narrow that it was a toss-up whether we capsized or maintained in balance.

"What should you do, Persimmons," said I as calmly as I could, "if you should meet a wagon?"

"Gawd only knows, ma'am," was the comforting answer.

It is a curious thing to be jogging along away low down on the road and all at once to see a big schooner coming at you all sails set, like a big blue eagle that meant to gobble you up without a moment's warning. All at once as we turned a bend in the road a mournful cry sounded across the silence, as dismal as the note of a loon, and there shot into view, apparently swooping down on us, a big schooner with red Venetian sails puffing in the wind. In the stern sat two or three blue-shirted men, and as the sails swung aside with the luffing of the vessel, the Sicilians, all copper red, seemed limned like Italian mosaics into the soft, shadowy, red background of canvas.

Ropes and clothes, and a vast deal of cordage hung on every available pole or place, and the red sails were patched with white and gray and brown so that they seemed tattooed. She looked lovely and quite like a trawler painted by Wikstrom.[5] On her decks were piles of melons and round baskets bulging with peaches. It was Banana Joe's fruit schooner that plies the bayou, even down to the Gulf islands.

Banana Joe turned a face like a Cellini bronze, earrings and all, darkening to the water. Not long since, Banana Joe's brother was drowned in the bayou. Search was made for the body, but it was not to be found. Then Banana Joe brought out a board stuck full of lighted, blessed candles. Was ever a stranger craft set afloat on so gruesome a mission? Slowly it floated over a swirling tide, the waters whispering in its wake. Finally, it turned to an eddy close in shore and there tugging, as if at a tether, the candles burnt low, casting white gleams on the sad waters. Just before they burnt out, the water was dragged and the swollen, hideous corpse was pulled out. The blessed candles, according to an old tradition of Italy, had come to harbor above the dead man's breast.

As we passed the schooner I noticed that the sky had turned absolutely violet. It was as purple as the velvet we see on king's thrones in the theaters. The green of the trees thrown into relief against this royal sky seemed to pale in color. A gull hurrying Gulf-ward shone in the sky like a star. The children belonging to a Negro school hurried roof-ward like a flock of blackbirds. Swifts zigzagged through the air in a panic of delicious joy. Superb blackbirds, with scarlet woven into their luminous black wings, tilted on the tasseled corn that bent before the coming wind.

A great blue heron, on heavy wing, as if evolved out of the violet mist, came flopping along the roadside. His pearl-pink legs dangled awkwardly and helplessly beneath his blue feathers as he plunged clumsily to a resting place in a brown, round pool all rimmed in with cattails and iris bloom. With the purple sky overhead, the red-sailed sloop fleeting in the distance, the wind shipping furiously over the seas of cane and corn, that stately blue bird Audubon called the Lady of the Waters made a picture of unforgettable charm.

Persimmons shut us in tight and rain-proof. We could only look out from the front of the carriage as if it were the mouth of a cave. Now and then the flash of a tremendous burst of lightning lit up the carriage

depths. My small maiden cowered at my side, loudly repenting her innocent sins, while Persimmons further tempted providence with his
unique blasphemies. The horses plowed on through mud and slush,
nine times out of ten being in that position of strain that you would
think must break the harness. The violet sky was a wall of livid light, and
across it, as if written with a pencil of flame, the forked lightning spelled
its eerie message of storm and danger and disaster.

Like a train rushing through the farther end of a tunnel, we rushed
from the mud and rain into a land of dust and dryness. The horses' fore-
hoofs literally struck dust while their hind feet were still in the mud.
Even Persimmons in an excess of joy—for no one is so afraid of thunder
as a small darky—changed the nature of his vituperation of the gray
mare. We put back the curtains, and as there was no longer any danger,
recovered our courage and self-reliance. It is ever the old story of "the
devil was sick, the devil a saint would be; the devil got well, the devil a
saint was he."

At the hamlet of Labadieville we crossed the bayou in a flatboat to
the Napoleonville side, and found ourselves in Assumption parish. This
famous sugar parish is composed, over all its 327 square miles, of good
alluvial land. Napoleonville, named many years ago, not after the great
emperor, but after an early settler, one Monsieur Napoleon, is a quiet,
pretty, very French little village, strung out all in a row like country
Mary's cockle shells, along the bayou's bank. Pretty turf-clad streets,
almost no thoroughfares, in their sweet cleanliness and dewy prettiness,
run inland at intervals, and are bordered by neat homes under the shade
of remunerative pecan trees.

Napoleonville has several large stores and a good hotel; it is the parish
seat and has good schools and churches. A canal runs across the country
to the bayou and lake at the West, and along this are pleasant homes, the
corporation finally falling off into the green fields of the planters.

It was getting on in the afternoon when Persimmons drew rein at the
hotel, and we emerged from the carriage at once mud-flecked and dusty.
A ferryboat was just crossing the river. It bore a wagon, some cattle and
half a dozen of the ebony peasants of the South. An idle group of look-
ers-on stared alternately at us and the flatboat. It was long past any rural
dinner hour, but we went at once to a big, dining-room and were properly served.

From the ceiling were hung at regular intervals a series of wooden aprons fastened to the ceiling by loose hinges and from one of these descended a rope. When we were served the waiter caught hold of the rope and began to drag it back and forth, thus setting all the aprons in motion. I do not know if this antebellum arrangement bothers the flies, at least it did not seriously incommode them, but it set loose in the silence a pleasant, drowsy creak, creak, that would have put us soon to sleep had not the puller waked up enough to give us our coffee. The liquid was the ideal coffee. Sometimes I think coffee must have been invented to recompense women for not having tobacco.

To me, paraphrasing a poem of an American poet, it is the benediction that follows after dinner. As we sat over our perfumed cups unpolluted as they were by sugar or cream, the silence of the place, that peculiar rural stillness, accentuated by the creak of a country cart, the clump, clump of an oar in its row-lock, the soft splish of a well-feathered oar, seemed to take possession of us.

"Could anything have ever happened here," was manifestly the thought of my small, town-bred lassie. She looked up at the waiter.

"Perhaps," she said kindly, "you all haven't heard yet who was elected governor. We are just from the city, and if you care to know we can give you the latest returns."

My idea is that she meant this for sarcasm. It is a bit difficult for sweet sixteen to adjust itself to silence. But, if so, she got paid back. The waiter was that incongruity, a black Democrat.

"Lors, missy," he answered briskly. "You alls can't tell us 'lection news. We makes gov'nors in our parishes 'thout pendin' on de city."[6]

On the levee front just beyond the hotel and office of the brisk little newspaper of which Mrs. Dupaty is the clever head, assisted by an excellent and careful masculine editor, Mr. Shepard, stands the courthouse.[7] It is one of those Grecian stone buildings which contribute so much to the architectural beauty of Louisiana. These fine and noble public buildings are too valuable and too picturesque to be allowed to fall into ruins. They should be preserved at any cost. Their architecture is the most superb; their masonry the most solid. No state in the union has so many fine old public buildings as Louisiana, and they belong really to the history of America. Nearly every town in the state has one of these.

Just beyond the Napoleonville courthouse, is Christ Church, the Episcopal church of the parish, and one of the most charming buildings in all the South. Barring brasses and lordly tombs, it is almost a facsimile of Charles Kingsley's church at Clovelly, England. It has been a church for more than half a century. During the war, this noble building was used as a stable, and the marrings of hoof and tooth are still on the deep window ledges.

On the bank of the bayou, a mile below Napoleonville stands one of the grandest plantation houses in the state, Madewood, put there three-quarters of a century since by a member of the Pugh family. The house with its noble front resembles accurately a Grecian temple. The peaked roof of white stone rests on six enormous Ionic columns of white stone. Behind these are broad stone porches as wide as the arcades on the square of St. Mark's in Venice. On either side of the house are miniature wings. The chimneys sprout up stately, as if they were the roots that had given birth to all. The residence contains twenty rooms exclusive of servants' quarters, three wide halls downstairs, a grand staircase with picturesque landings opening out through a rounded doorway upon a broad gallery, and a dining-room that is quite half the size of the East Room in the White House.

This stately house, that has not its superior anywhere, should be the model of the Louisiana exhibit building at Chicago.[8] It stands in a noble park of oak and pecan trees. Behind the house is a rose garden, now one sweet, tangled thicket of briar and bloom, with passion flowers, purpling on the fences and four-o'-clocks opening their mild blue eyes as irrelevantly as if time were dead, and stone-crop creeping over all the tall, ruined towers of the dismantled cisterns.[9]

Beside the rose garden is the beautifully kept family graveyard. The low table graves grow all about a central monument; the grass spreads like a soft, velvet pall, and white roses rain down their fragrant petals as if they were angels telling their beads. We climbed over a stile to reach this bit of God's acre, perhaps frightening away a pretty, harmless pink chameleon taking on the hues of the crepe myrtle tree that crooned its pink plumes in the wind and shed its rose-red to mingle with the snow-white of the roses above the graves. Here were slabs into which were cut dates three-quarters of a century old. A close clinging gray moss of time had embroidered itself over the stones above these dear remembered dead. Along all the brown bayou's brim there is nothing more lovely to the eye than that quiet graveyard with its old gray table graves and its shining white tablets of Carrara, sacred to sweet memories and names.

The present owners of Madewood, young, genial and hospitable, are Mr. and Mrs. Llewellyn Pugh.[10] The plantation is finely conducted; this year, it is estimated, it will yield two million pounds of sugar. On Madewood there are old pensioners, slaves left over from before the war times. These have never left their home since they were born. Among these is an old blind woman who, in her young days, was a seamstress for the mistress of Madewood. But she hated to sew, and the story runs that with a needle she put out both her eyes. At any rate, to this day she is a pensioner of Madewood.

When we arrived to swell the number of guests at Madewood, the house party was like that at some English hall. All the long, wide rooms were superbly decorated with moss, crepe myrtle and magnolia. The great dining hall was tented over with green branches—in the niches of the great stairway were shapes of green, and through the halls, and up and down the staircase beautiful girls—innocent, frolicsome as lambs and sweet as primroses at evening time—were flitting.

At night there was a ball, and other lovely girls and gallant young men came from up and down the bayou. The bonnie young mistress who might so readily and gracefully have posed as a statue of welcome stood in the wide hall, as young, as sweet and charming as any girl in her garden of roses. I think someday, after that week at Madewood, I shall write a story and call it "A Study in Pink and White."

By and by the Bayou Lafourche Band trooped in and were given places in one of the halls. They ranged themselves out against the wall like bas reliefs done in clay, their sad Africk faces insensibly softening under the caressing croon of their own weird music. Where else but in the South could one hear such music as was played by that band of Bayou Lafourche? I am amused and yet saddened to tell what instruments they played on. To me, there is something pathetic in the mere enumeration of them. Well, there were two mouth harmonicas, a guitar and two cornets, the latter fashioned rudely out of a coil of gas pipe and a section of sugar-house pipe.

I may not describe, tried I ever so hard, the buzzing, booming rhythmic sounds that came from those odd pipes. But I may not forget the tall blonde and brunette girls, the pretty chatelaines, the winsome lassies and the lovely young matron—like roses in a vase filling Madewood with beauty. It was past midnight when I stepped out on the cool stone porch to be alone with the night for a moment. Under the trees horses ˙ impatiently neighed and pulled at their tether. All along the house wall lay a number of olive and ivory and ebony-colored cherubs. I think every little darky and Italian child in Assumption had been attracted, like a moth to an electric light, to that ball at beautiful Madewood.

TERREBONNE PÁRISH

As Martha Field prepares for yet another journey, she creates for her readers an atmosphere that makes travel something intimate, personal, and inviting—"a nice going away feel that is . . . irresistible." She loves the adventure of all new things, major and minor. Travel, she explains, is also a builder of character. Its hardships create compassion and empathy for others—a particularly feminine observation for this era.

Her destination is a turtle farm at Dulac, one of the last pieces of firm ground north of the Gulf. Her account of the capture of thousands of turtles to make soup for wealthy Northerners strikes a modern reader as a description of the worst kind of exploitation of what is now an endangered species. It is, however, in keeping with Field's constant search for new commercial opportunities for Louisiana. But even she has reservations about the viability of turtle farming when she learns that a baby turtle showed no noticeable growth in a year. (*Picayune*, July 17, 1892)

Whenever I am going away anywhere I always get up at daybreak. In this way, I see the sun rise, and also never miss a train. It is true, my train may not be leaving until sunset, but the getting up early, the rushing around after things, the throwing the entire household into a hullabaloo of excitement with dogs scampering everywhere, particularly under one's feet, has such a nice going away feel that it is irresistible. In this way I get just as much pleasure preparing to go to Handsboro, Miss., as to Genoa or the Yosemite.

I have a friend whom I predict will die of heart disease, contracted from running after trains. But there isn't any very wild pleasure in reaching a station after the train is in motion, and in throwing yourself on the rear platform as if you were a rubber ball, to sit for an hour afterwards with your heart pounding in your ears like a convict breaking rocks, or a troop of soldiers marching over a plank walk.

But this morning I *had* to get up early; there was no particular virtue in it, since my train for Terrebonne Parish left at an early hour and there is a matter of ten miles between my home and the Morgan ferry.[1] Truly enough, New Orleans is a city of magnificent distances.

After all, the great charm of life is experience, or rather, I should say, experiences. If they end all right like a proper sort of novel no one need regret them. If you haven't starved yourself, known what it was to be without bread, how can you feel for the famine sufferers of Russia? If you have had no pain yourself how can you sympathetically ache over some other's wound? I have no patience with the philosophy of those sofa-cushion sort of ladies on whom the winds of heaven have never blown too roughly, and who never have seen beyond the shadows of their own front doors.

While I was thinking this, my head was hanging out a car window at the Morgan station and the thought had something to do with the fact that a new experience was before me. At any rate, I was to go into an unknown land, and I got out my map and admired the fascinating out-lines of Gulf-girt Terrebonne, with its sea marshes and twisting bayous, its long, wallowing lakes and scalloped coast, set about by Little and Big Caillou (pronounced kigh-you), by the Timbalier and Isle Derniere, that fateful "Last Island" whose very name seems enough to Jonah it for all time.

It is a very pretty place, that Morgan Road station. The car-house is made to look like some grand old English edifice, being covered over all its walls and heavy buttresses quite to the roof, by a magnificent mantle of ivy. The yard is as well kept as any lawn on St. Charles Avenue, and beautiful flowers bloom everywhere. In a way, this station puts quite a pleasant taste in one's mouth.

On a neighboring guide post, as the train moved slowly off, I caught a glimpse of the words San Francisco, two thousand two hundred and something miles. What an invitation it seemed, that legend of the guide post, but it looked as far away as the moon when I reckoned up the modest fifty-miles I was to travel to Schriever, where a branch road would take me down to Houma.

At thought of the branch road I brightened up. Branch roads are always entertaining and sociable. The cars go slumping along in a free and easy sort of way; like as not the engine will be hitched on hind part before. The conductor will know everybody in the train but you, the passengers will pleasantly chaff each other and every stop at a station partakes of the nature of a social visit to a friendly neighbor. After that I looked around with a good deal of equanimity on the people in the sleeper who were going to make the Overland trip. It was easy to pick them out, by their huge hampers of lunch and their cretonne-colored pillows.

At this moment, the buffet porter came around with his high-priced menus. The printed list was tempting, but as an old traveler I know that the actualities resolve into beans, eggs, and sandwiches, with occasionally milk. Naturally, the menu was flung at me in the surly, sullen fashion that characterizes the behavior of almost all sleeping car porters to women who travel alone. It never enters the dense brain of a porter that a woman is good for a fee.

During that *mauvais quart d'heure* before a train arrives, while the porter solicits ostentatiously with his whisk broom to relieve travelers of dust, and silver quarters—no one adventures to offer a sleeping car porter less—he deliberately passes by the women traveling alone. Now, my sex is not mean; we can tip as generously as the best man alive, when the tip has been earned. Often, I have taken occasion to tell these short-sighted servitors that they lose money by their inattentions. It does me a sort of moral good to throw this up to them, and it also saves me many a quarter dollar.

And then I was transferred to the branch road. It is a pretty little branch road covering the fifteen miles between Houma and Schriever and it proved to be up to my ideal: social conductor, chatty passengers, engine hind part before and all. I liked it so much that I really had a pang when I learned the freight charges on this little road are really too awful and exorbitant to be endured. If things in this respect are not improved it will certainly end in the development of Terrebonne Parish being reached by means of a regular and rapid boat service via the bayous and Gulf of Mexico.

It seemed to me as we started off that I could already sniff the salt breezes of the Gulf. Certainly our route was due Gulf-ward, the feel of things was extremely southern and seacoastly. We seemed to be in a valley of prosperity—a little pale green island of cane, flecked here and there with the delicate amber of corn tassels—surrounded by a great shadowy, far off, black rim of forest.

In that forest here and there a taller cypress rose above the common hordes of trees. Its wild, ragged branches, from which flapped tatters of Spanish moss, made it look like a wrecked ship. Here and there the forest obtruded and came close to the train. It showed smooth lawns and tall trees and a jumbled array of dagger plants and latania darting obliquely out of the ground, and so like to Japanese fans that it looked as if nature had gone into the shop business, and that presently we would see Mme. Chrysanthème with "the form bent forward to make a graceful bow, that sash knotted behind in an enormous puff, those large flowing sleeves, that gown with the little train," coming to price one of the beautiful green fans, or else gather water lilies from the lips of the still pools to put in the vases at home.[2]

Every time I start off anywhere to make a real idle journey into a state that, to me, is the grandest, beautifulest, and best of all the states in the union, and when I am enjoying myself outing in my own peculiar fashion, conscience runs after me, reminding me of a duty I owe the state, as a good citizen, to tell at all times and whenever I can the wonderland story of its riches and resources, and to say my say in behalf of immigration.[3]

Now here is the parish of Terrebonne. In the old days it used to be "Lafourche Interior."[4] In my mind's eye I can see how that parish of Terrebonne has its beginning, how slowly like the ridged back of a turtle the sandy half-land rises above the level of the oyster-gray waves, how rushes grow, gray, green and hard spiked, how finally they feather into cat-tails, and iris blooms and a coarse sage brush appears, rimming the deep pools of water, and how finally bayous like broad bands of ribbon wind in and out among the rushes, showing the land is formed at last. How oak trees appear like out-sentinels, presently forests of them and finally the wide fertile fields to be dedicated to the corn and cane that are the great crops of this plenteous parish.

An enumeration of the resources of the parish will show sugar, molasses, pecans, corn, melons, figs, grapes, peaches, rice, tobacco, lumber, oysters, fish, turtle, moss, sweet potatoes, as among the chief means of making money. The total acreage of the parish is 436,980 acres, of which 40,000 are under cultivation. The assessed value of lands is

$1,644,938; of personal property $282,381. There are 72 Indian voters, 2,072 white, and 1,992 Colored voters, while the total population of the parish is 20,451, with 10,574 whites, 9,541 Colored and 336 Indians.

These suggestive figures were furnished me by perhaps the best informed man in the parish, Mr. E. W. Condon, of Houma, for sixteen years clerk of the court, who has the history, resources and possibilities of Terrebonne at his tongue's end. The average price of improved lands may be set at not more than $30 an acre. Not long since, a prominent planter sent some earth to a famous Boston firm for analysis. Their report was that it contained the very best materials for vegetable supply, and that if contiguous to Boston it would be worth $250 an acre.

"I can always tell when the yam crop is fine in Terrebonne," said a handsome gentleman on the train talking across the aisle to a neighbor. "When the crop is fine he goes to town and buys a buggy. When it's mighty fine he blows in a carriage, and when it's mighty poor, he eases off with a sulky. That's why you don't see many sulkies in Terrebonne. The yam crop never runs that low."

This becomes intelligible when we learn that sweet potatoes sell at from a dollar to a dollar and a half a barrel, and that the ordinary yield in this parish is, of the California variety, sixty barrels to the acre, of the yams thirty barrels. An acre of land that yields an income of $45 a year on so easily cultivated a crop as yams, is certainly worth more than any fabled prairie of the far Northwest.

The pretty and peaceful town of Houma, the most southern town in the state, is an ancient settlement, getting its name from the tribe of Houmas Indians who first had their wigwams on these fertile prairies, and who now survive in a few families living in palmetto huts on the bayous near the sea marshes.

Houma has a population of about 1,200. The streets are wide and grass-grown. Plank walks keep the town out of any inconvenience from mud. The courthouse is now being rebuilt at a cost of $17,000.[5] It is a picturesque red-brick building with a fine tower and a belvedere tower, and when finished will be one of the most decidedly ornamental modern buildings in the state. At the same time, the newly-organized Bank of Houma is erecting a fine building, and the Episcopalians are putting up an extremely pretty church. The Catholic church, under the care of its new and progressive rector, Rev. Father Laval, has been made new and beautiful, an artistic rectory added, and the churchyard embellished so that it really becomes one of the pretty showplaces of the parish. Houma has about twenty stores, a post office in which is located a first-rate newsstand, an excellent hotel most hospitably managed by Mr. Clifford Smith, with good schools, and two newspapers, the *Houma Courier* and *Houma World*, devoted to developing the resources of a parish that could easily be made one of the richest and most productive in the state.

Dinner, that rural midday dinner that is always so good and so wholesome, was just over and I sat by the front window of the hotel trying to adjust myself to the present order of things. I had been for a lonely ramble over the pretty town. It was as pink as Genoa with its crepe myrtle and as fragrant as the Rhine with its arbors of purple grapes. Every house seemed an incipient vineyard, and in the tawny grasses by the gray fences the petal of crepe myrtles lay heaped like a pink foam of a sea wave, or the rose tipped scallops for a seashell.

Across the way, at a livery stable, a multitude of little darkies were chaffing and loafing and waiting for orders to hitch up horses. From a room near the parlor came the droning sound of a voice that had been monotonously at it for hours. I recognized it as the voice of a drummer who was busy drumming. In the middle of the street stood a country cart piled high with melons. To me, as a stranger, it appeared an excellent advertisement of the parish resources that the average weight of those melons was thirty-five pounds. Naturally, there was a black halo of darkies about the cart, and a great bustle and sensation every time a sale was effected. The rain was pouring down in torrents. I expressed a regret.

"What can you expect," said a farmer who stood under the window and with whom I had scraped acquaintance. "It rained on St. Swithin's day. It will sure rain for forty days, so we must have patience."

A buggy came sloshing along. I knew from the very jog trot it was a doctor's buggy. Yes, on the seat were the leather saddle-bags. I could fairly smell the calomel. God bless those country doctors, not for their calomel, with which, thank Providence, they have not as yet salivated me; but for their politeness, their patience, their culture, their hospitality, their intelligence. With how many a one have I not been doctoring; what recollections I have of Caruth of Pointe Coupee, of McKittrick of Baton Rouge, of Sexton, then of Wesson, Miss., now a professor at Tulane; of Pugh of Lafourche and Perkins of Feliciana. I cannot imagine a better way to study a parish than to go a- doctoring with the favorite parish physician.

Next door a horseman was emptying a sack of dried shrimp into a big homemade basket. They smelled saltily of the sea.

"Gooda," said the Italian vendor as I drew near. "They first we gotta dis year. Gooda, cheap-a."

The great pink crescents lay piled high, emitting a salty, fishy smell. I did not care for them, but somehow they made me long for the sea marshes, and I fell to thinking on the land as it dribbles off into the Gulf; of the widening bayous, where the redfish come to be caught; of the long, dun-colored sand dunes, where the Malays leave their shrimp camps, where they set up big kettles like open sugar kettles, under which they light fires of wreckage, in which they parboil the pale gray trophies of seine and net until they turn rose-red. They then spread the shrimps on the sands and dry them in the hot, tropic sun until they are fit to sell in Houma or ship to China, where millions of shrimps are sent each year from Louisiana.

I wonder what it is in me that irresistibly draws me seaward! Why, the very sound of a conch is enough to set me thinking on a voyage; the smell of shrimp makes me long for a sail around Little Caillou. It must be that I had a sea king for an ancestor. Did not a fortune teller tell me not long since that when I am ninety years old I am to nearly lose my life at sea?

Somehow, everything else in pretty Houma paled beside the pink fires of those sun-dried shrimps. I could think of nothing but the islands where they were dried until the very moaning of the storm wind howled lonesomely in my ears.

At that moment a little lad came in with a basket woven of cane on his arms. He was like a little mannequin cut out of nicotine-stained meerschaum. I said as much, in other words, to my pretty hostess, Mrs. Clifford Smith.

"No wonder," said she. "He was saved from the storm of '88.[6] When my sister found him he was eating raw crawfish and live shrimps. My mother adopted him and today little Emile, of whom so much was said in the newspapers, comes to us not with a message of the sea, but with a basket full of the purple grapes of Terrebonne."

And she lifted into my lap a huge cluster of grapes, whose perfume was like willow buds; but little Emile, like the nicotine-stained image of meerschaum, forlorn little flotsam of the sea, leaned out at the door and smelled hungrily at the dried shrimp on the barrel top at the Italian shop.

Almost every intelligent Louisianan has heard of Southdown plantation, the estate of Mr. H. C. Minor, which has been one of the great plantations of the South for nearly a hundred years.[7] The noteworthy place is really a most typical plantation home. The big plantation house, with its wide hall and large rooms, its broad galleries and richly-carved colonial furnishings, is indescribably lovely. On the walls are portraits by Gilbert Stuart and Jarvis; in the oak cabinets are treasures of Delft-ware and Sevres, of old English and Willowware, of quaint silver and priceless crystal, that may never be replaced.[8]

The kitchens and house servants' quarters are near. At a distance are the stables and barns, and still further off, but connected by telephone, the sugar-house with its own colony of quarters and boarding houses or "hotels" for the extra men needed during grinding.

Such a plantation is like a little village. It gives regular employment to 150 men. These are paid by the day. If they have families they are allowed a house to live in, enough land for a garden and the use of a mule and plow, or a mule to draw fuel from the forest. It has been said that it takes thirteen months in the year to cultivate a sugar crop. This year the rain keeps the hands idle. But they cannot starve, and so the planter must make work for them. He must give them wood to cut, fences to mend, bridges to fix, machinery to clean.

Perhaps, roughly guessing, the payroll on a place like Southdown during the rainy summer months, before the cane is "laid by," will be $450 a week. During grinding this working population is swelled to 500 souls, and if all goes well the crop will be five million pounds of sugar.

On the lawn at the rear of Southdown House is an improved "scratcher" for stock. It is made of latania and cross-boards, was invented by Mr. Minor, the genial and accomplished owner of these vast fields, and is a humorous but real blessing to the stock that patronize it.

Once I stayed a week at a western farm. The farmer tilled 500 acres of land. He worked like a Trojan; so did his family. I can never get out of my mind the ache of those weary women, who cleaned, milked, cooked, churned, sewed, scrubbed, and who had no time to live, to think, or to be. A dimmed remembrance of that farm life in the blizzard country came back to me as we sat that night at supper in the big dining room at Southdown House, where no one was so much at ease as the beautiful and charming hostess. Books, magazines and newspapers were everywhere; an open piano, an organ and flowers gave further evidences of taste. The mistress had shown me her kitchen, pantries and dairy. Surely, life is at its best on such a sugar farm as Southdown and in such a refined and cultured home as Southdown House.

"Well, if you go, I only hope you won't drown."

The speaker was the genial host of Smith's Hotel. The person he addressed was me, huddled up in the corner of a buggy, while a mahogany-colored lad of fifteen years held the reins over a tall red horse, got up as regards tail and mane for wet weather.

Twenty miles south of Houma, at almost the extreme point of real solid land in the state of Louisiana, one of the most progressive, intelligent and prosperous men in the state has his home, store, and farm. This gentleman, Mr. Frederick Lottinger, has located himself on the broad prairies and salt water marshes of southern Terrebonne, with the Bayou Terrebonne clasping his lands and giving him a cheap and easy transportation for his crops and produce to the city.[9]

Before the war this was the Pelton plantation, and was the extreme point of sugar culture in the state.[10] Indeed, this is so today, and there are croakers who contend that sugar cane never grows sweet on these wide saltwater marshes. The old Pelton house must have been in its day a fine affair of red brick, with great fireplaces and large, hospitable rooms, the whole set in a grove of orange trees. But now the house, all tumbled and worn, is a public schoolhouse, the most southerly in the state, and the salt winds from off the marshes have worn the bright-red bricks into the most curious shapes—just as water wears into gnomes and elfs the limestones in a cataract.

It was twenty miles between Houma and Dulac, the home of Mr. Lottinger, for which we were bound. Twenty miles of blinding rain that wet us to the skin, that blurred our outlook, but was still not wet enough to dampen my interest. We rolled the tarpaulin high up before the buggy, but still the rain came rushing in, half-drowning the forlorn little darky driver, who like all darkies, could stand neither cold nor wet. It brought with it a swarm of mosquitoes that if I tried to describe would imperil my veracity as a newspaper correspondent.

The wind boomed and howled around the vehicle with a chill, depressing Novembery howl that sent my mental barometer to the lowest ebb. For the full twenty miles we had the rain in our faces, the cane fields on our left and the swamp at our right. The horse plowed on bravely through mud up to his knees. Now and then a water moccasin swished out of the way, and once a long, black thing, twisting and squirming, got tangled up in the wheel and went whirling around until it was beaten into a shapeless mass.

Often we met small boys, knee deep in the watery roadway, catching with hand nets crawfish for the Sunday dinner. Could life be easier than in a land where the small boys take to the public roads to collect the material for such a feast as might surfeit a king?

How it stormed! Surely, every bolt of thunder seemed to be making a dead set at the buggy. I saw Charlie surreptitiously crossing himself. Certainly the sky was enough to give one the blue devils. Suddenly a cow jumped up in the swamp by the road; our good Sam, whose nerves, like mine, were already strained to the breaking point, jumped and plunged furiously, and managed to break the shaft. No woman on earth could be expected to endure more. I climbed down into the water up to my knees. A moccasin snake slipped over the instep of my low-quarter shoe. I think my ebony driver thought that between the storm, the snake and the broken shaft, I was going to faint.

"Charlie," said I sadly, "do you think we can get anything to eat over there?"

"Lord a massy, madam, I'm glad youse coming too. Of course we kin git grub ef we kin pay for it," said Charlie, as he groped around in the storm's semi-darkness, mending the harness and soothing the horse.

I wish some of our detractors had been along. I wish they had seen with me that clean, contented plantation cabin home where Charlie and I had hot corn soup, corn bread and black coffee fit for the emperor of the French. A parlor could not have been cleaner and surely no bouillon could have tasted as finely as did that corn soup served in a yellow bowl and eaten over an open fire of cypress logs in a cabin home on the banks of brown Bayou Dulac!

I had traveled twenty miles in order to have a look at Mr. Lottinger's terrapin farm. Six months ago, Mr. Lottinger, who owns a plantation on the edge of Bayou Dulac, established a terrapin farm. He fenced in a section of shell banks, sea marsh and bayou and then began to buy the diamond-back delicacies, those famous terrapins which millionaires are always willing to pay as high as $200 a dozen in order to provide their ball guests with terrapin stew.

Mr. Lottinger has been buying diamond-backs at the rate of $4.50 a dozen. He now has penned up no less than 5,550. These are fed two times a week on small fish, sardines, etc., and as they are very fat and frisky will probably be sent to market this winter.

The terrapins are only to be caught during the egg season—May and June. Then they come out on the sand banks when the fishers, after they have laid their eggs, catch them either by hand or with nets. Sometimes, near breeding time, fishers seine near the banks for them and catch a great many. When a terrapin is going to lay eggs it crawls up on the bank, provided no enemy is near, and with her fore-paws, using them alternately, digs a funnel-shaped hole in the ground. Then she sits over this and drops in one of her soft-skinned eggs, then another and another.

Occasionally she stops the process of laying to properly place the eggs. Her litter of eggs, from ten to twenty, is laid in one day; the time occupied is never more than an hour. Then she scratches the earth over the eggs, flaps it down tight and goes away, leaving the earth and sun to do the rest. The greatest enemies are snakes, and Mr. Lottinger has killed in his pen many reptiles that were too manifestly nosing after eggs.

Mr. Lottinger has so far been able to obtain no statistics concerning the age of terrapins. A dead one, found in the pen, that had just laid a nest of eggs, was found to be full of eggs, presumably these were for next year. An experiment made with a diamond-back raised from the egg showed that it had not perceptibly grown in a year. If this is so, it will certainly place limitations upon terrapin farming.

In addition to his diamond-back turtle farm, Mr. Lottinger has converted his sea marshes into an admirable stock farm, where the average weight of his two-year-old beeves is 800 pounds, easily sold in the Houma market at $17 and $18 a head. This, without any expense of feeding, is indeed a capital investment for money.

It was nine o'clock at night. Still the rain poured down in torrents. I and my hospitable hosts of Dulac plantation, Mr. and Mrs. Lottinger, sat in the wide hall of their pretty home. The wind threshed through the grand old oak trees in the yard before the house. The cattle on the prairie marsh howled dismally. The rain, like a fog, melted into the tree tops, and at that moment a wild cry filled the silence of the night as wind fills a sail at sea.

"In heaven's name, what was it?" said I, a little awed anyhow by the silence and farawayness of the place, by the mournful wheeze of mosquitoes, the low of a cow, the whine of a dog.

Again the eerie sound crossed over the night.

It was a conch shell blown by a luggerman. He had come up the bayou in search of shrimp and redfish, which he would catch and dry to ship to China.

Truly, Terrebonne, sending its delicate sugar to sweeten the chocolates of European princes, sending its rice to Manitoba, its tobacco to Maine, its shrimp to China, may be said to touch the limits of the universe.[11]

Somehow, next morning, as I rode along its wide country roads, where Sam plowed knee deep in the country roads, where the blackbirds rose in the air like rubber balls tossed from the hands of a magician, I could not but think that neither Dakota nor California could yield better returns than Terrebonne, with its cane fields and its fabulous fishing grounds and terrapin farms.

MORGAN CITY: A COUNTRY WEDDING

In the course of her wanderings through Louisiana, Catharine
Cole met with varying reactions when she showed up unannounced
in thinly populated parishes, usually accompanied only by a boy
buggy driver. At the mansions of the plantation aristocracy she was
greeted with the hospitality afforded well-born ladies. In small towns
on the road, women welcomed her as a popular writer to be admired
for her pluck. Men were often a problem for her, however, particularly
working-class men.

In this column she is rebuked by a black porter for her feminine
indecision, and insulted by a newspaperman, who would be expected
to be sympathetic to a fellow news writer in search of an interesting
story. He refuses to acknowledge her as a working journalist, capable
of enduring the hardships and discomforts that come with the job.
A Southern man, she concludes, will not accept that a woman can
endure "mosquitoes, grease, and other discomforts when in the
pursuit of useful knowledge." It is a lament repeated throughout her
writings.

In this episode she travels by canoe through the marshy waters of
Grand Lake to attend a Cajun wedding on one of the islands in the lake.
She is readily accepted as a guest, and she in turn idealizes the primitive
lives of these moss gatherers, fishermen, and farmers, describing them
as Rousseauistic nobility. Country maids are "beautiful, buxom lassies,
with eyes like black stars and cheeks like pomegranates," and rustic
violinists are "like two portraits by Rembrandt." Field typically
views the rural Louisiana subjects of her writings through lenses
coated with rosy tints of nineteenth-century romanticism. (*Picayune*,
July 15, 1888)

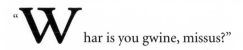

"**W**har is you gwine, missus?"

The speaker was an old shiny-faced white-wooled, black-skinned Negro baggage-master standing on the baggage shed at the Morgan Depot in New Orleans.

The morning was hot and the steaming locomotives, the creaking freight cars, the noise of tumbling trunks, bags and boxes, and the general din and uproar of the river added to the heat and my dismay. Over under the long lines of trees on Esplanade Avenue things looked cool and peaceful, and down on the yellow river—that morning as yellow as the Tiber—the wind flipped the white and brown sails of the blue-bellied melon boats and sent the smoke of the tugs puffing and curling across the water.

Across the river a rim of willows made a harsh, bright green band of color. A steamer with an honorable crust of salt high up on her red smokestack moved silently upstream toward her berth. In the railroad depot passengers were collecting, buying tickets, consulting maps and trooping on board the big transfer-boat that was to convey us all over the river to the waiting train.

Time was nearly up—"all aboard" had been cried—but I still sat dubious on the lid of my tin box trying feebly to make up my mind where it was best for me to go.

"Fo' Gord, Missus, where is you a gwine to, honey?" said the old baggage-master, anxiously fingering my English "box," and trying covertly to "histe" me off of it. I looked up into his black face, and smiled at him in a friendly fashion.

"I'm going for an outing in Arcady. I'm going in search of happy islands, where the shells are white as the shore. I'm going to find out where the sea gull lays her eggs. I'm going to hunt the white crane and the big pelican and the lost Evangeline," said I slowly.

"Does you want to go to Morgan City?[1] Then you kin take de boat and go up de bayou right smack to de place," and before I knew it I was off that tin box and on my way to the boat with a brass local check in my hand.

It is not wise to romance with an old darky baggage-master, and he being used to the vagaries of lone women travelers; it served me pretty much as I deserved. It is not in the masculine mind to calmly endure a woman who is subject to indecision.

Years ago, Morgan City was a great shipping port, but when the Great Southern Pacific Road was completed and the daily line of steamers to

Texas was discontinued, the brisk little town on Tiger Island, whose country roads are waterways and whose country carts are pirogues, and sloops, and luggers, and skiffs, began to fall off.² Now the pretty little place, with its wide, grass-grown and unfrequented streets is waiting for the new boom that some day is certain to overtake it.

Some time ago, an enterprising man came to Morgan City, put up a little flatboat warehouse on the bay, tethered it to the white shell heaps on the shore and went extensively into the catfish trade. The fish were brought to him daily by the thousands, skinned, cleaned, packed in ice, and shipped by the carload to Texas and the far West where they are sold and eaten as the best tenderloin of trout. In the summer this trade naturally languishes, but it is certainly suggestive of a lucrative industry.

Three or four wide, rambling streets, shaded by beautiful trees; some sweet homes, and rows of shops, and big, well-stocked stores, several pretty churches, a couple of dingy, gabled-roofed hotels, a sash factory, a newspaper office, a custom-house, the oyster packeries, and the railroad offices, etc., make up all I had seen of Morgan City after an hour's ramble.

Go in whatever direction I chose from the hotel, I invariably found myself seeing the beautiful bay, and looking with longing eyes upon the green schooners, the lazy oyster boats tied up for the season, and the two or three lumbering, old, black sailing boats, of whatever kind, that tumbled about in the bay, pulling at their tethers fretfully. Here and there an Italian sailor and fisherman was lolling on his little deck, or hanging his blue shirt out to dry on his white sail. A nipping, sweet delicious salt wind rushed up from the bay. I could taste it on my tongue, and feel it in my hair. It blew in ceaselessly and made one forget the hot sun overhead and long for the happy islands where the shells are white on the shore.

Over in a big job-printing office where the Morgan City *Review*—a very good paper—is edited and published by a very good man, I found Mr. Jolley the editor and told him in substance the rash assertions I had made to the baggage master at home.³ As I chanted them over, my host shook his head solemnly.

"You can't go there," said he when I suggested Last Island, *Isle Dernière*.

"Belle Isle?"

"Mosquitoes will eat you up."

"Vermillion Bay and Abbeville?"

"Boat just gone."

"St. Martinsville and the Teche?"

"Boat left an hour ago; be back next week."

"What's the matter with taking a timber-boat and going out into the swamp after a raft of logs?"

"Boat's too greasy. You can't go in that dress—mosquitoes will eat you up. Besides, the boat has just gone."

It is too bad, but it is impossible to get a Southern man to realize that a woman may not mind mosquitoes, grease, and other discomforts when in the pursuit of useful knowledge, and that it may not be convenient or possible for her to sit on a cushion and sew a fine seam and feed upon strawberries, sugar and cream.

The day, or all that was left of it, crept along slowly. I sat up in the parlor of the hotel, in lonesome state, and read the poems in the autograph albums belonging to the bonnie daughters of the house. Occasionally there was a passer-by—a handsome man, exquisitely dressed in white linen, a tropically-looking Colonel, as if freshly arrived from the Indies. Once or twice, when the poems began to indigest, I ran across the railway, or under it, to a big drug-and-book store and bought me a magazine or a novel or an illustrated paper.

Talk about being lost in London or in some occidental desert! It was nothing compared to the charm and novelty of being lost in Morgan City. Silent? It was like some all-but-deserted village save for the knocking of hammers where a new building is going up, the cry of a passing fruit peddler, or the song of some fisherman down in the bay. It was like some tiny Venice—water all around—and there was an unmistakable charm on being in a town where neither carriages nor carts of any description are seen, save those in use by the merchants and carriers of the town.

The exits and entrances of Morgan City are all by waterways; the farmers living on the island, or up the bay on any of the islands, get to town in boats, and carry their splendid melons, potatoes, corn and other vegetables to market in boats. It was plain that if the boats I wanted were all gone, they must come back again—no matter what Mr. Jolley said— so I arranged my room to give it a lived-in look, put out my belongings and prepared to wait with a faith that nothing might disturb, hoping in the belief that before long something would turn up.

That was two days ago, and since that time I have been to a wedding in Arcady, and have seen the meeting of the waters, where the brown Teche flows into dappled Atchafalaya, and have had a boat trip up the American Thames to New Iberia and back again.

It was four o'clock in the afternoon when, in company with the judge and the judge's charming wife, I stepped into a boat and we set out for Three Islands—those lovely, densely forested round islands lying in Grand Lake, half a dozen miles away from town. Beside the oarsmen, our own party and a small lad, we carried the bridal bouquet, a barrel of beer and a sack of ice. The sun shone hot and the reflection from the cane fields of the famous Pharr plantation, where, it is said, the frost never falls, hurt the eyes.[4] A stiff wind came whipping up, and now and then the lips of a tawny wave curled over the side of our shallow craft.

A huge, heavy-winged bird or two floated overhead; down in the bay an occasional water snake swam past us. On the distant shores, for the waters widened as we went, were dense swamps; a splendid mingling of gray and green and brown. The air was delicious with the scent of the willows, floating over this broad expanse of water; the luminous blue bending above us, the circle of forest closing about us, the soft salt wind refreshing us, was a pleasant way of getting rid of a July afternoon. It was better than Waukesha or Saratoga, and quite as good as Colorado. Now and then we saw a "dugout" tethered in the shade under the willows and an old darky catfishing for his supper, or we heard a crash in the forest and presently could see a moss-gatherer at his gloomy task.

He goes into the swamp where it is alive with reptiles and pulls the moss from the trees. In order to cleanse it, he digs a hole in the ground and buries it. In a month the outer gray covering will be rotted away; he then digs it up, shakes it free of dirt and its own refuse and carries it to town where he can sell it for about a cent a pound. There is an old saying in this country that when a Negro wants meat he goes down to the bayou and traps a "cat," when he wants fuel he cuts him a log, and when he wants bread he pulls a bunch of moss off a tree, takes it to the nearest country store where he exchanges it for a loaf. Surely, life is easy in this country, too easy by far.

The sun was down, and the red and purple afterglow made the dimpling expanse of Grand Lake gleam like a Mexican opal. Just ahead of us, a mile or two away, the graceful outlines of the first of Three Islands could be seen. Its giant trees all strung with moss, lifting their cypress crests high in the sky, looked like huge clusters of giant ferns. They were limned against the delicate semi-green and yellow of the sky like the beautiful sprays we find in amber or agates—enameled as it were into the matchless purity of the blue, and yellow, and silvery shield of the midsummer sky in Arcady.

No roofs were in sight, nor a friendly pennon of smoke, but from all parts of the lake, starting forth as it were from the haunts of the hunted alligators, were strange craft, all apparently in chase after us, and rapidly closing around us. A curious rigger or socket was fixed up in each boat and a man stood up rowing at a great rate, his body moving at his task as a wash-woman's does over her board. Each oarsman was bareheaded and in his shirt sleeves, and the spectacle of all these boats scudding towards us, the white shirts shining in the sunset, the wind puffing the sleeves full like sails, was as curious as pretty. These were all guests hastening to the wedding. By and by we overhauled a big schooner laden with people, and then, as darkness closed about us, a deft stroke or two turned us into shore and we landed at the island.

Here were two or three schooners and luggers, a big black vessel called the *Spectre,* her sails hanging idly like broken wings of a sea gull. Here were a dozen or more canoes and skiffs, and on the bank walking about, playing at such games as pole-jumping and distance leaping, were scores of manly, sturdy, sun-burned young men. Two or three neat houses faced the water, and in one we could see billowy, moving masses of white, and pale-colored fabrics, showing that it was full of women.

"Really, my dear," said the handsome judge to his wife, "I ought to have worn my dress coat"; and I do not think he got over regretting it all evening.

It was a simple home; but we were made welcome with a hospitality that would have been royal in a palace. The floors, ceilings and walls were all of oak and cypress, and under the soft glow of the lamps and candles the beautiful colors and grain of the woods made the bare rooms grateful to the eye. Chintz curtains hung at the doorways, and behind one of these, in a room, a bevy of girls were dressing the bride. In the largest room, someone ranged chairs along the wall and covered a table in the center with a white cloth, and presently, hand in hand, in a pretty, old-fashioned way, the young bridegroom and bride and their attendants came trooping forth.

What candid, kind young faces those were, uplifted to the judge's own; how sincerely and simply they answered "yes sir," to all the questions put them; how pretty it was to see a big sister of the bride standing behind her like a gingham-gowned guardian angel dutifully fanning the couple all during the ceremony; how pretty the bride looked in her finery of lace and ribbons, I need not tell.

"And so they were married," and out in the big kitchen, at a long table islanded all over with pound cakes, elaborately decorated with sugar lozenges, the first of the feasting began, or not the first, for during the day there had been a great dinner at which were several dozens of chickens and turkeys and a roast pig.

Guns hung on the amber-hued wooden walls, and hunting bags and horns; pink-lipped seashells propped open the doors. The patriarch of the family sat in his chair in the corner, and when one wanted to drink the bride's health one dipped a ladleful of creamy milk from the generous crocks that stood on the corner shelf. Time went on, and by and by the young bride went up and kissed her old grandfather goodnight, and then hand in hand, like couples in a minuet, the bridal party and all the guests went down the steps and across the pasture land to the new husband's home where the "infair" was to be held and where more than a hundred guests were already assembled.[5]

The star-powdered sky was like a fabric of blue and gold, the island opposite was like a blot of black enamel, the lake was like a veiled mirror and the sloops and schooners at the bank were like ghosts of boats. The very thinnest rim of a moon was in the sky; it looked like a worn out wedding ring. Across the blurred field the ghostly procession filed slowly; the white veil of the bride floated out on the breeze and made it appear that she skimmed over the earth.

The partitions were not all up in this new house, and the oak rafters in the roof were like those in some old Swiss farmhouse. The front of the house, thus left in one large room, was bare of furniture save for improvised board benches along the walls. In a corner upon a high table, seated on chairs, were two fiddlers, playing away mightily and most sweetly a dreamy, crooning, bee-buzzing, katydid, croaking, mimic-toned tune that was wondrously sweet to hear, and made me think of

Mrs. Pemberton-Hincks when, with her glorious eyes caressing you, she sings her Spanish song with its strange refrain, beginning "lal, lal, lal."[6]

Over the lintels of door and window, candles were placed; around the room were beautiful, buxom lassies, with eyes like black stars and cheeks like pomegranates; mothers, with plaits of black hair that rival in splendor a duchess' coronet, hushed their babies and reminisced about their own wedding days. The musicians, two fine-faced fellows with tawny mustaches, drooped over their violins, sawing out the crooning melody, keeping time on the table with their feet. Up under the flaring candles they looked like two portraits by Rembrandt.

In the center of the floor the young ones were dancing a pretty dance, as only the French can dance. Arm in arm, the couples would whirl along and then suddenly as the crooning music deepened, the youth would slip his arm about the girl's waist—hers went up over his shoulder—and like young lambs in springtime, with a joyous, graceful motion they would skip side by side across the room. Nothing could have been prettier, and when we came away, long past the midnight hour, and took our canoe for the homeward trip, I carried with me the imperishable picture of that "infair." Of the pedestaled musicians sawing away in the corner; of the burly dance director calling out, "Swing to your right, sashez all around. Do-re-do, swing corners. First fo' forward." Of the wide-eyed belles and trim gallants, of the myriads of children and their few mothers, of the young bride skipping down the room on her husband's arm.

Chickens were crowing for morning when we stumbled over the shells of the wharf at home, and as one toiled up the dewy street the judge's wife, remembering the Three Islands, said to nobody in particular, "And so they were married."

ST. MARY PARISH

Catharine Cole visited the town of Franklin shortly after its most famous citizen, Murphy J. Foster, had been elected governor in a hotly fought contest. She was welcomed as a guest at the Foster plantation house, for her name invariably gave her entrance to the homes of the state's elite. Except for their attention to women's issues, Cole's columns are usually free of political references, and this one is no exception. It is clear, however, from this and all of her other interviews with Louisiana's politicians, that she is comfortable with the state's so-called "Bourbon" oligarchy, the group of planters, bankers, and businessmen that maintained a tight control over the state during the post-Reconstruction era until the arrival of the populist Huey Long. Martha Field loved to cast a line and enjoy her catch, but one suspects that the Kingfish would not have been to her taste. (*Picayune*, July 31, 1892)

S t. Mary Parish is a scroll-shaped treasure of land and water that lies southwest of the Mississippi River, and whose richest portion contributes to form that wonderland of Arcady known as the Teche country. The parish is distinguished almost above all other sugar parishes by its beautiful and numerous plantations. It possesses at Franklin the largest and finest sugar refinery in the South, the Caffery Refinery, erected a year ago by Mr. John A. Morris, on the Don Caffery plantation, Bethia, at a cost of a million dollars.[1] It has added enormously to the sugar culture on St. Mary. Now, every little farmer within hauling distance knows he can sell even an acre of cane at the refinery. This establishment will this year make ten million pounds of sugar.

St. Mary Parish is in a political sense the banner parish of the state this year; our gallant Governor Foster having been born and raised near Franklin, now has his pretty home on the Dixie plantation, one mile from town.[2] Hon. Don Caffery, one of the most popular and genial gentlemen in all southwestern Louisiana, has also his home in Franklin in a fine old colonial residence.³ Another prominent and well-beloved citizen is Col. John A. O'Niell, parish Treasurer, an influential politician, a man of general popularity, with a stainless record, who has made his home in St. Mary parish for much the best part of half a century.⁴

There had been a heavy shower and the sky had that clean-washed look of brilliant blue, with soft white balloons of vapor hanging low over the forests, when our train slowed up for Morgan City. Morgan City belongs to St. Mary. It is its seaport, and formerly great ships entered here via its Atchafalaya River and Bay. The storm of 1888 and last year's fire swept the town like newly-appointed scavengers, and since then new and handsome brick buildings have been erected, with many charming homes, to give the place a tidy and progressive air. Here the river is almost half a mile wide, and the fine bridge over it—it is now called Berwick Bay—rests on pilings eighty feet deep.

The Baron Natili, the genial raconteur and bon vivant, who keeps up a private terrapin farm, and whose entertainment of strangers is always as unique as it is hospitable—who fixes up pie-eating matches and cake walks highly colored for their amusement, has here his pretty home. The bay shore of the little island city—for Morgan City is on Tiger Island— is lined with catboats, luggers and schooners, and in all the handsome stores are the signs of a seaport: pink conch shells, alligator hides; cups of carved coconut, skins of shark and pouches of pelicans.

It is here the merchants ship fish to the far West, and white aigrettes and gray- plumaged terns to Paris. The railroad is placed on a high trestle far above the town, and as we look down beyond the pretty station-house we see pink-plumaged parrots from Brazil, balancing like bird acrobats on their hoops, hammocks to tempt the seamen, a child cradled in the big, scaly, yellow shell of a sea-turtle, and Sicilian fishermen passing, lank and long-legged, calling out their wares of dried shrimp and jewfish. Given a capital of five dollars, any lad who chooses to fish for a living can easily earn it if he casts in his fortune with this pretty, progressive seafaring town of Morgan City.

And then the train skims over the big red bridge and cuts a sort of pioneer path through the forest. Could anything be lovelier than this wooded wilderness of Arcady? Earth, got from somewhere, has been thrown up in high levees broad enough to hold the railway. On either side the forest spreads. The swamp waters are brown and in the sun, luminous with light. All is silence; the very caw of the rook or the flight of the redbird seems but a lost chord in this harmony of nature.

The train shoots out with electrical effect into the high ground and farming land of St. Mary. On either side are broad fields of rich pasture land. They are knee deep in tawny, sweet-scented grasses, and are dotted here and there by clusters of trees, that under the haze of a hot sun have the hazy, floating appearance of oases in a desert. Trim board fences in good order cut these pastures into paddocks. Blooded cattle, sleek, combed Kentucky horses, dappled Holstein, amber Jerseys and speckled Alderneys lift their pretty heads and stare after the train. Under a grove of oaks the huge outlines of a plantation home gleam cheerily. The house fronts towards the train, and if its front and back hall doors are opened we look on a silvery wedge of Bayou Teche that flows behind the house, so close that it presents the curious appearance of being a looking glass framed in by the plantation doorway.

You know that this is a famous parish for milch cattle and for good horses. Why, the state's chief executive makes a specialty of blooded stock, and you view with interest the scampering herds, or the blue-shirted man letting down the bars, over which the soft-eyed milking cows step docilely and file away under the trees until the farthest one, lost in the distance, seems no more than a little red figure out of Noah's ark.

I think the parish statistics give 40,000 barrels of rice as the crop for last year. That means more than a quarter of a million dollars, and a prettier crop was never grown. Six men can cultivate 300 acres of rice. When the land is plowed it is sown broadcast; after it is well out of the ground it is flooded with water, and its after-culture, save once going over for weeds, is merely a series of floodings. A rice plantation is cut up into squares like a checker-board, with deep ditches. The water is pumped up into a flume by means of an engine, and let off into the fields, where it can be fastened in by wooden gates across each ditch.

It is kept at a uniform depth of two feet, perhaps, and at intervals is run off to the next field. Just before harvesting the fields are dried and the ground becomes hard enough for the horses and mowing machines. Rice harvesting begins early in August. The ripe crops are as lovely to the eye as wheat. Rice culture is almost clear profit, and in a rainy season, when nature politely floods the fields, the expenses are materially reduced.

One of the oldest and most aristocratic towns of the fabulous Teche country, the pretty little town of Franklin, the county seat of St. Mary, issues its invitation card at the depot of the Southern Pacific, that great railroad that has the peculiar taste to keep on to California, but which at least makes up for it by coming back again. About in the heart of the parish, Franklin is at once on the railroad and on the brim of Bayou Teche. Its wooded shores slope as gentle as the meadows of Warwickshire do into the Avon down to the lapping, storied, limpid pools of the Teche. The great oaks lean waterward to regard themselves in its broad mirrors, and wild briar roses adventure mighty near, as roses are not wont to do.

And then, like a wonderful scroll, all illumined, and with marginal notes of bloom, all thick set with Cherokee hedges and rice, with may-pops that come in September, playing a game of greenball through the fences, the fertile fields roll up and away from the picturesque river. With stretches all carpeted in the sober shades of cow peas and yams, these fair and fertile fields of St. Mary roll away Westward to the cypress swamps. In those marshes are great hill islands of fabulous value—Cote Blanche, Grand Cote, Avery's Island, Jefferson Island—that are the puzzle of scientists and the delight of travelers.[5]

It is on this beautifully set stage the pretty, artistic village of Franklin, as pretty and as full of charm as any little town in England, has its habitation. Franklin's main street runs parallel with the bayou. It is an avenue about one hundred feet wide, tree-planted and lined with stores for a distance of half a mile. The goods displayed are elegant, fashionable and of the best. They give a stranger the cue to the social status of the people who buy them. The contiguous streets are broad, well side-walked and lighted, and they lead the way to well-kept homes that have the unmistakable air of refinement, thrift and comfort.

Accompanied by my genial and witty host, Col. John A. O'Niell, one of the most progressive merchants of Franklin, we plowed a way through the mud to Dixie, the country home of Murphy J. Foster, our governor.[6] If facts were needed to prove the simple, unaffected citizenship of Governor Foster, his plain farming life, his refined family circle and pure domestic relations, one need only visit Dixie.

It is a big, gabled, two-storied house, turning its back on the bayou and shaded under many trees. In the yards are Pekin ducks, turkeys and geese. At one side is a wondrous rose garden, one of the finest in quality in the state. The pretty and charming young chatelaine of this sweet home we found at a woman's best if most tiresome vocation, nursing the baby and getting ready for removal to Baton Rouge.

When Mrs. Foster goes to Baton Rouge to live she gives the promise to becoming as popular in a state way as Mrs. Cleveland is in a national one.[7] She unaffectedly says the governor's mansion is to be a home for all the governor's fellow-citizens. It is evident that, herself a happy woman, she will give a happy, womanly welcome to all who come her way. Under the care of Mrs. Foster, the executive mansion is almost certain to become one of the most popular homes in the state.

In the parlor at Dixie were preserved every eloquent trophy of the late campaign that came Governor Foster's way, from ships of state down to those simple souvenir cards shyly and anonymously inscribed "from a humble admirer."

There are 60,000 acres of idle land ready for the plow in St. Mary. It can be rented at $2.00 an acre, worked on shares or bought outright. It will yield money: clothing from its cotton, moss for mattresses, fuel for the winter, fruit for winter nights, rice for jambolayas, sugar for taffy candy, wine for birthday feasts, and yams to roast with the possums that are to be caught in the forest. Neither sapphires, rubies, nor garnets are to be spaded like goober nuts, but if I were a young fellow, with my way to make, I should like no better start in life than a cottage and twenty acres of land in the rich heart of the country of Arcady, the Teche country of Evangeline.

LÁST ISLÁND

This account of a glorious sunswept holiday of fishing, swimming, hiking, and sunbathing on Last Island (*Isle Dernière*) is set against the fading history, like a dimly remembered nightmare, of the hurricane of 1856. The hurricane became one of the most infamous of Louisiana's many tropical cyclones because its winds, waves, and storm surge buried the island in water and took the lives of some of the state's most prominent citizens. Many were dancing at a ball when the winds began to howl. As Martha Field discovered some thirty years later, the island never recovered; it was reduced to bare, broken spits of sand, and remains so today.

In this travel account, Field is not a mere passive observer, but an active participant in a physical, visceral experience. There is no romanticism or sentimentality here; she describes the preparation of birds killed to decorate ladies' hats with cool, scientific detachment, with not a trace of feminine squeamishness. She describes herself as "an amphibiously-inclined person" and is quite comfortable roughing it in the surf, fighting a huge redfish, baking in the sun in salt-water-stiffened clothes, and wolfing down fish dinners with the appetite of a day laborer. She seems very much like a modern woman. (*Picayune*, July 29, 1888)

"For a person to travel around and have a good time in this particular part of our state," observed a hospitable lighthouse keeper with whom I was dining the other day, "he or she must be more or less amphibious. I calculate that you are somewhat amphibious, are you not?" he questioned.

I looked down at my sun and sea-blistered wrists, at a gingham gown stiff with repeated duckings in brine and bayou, at the battered wreck of a once-beribboned palmetto woven by the deft fingers of some dark-eyed island beauty. I looked out at the lighthouse boat by which my host had just arrived on furlough, at the family lugger and the less conventional pirogue, at our own canoe—all hitched up to the front gate—out through the gaps in the rushes at the unrumpled expanse of water where our schooner was lying becalmed. I looked on all this, I say, and I felt free to admit that I was "more or less amphibious."

To have a good time in Louisiana there is no better way than for an amphibiously-inclined person to take a sloop, a catboat, a lugger or a schooner and voyage among the wonderful, desolate, but picturesque islands that fret our Gulf Coast. He will get amongst people whose total belongings are a roof-over-head of palmettos, a cast net, a pirogue, an iron pot, and an accordion. He will see grizzled old men—a hundred years old, maybe—come out of their huts in the morning barefooted, get into their pirogues and paddle away to throw a cast net and fish up a breakfast.

He will see youngsters, not able to talk plain, doing the same thing. He will hear legends of storms, and stories of sea ghosts, and of a horrid devil fish that haunts the Gulf and sometimes drags a schooner or a lugger away, away out to sea, and then down, down to the bottom of the ocean.

Once a lighthouse-keeper was on his way to Timbalier in his catboat. He was seen crossing Vine Island Pass—and never again. Perhaps a storm came up and drove him out to sea, but there are those who shrug their shoulders at this and say: "Yes, a squall indeed! Very likely! He was caught on the horns of the devil fish more likely."

Inhabitants on these islands are truly few and far between, but mosquitoes are plenty, and here the pelican and gulls are to be found, and the redfish leap in the sea, and schools of giant shrimp crumple the surface of the waters, and sharks are sometimes to be caught, with hooks half a yard long, fastened on iron chains—so that to cruise among these islands is very good sport indeed during these summer months before the islanders begin to live in fear and trembling of the storms.

The fashionable hotel, the latest cut in bathing suits, the six o'clock dinner and the Saturday night hop are all very well in their way, but to my mind they do not compare to the pleasure of the surf dashing furiously over these gray and bleak shores, to a tremendous squall with no shelter nigh, to the mad tug with which a fourteen-pound redfish runs away with one's line, to a night's sleep under the stars on a schooner's deck, to the morning surf bath and the breakfast of fried trout and salt meat and coffee by a camp fire, or on the schooner's hatch—to say nothing of the cheapness of such an outing.

A lugger that will accommodate six or eight can be hired with the services of a trusty sailor and a captain, who is a famous cook as well, for two dollars a day, and to this must only be added the expenses of provisioning the boat.

Some twelve mornings ago, when the sun was yet low in the blue and the dew still beaded on the roses, I went across the streets of the little seaport town of Morgan City to a rotting wharf at the further end of the town, where the *Julia*, a schooner that I had hired for a trip to the islands, was ready for sailing. She was a beautifully-shaped, dingy-green vessel, with gently curving breasts, floating on the water like a pelican. Her sails were tied up, a tent covered her deck, and under it were all the crew assembled waiting for me, and eyeing me reproachfully as a person who did not mind keeping a boat waiting two long hours beyond the appointed sailing hour.

Through the thoughtful courtesy of Mr. Kock of the Morgan Road, the tugboat *Cricket* was to take us to the mouth of the river and in a few moments we were lashed to her side and were on our way.[1]

The *Julia* certainly looked provisioned for a cruise. Tubs of vegetables, piles of lemons, coops of chickens, a little green hillock of melons, and groceries stood about among the anchors, chains, ropes and piles of spare sails. It was a comforting-looking disorder, but the captain's wife and daughter were gradually getting things to rights so that by the time the *Cricket* gave us a farewell salute and her clever and entertaining Captain Smith, a hero in many sea adventures, had waved us goodbye we presented quite a ship-shape appearance, and the crew, with all sails set, had settled down to the peacefuller occupations of sorting fishing lines, mending casting nets, cleaning guns and getting dinners.[2]

Captain Siegfried and his family live on board the schooner and during the fall and winter hunt birds, coasting among the islands for gulls, terns, and pigeons, which they skin, stuff, pack in paper cornucopias and ship to France by the thousand. Last year, they shipped 5,000 birds. Miss Lena, the brave young daughter of Captain Siegfried, who can sail the *Julia*, pull a canoe, kill a shark, land a mammoth redfish, skin an otter, and kill a laughing gull on the wing, can also skin, dress and prepare for shipping no less than forty birds an hour.

It was an almost perfect day. The wide river on which not a rippled wave beat shoreward, was like a shield of quicksilver. The canopied oaks and cypress trees looked up at us from this strange mirror and out at us from the banks where a jungle of lush marsh grasses, yellow reeds and spiked fans of green palmetto grew about their roots. The sky, pale blue almost to whiteness, held not a cloud, but glittered like burnished metal, and to gaze up into it made the eyes sting and blurred and blinded one's vision.

In an hour there were no more oak trees to be seen—only here and there a straggling willow and broad, bronze-yellow and coppery reaches of marsh reeds with amber crests of feathery bloom like myriads of butterflies poised for flight. The land had dribbled down into the desolation of the salines, and already here at the mouth of the Atchafalaya we were nearing the haunts of the pelican and the blue crane and the grosbeak.

At our left was Deer Island, an irregular shape of sea marsh, with the twisted skeletons of dead oaks rising here and there, curiously like the huge antlers of deer. Within the memory of the oldest sailors these dead trees have stood on Deer Island; from their resemblance to antlers probably giving the island its name, although it is said that hereabout deer, as well as wildcat, abound.

Down in the cabin, where clothing, provisions, cooking utensils, shooting things, etc. were stored, and where the cooking-stove was, the heat was something terrific. The wind that filled our sails was hot and came in puffs. Dinner, that had been served on the hatch, was over, and we sat around, like fish out of water, gasping for breath. The sun seemed to have melted all over the heavens. Charlie, patient, brave, skillful now as he was on that first dry day of our voyage, said the sun made him grin. It was true. It shone so fiercely out of that white, molten silver sky that we all "grinned" under its glare.

We were in Four League Bay, and off in all directions a horizon was made of ragged fringes of brush, and sage-like bushes that in this luminous atmosphere upreared like giant trees. Down in the cabin the thermometer stood at 120 degrees Fahrenheit; on deck it was 105 degrees. Now and then, the glistening sky seemed to crack and we had a flash-view, too quick for eyesight, almost too swift for thought, of some vivider brightness that was frightful.

"What is it!" I asked Charlie, getting under the small canopy rigged over the steersman.

"Sunshine lightning," said Charlie, and just then, off in the distance, the low growl of thunder began. The luminous atmosphere in a moment turned yellow—the greenish yellow of sulphur—the bay was like an olive green ink, thick, muddy, and as the sky turned from yellow to green and from bluish black to violet, the lightning could be seen not in one place, but everywhere. It came like harpoons of fire cast at a whale; it was thrown, here, there, everywhere about the boat like the broken spears of maddened warriors.

There were still no clouds, only this violet dome pressing down on us and deepening in color every moment. Then the rain began, not as it rains on shore, but as it rains only at sea, a white wall of water falling solidly, shutting out the rest of the world, and so thick that from where I sat the jib was scarcely visible. The captain, unable to see his way and fearful of being stuck until next tide on an oyster reef, hauled the boat round and let go an anchor.

We all huddled down in the cabin, leaving the steps in and the door open, watching the terrific sky and the white sheets of rain. Suddenly an enormous fish sprung far into the air and landed plump in our canoe, tied alongside the schooner. It was a hundred pound silver fish, and in no time at all, and before Charlie could run at the canoe with an ax, it had broken loose the nailed seats, sent oars adrift, and filled the canoe with its own blood.

"He's broken his neck," Charlie cried above the roar of the rain and between the poundings of the thunder, and then he climbed into the schooner again and prepared to go after the oars that were already out of sight.

"Wait a bit," said his father, and Charlie sat down, dripping, on the cabin bench.

"It's the worst storm"—bellowed the captain looking out at the emblazoned sky now written all over with the terrific autograph, but he never finished the sentence, for there came into the cabin, seeming for a moment to cut the boat into a hundred parts, such a splendid, frightful flash as cannot be described. It cut here and there. There was a tangle of its fierce spearheads among the guns in their racks, and quick as the lightning, I knew we had been struck by it.

The electric shock threw Captain Siegfried on his knees, took me in the back of the head and the others also in the head and face. Momentarily, and while the crashing noise still boomed in the cabin, we were stunned and then half dazed and wholly alarmed. We sat up and began looking about, expecting to find the *Julia* a total wreck. No serious damage was done however, and with that fierce attack the backbone of the storm was broken, the lightning retired like a growling lion, and in another half hour the pale whitish blue sky, with a tender, repentant rain-drenched face, shone down upon us, and Captain Siegfried was beating about in his pirogue far astern, looking with German thrift and patience for the lost oars.

The exit from Four League Bay is through Oyster Bayou, a winding uncertain oyster-reefed lane of salt water where sea-cat and sharks and the big silver fish abound. It is only two miles long but a lugger has been known to take twenty-four hours or more in getting through it. On either side are sea marshes, a rotting, porous, fiddler-eaten crust of half earth, half sand, sown thick with a rank, coarse growth of sea rushes sharp enough to stab a murderer to the heart if daggers are scarce, hollow enough to serve a peaceable Isaac Walton with a pipe stem.

Deer are sometimes seen in these marshlands and wildcat often enough. As we drifted out, the wind, having failed almost entirely, one of these deer, a gaunt thing with mad eyes, peered out at us from the rushes and then crashed away, rustling through the brakes. Something dark blue and plumy swung overhead and dropped down in the rushes.

"It is a blue crane," Lena said.

"Where?" asked I, my untrained eyes failing to locate the bird.

"There," said the young huntress, "just beyond the grave."

The sky was darkling over for night; already silvery mists were rising out of the marshes—mists of malaria and mosquitoes and myriads of gnats and other small winged insects of the night. With only those treacherous marshes in sight, and the salt waters of the Gulf, to have Lena pointing a long forefinger at a blue crane hovering over some dead man's grave was not pleasant.

Just above the feathered tip of the rushes that grew highest near the bank, I could make out in the somber evening light a weather-beaten cross. A dead man's body had been found floating here years ago, and some fishermen had buried him in the marsh, and put a notched stick to mark his grave. It was low tide, and the black-teethed, jagged combs of the oyster reefs showed above the wimple of the bayou, or we could see a brown stretch of sand and mud that the tide had sucked dry. Some slender birds, with soft brown or gray plumage, were picking about on these sand flats, and Charlie, promising us prairie chickens for supper, took his gun and crept off in his pirogue after them.[3]

Half a dozen times his gun was fired and the pretty things dropped one after the other. One, wounded, ran fleetly with broken, trailing wings off far into the marsh, and when our boy hunter came back and slung his three brace of birds upon the schooner's deck he only said he would "rather have not shot any than to know that one of them pretty little things was bleeding to death out there in the salt mud and a-makin' no cry."

These harvesters of the sea, what strange fruits they bring home! Charlie and his pirogue never failed us in surprises, and on this first hunting venture of his, as well as prairie chickens, tender and delicious, he tossed on board a big brown flounder, knocked in the head with a paddle, and enough salt, fine, fat oysters to make that famous mess so dear to epicures: macaroni, tomatoes, red peppers, and oysters.

The stars were out when supper was set forth on the roof of the cabin—a meal of boiled flounder and prairie chickens, tea and a crusty loaf, and as if to hearten us up still further a lusty wind came zooming up and we went flying through the crackling waves, all sail set, and Aleck up in the anchor chains making the dewless, salty July night sweet with the music of "Annie Laurie," played with many a flourish on the *Julia's* best accordion.

It was ten o'clock at night. The *Julia* flew through the waters, the spray drenching the musician tangled up in the anchor chains, when a flash of light showed off far across our bows.

"Ship Shoal light," said the captain from the tiller, the lonesomest, most man-and- God-forsaken place on the coast, twelve miles from any land, and the nearest land is that sand island with the curse upon it, that place of the great storm—Last Island. The jib came rattling down like a white sheet of rain, the topsail fell like a white pigeon wounded to the deck, the anchor chain jingled and clinked, and the *Julia* gave a lurch forward and then rode peacefully at anchor off the east shore of that fated Last Island, whose horrors are not romance to the people of the Teche country.

Here in this particular part of the state you may perhaps meet one with sad, frightened eyes, that if a storm be brewing will glare and flash like those of a wounded animal brought to bay. You may not ask with half careless, conventional courtesy if this one is afraid of storms, for someone will pluck you by the sleeve and say, "Hush, she was saved from Last Island," and here you may meet many a person of whom you will be told, "You see that one there? Well, all his family—his father, mother, all—were lost at Last Island."

At Tigerville, I think, there lives, or did live, the man who was saved by a billiard table. It floated in with this man and a Colored woman upon it, and during that terrific voyage (the storm, I am told, culminated in the daytime, not at night) the woman gave birth to a child. But these are old stories—the classics of St. Mary parish—the legends familiar to you as to the child at your knee.

That night, as we rode at anchor I lifted the flap of the tent—for we all, captain and crew and bos'n too, slept on deck on feather beds, our cheesecloth mosquito bar rigged up on poles and ropes—and looked out at the mysterious island. A long, narrow, level stretch of sandy soil, barely rising above the sea, with only brush and bushes and rank rushes growing on it, or here and there at the edge of Village Bayou a stunted willow tree or two, with a projecting beach or shelving sand like a long underlip.

Last Island might almost, in the midnight gloom, be mistaken for the back of some dreamed of devil fish, or some fin of a giant, stealthy shark, or even what it is—the island of the curse of God—where flowers bloom not, where no clean nor honest life is, and where even the bird hunters camp with fear and trembling, because of the ghosts of those who were drowned here during the storm of '56.

Later storms have cut the island into two parts, and no one lives here save the black inhabitants of two miserable huts made of wreckage, and built up in the air—like cranes standing on long legs in the rushes. There are some cattle on the island, wild, wide-horned, scraggy little beasts, fleet of foot and fierce of blood, and there are sheep—white, woolly beauties.

The Last Islanders have a dreadful name. One, it is said, stole his sheep stock from the mainland by the lugger load. We saw one of the men—a big, black-faced, black-bearded man of the sea, with shoulders like those of a huge dolphin, and a dull face. He sat low down in his lugger, well in the shadow of its bright, red sail. Presently he lifted a conch and blew three signals—three telegraphic notes of minor-toned mournful music.

Afar off from the rushes or from the waves or from the desolated sand flats of the beach, with its moving surface of black and yellow fiddlers, there came bleating back a mournful answer. Apparently it satisfied the black man in the lugger, for he turned his red sail, like a sea warrior's shield with dry blood on it, and away the small craft bounded seaward.

Like the snout of a swordfish the east end of Last Island, a long wedge or knife of yellow sand, runs out a quarter of a mile into the sea. There are no rushes here, only sand and hundreds of birds—nay, thousands have their nests here. As we came ashore and walked along, the yellow fiddlers swept away before us like a receding wave of the sea. One could not put feet down without crushing these helpless, silent, harmless little bodies moving like soldiers in retreat.

Overhead the sky was darkened by the birds—laughing gulls, terns, and pigeons. They screamed at us, the breath of their wings beat down on us, the long, scarlet scissors of their fierce beaks were close to us, their shrill cries split in our ears. Over on the sands just beyond high tide were the eggs of these birds—four together and so thick that one might have gathered a dozen barrels of them. The eggs were just hatching and one had to step carefully and look keenly to keep from crushing the sand-colored young, so closely do they resemble the sand that at a distance of three yards a young tern or gull will be invisible. The wind blew saltily off the green Gulf, the surf tumbled in superbly. The surf bathing at Last Island is said to be the finest on the continent, and before we knew what we were about, our entire crew had joined hands and we were facing and awaiting a mighty wave that came frothing and curling at us, beating us down into the sand and leveling us for the moment like so much flotsam on the shore.

During storms the waves will wash over Last Island, and few would venture to stop there without a trusty boat near at hand. There are other islands just as dreadful and desolate and insecure, but none with the curse of God on it as this one has. Only the fierce-winged gulls, the half-wild cattle feeding on salty rushes, and the half-wild inhabitants of the two little perches up in the center of the island may be said to live here.

But the redfish come in close to shore—and the man-eating sharks as well. Not long since one tore a pound of flesh from the side of a swimmer. The shore is crusted with beautiful shells—some pink as the sunset, some with shallows like silver, some like the scaly moons on the silver fish, and others brown, horny hulks crawling about with now and then a hairy claw protruding so that the beach seemed alive.

Last Island is a favorite camp for bird hunters. Here the gulls and other small seabirds of most beautiful plumage have their homes and deposit their bluish eggs, splotched with dark brown for the sun and the warm sands to hatch. These birds with soft gray backs, black heads and lovely mottled wings are worth, the smaller ones, according to the fashions, from fifteen to thirty-five cents apiece. They are shot on the wing and one of the hunters follows the gunners picking up the dead birds and hanging them by their slender, pretty scarlet or yellow beaks on wire racks made like big square footstools, covered with wire netting, from the under-side of which the hooks project.

To skin them the legs and wings are broken, a slight cut made in the underside of the body, the skin is turned down from the "drumsticks," which are cut off with peculiar scissors, and deftly the skin is pulled inside out from the flesh. Plaster of Paris is thrown on the bird's flesh, which dries the blood immediately and keeps the pretty plumage from being stained. The brain is cut out, but the top of the skull is left, and all bony and fleshy parts are rubbed with arsenic.

Wads of cotton replace the eyes, a false beginning of a neck is made of a roll of cotton, and the already-dry skin is slowly pulled back again, the breast is plumped with cotton, the helpless wings are folded back, and that which ten minutes ago was a feather-light creature of lovely shape, beating in the sunshiny air on joyous wing, lies in a little white paper coffin, ready to be sent across seas to Paris, where it is wired and eyed, ready for the garniture on *ma belle's* ball gown or to be poised on her dainty bonnet.

Pelicans are killed for their pouches, of which purses and tobacco bags are made, and for the snow-white down on their breasts, of which powder puffs are made, and for the bones of their strong wings, of which pipe stems are made.

The white cranes are killed by the million for the aigrettes that grow between their shoulders; a white crane, indeed, is called "an aigrette" by the hunters; fans are sometimes made of the blue crane's wings, but the cruelest slaughter of all seems to be that of the aigrettes and the laughing gulls.

That night, tired out from surf bathing and shell hunting and fearful trips through the edges of the marshes towards Village Bayou, that silvery stream of silently flowing waters where the *Morning Star* was wrecked in 1856, when 300 rich and fashionable summer visitors were wave-beaten to death, one slept well on the *Julia's* wave-beaten deck. All night the surf pounded and moaned over the beach and filled the night with a howling like the baying of distant unkenneled dogs. All night the wind rustled among the reeds and grasses, and bruised out of them a salty fragrance and a chinking kind of music like the rubbing together of three silver coins.

Once in a while a belated pelican swept by, beating the air with heavy, hurried wings, or a tern screamed like a shrill sea witch. It lacked but a few days of being the anniversary of that fearful storm that made the history and the tragedy of this most desolate spot, and, remembering this, it was long before I could sleep, just for listening to the moaning surf, to the growling of far-off thunder, but at last a sleep came, and when I awoke it was half-past four in the morning. Lena was handing a cup of coffee under my mosquito net and was saying in her pleasant way: "It is breezing up, and if you will get up so the mainsail can be set we will be getting away to Timbalier."

I tumbled out; in a jiffy the tent was down, the beds rolled and stowed below, and our boys, Charlie and George and Aleck, all of whom are "sailorizing," had up the anchor and the sails and like a white gull on the wing the *Julia* was running before the wind, heading away for Vine Island pass, Little Caillou and Timbalier.

TIMBALIER ISLAND

This piece is ornamented by some of Martha Field's loveliest descriptive
nature writing. Her hired schooner and crew anchor off the desolate sands
of Timbalier Island where she visits the nearby lighthouse, endlessly fishes,
bathes in the surf, and walks the beaches. She is unexpectedly invited to a
Saturday night dance at a most unlikely beachfront "ballroom." Her adventure at the sun-drenched wilds of Timbalier ends hauntingly with an eclipse
viewed from the deck of the schooner, described with the eye of a poet.
(*Picayune*, August 5, 1888)

It was past noon, and for four hours we had been lying becalmed,
with the wind blowing straight down the mast and with no apparent
prospect of it ever doing anything else. A silvery haze of heat shimmered
and quivered over the dazzling sheet of motionless water. Far away, a few
straggling branched bushes rose out of an invisible shelf of sand. It was
the island of Little Caillou hanging on the sea like a dim, blurred, distant
picture in India ink.

In an oval frame of foamy, pink-rimmed clouds the quiet sky seemed
to sleep. It was blue, like the banks of forget-me-not blooms that are
sweet in the paths of far-off Irish Innisfallen. Not a sound could be
heard. It was the absolute unbroken peacefulness of nature in midsummer and mid-afternoon rest.

The sails of our boat drooped wearily. Life was as if we were lying in
the pearl and amber shallow of a huge shell—asleep. Every one on board
was asleep except myself, lying on rope-coils and canvas heaps. We had
whistled for the wind, scratched the mast and called on Saint Antonio,
but still the soft sweet amorous calm, the tender, flower-like serenity of
the sky, the waveless gleaming of the silver-green waters was all we got in
answer.

I leaned over the boat and looked down where hundreds of bellfish were floating by in their white palaces. How lovely they are and how perishable!—the most beautiful of all the jellyfish, I think. To look down in the water at these hundreds of bellfish is to fancy them so many rare vases filled with rarer flowers.

It is near six o'clock when we come to anchor at the mouth of a little silvery bayou or water lane that cuts Timbalier Island West, into two equal parts. It would be dull work enumerating the islands like Timbalier that lie along our Gulf Coast. They are flat, irregular-shaped expanses of sea-marsh covered with rushes, and here and there a ridge or hillock of solider ground, or perhaps an inner island in the marsh of good, tillable land.

They have no timber upon them, nothing more than situated willows and dreary prickly ash trees. It is said, however, that upon some a few oak trees grow, and the palmetto. In the bayous abound the finest crabs and millions of oysters. In the sand wells is a brackish water that at least will keep the wild cattle from dying of thirst. The scraggy bushes that have a fierce, weatherbeaten look are the coverts for grosbeak and prairie chickens, and ducks innumerable.

Shrimp are to be had by the barrelful just for the seining, and on Timbalier and other islands equally flat and dreary the Chinese make their camps over the old haunts of Lafitte, whose dark-eyed descendants will perhaps dance with you at some island ball. It is a great industry, that, of drying shrimp and salting down sea trout, and the Chinese understand both to perfection. The shrimp swim in shoals directly on the surface of the water, and are caught in cast-nets. They are boiled before drying.

The Orientals have a huge wooden box with a sheet of tin nailed over the bottom. They make a shallow trench for the fire, rest the box over it and boil the fish in it, afterwards drying them in the sun. A Chinese will insert his fingers in the gills of a fish, give a deft pull and bring out gills and entrails all at once. The fish, apparently whole, unscaled, is then salted down and ready for shipping—to China it is said. At this season of the year many Acadians visit the islands and Gulf, catching shrimp and salting down redfish for their winter stores.

The water in Timbalier Bayou was brown and limpid; it flowed out with a pleasant gurgle among the rushes that were so brown and so golden, so green and so silvery-gray, so yellow and lead-colored under the mellow sky and soft evening light. There was the whir of wings, and a flock of snipe arose from the rushes and settled further off. On the other shore some hunters had put up their tent, stained crimson and glowing cheerily like a vivid bit of Florentine mosaic in the intermingled richness and softness of the neutral tints that come from sky and earth and water. Just beyond the tent was an old house set in the sands, yet perched on stilts up in the air.

The board chimney leaned away from the house. A perch, or roosting place on the lopsided porch-way was placed high up in the air so that those who sat upon it would have to climb mightily. A fire of wreckage and dried bushes smoldered to windward so that the queer, doorless, windowless shanty was enveloped in a cloud of blue smoke, appearing and disappearing from this murky halo in the most vexing way.

Half a dozen men, a boy and two women sat on this perch, and one of them played on the accordion a wheezy, asthmatic tune that had no ending at all. A little lugger, her red sail trailing untrimly, pulled at a mud hook near the bank. Our pirogue floated idly on the oyster reef where Charlie was breaking off black ridges and tossing them into his boat as if they were so many rocks. Presently, he gave an explanation and sprang to the other side of the reef.

"What was it, Charlie?" we called from the bows of the schooner.

"Only a stone crab," he answered back.

A stone crab is a dark, snake-gray creature, almost invisible when it lies among the oyster reefs. It has one huge claw, with power sufficient to cut a man's hand in two or to break open oyster shells in search of the oysters. All unafraid of stone crabs or sharks or whipperees we took our bath in the salty bayou and came back to the schooner at dark, dripping brine and hungry as man-of-war hawks.[1]

On the cabin roof the pretty cups and saucers were arrayed, the pot of tea and the plates heaped with snipe and oysters. To pass all this by and reach out for fried salt side- meat and a cup of black coffee and a loaf of dry crumby corn bread was natural enough.

When I stood on the *Julia*'s cabin at Morgan City, saying goodbye to a friend or two, one of them said to me, "In a day or so you will toss your head at snipe and tenderloin of trout, and you will think that nothing in this world can be so wholesome or so good as salt meat, black coffee, cornbread and cold water." It is even so. Time and time again have I stepped up out of the surf too hungry to wait for dry clothes, and, disdaining all my hostess' dainty dishes, her salads and puddings and court-bouillon, have feasted with an appetite a king might envy on crisp slices of salt shoulder and a bowl of black coffee.

That night we had a mosquito pest. They came not as they do on land, but as only the mosquitoes can come when you invade them in their own haunts. Their buzzing was like the wind playing over a million strings of fine wire. I looked over at Lena and her face was black with them. She said mine was equally covered.

When breakfast was over the next day we women folk all went a visiting. Charlie rowed us up the bayou, and when it was too shallow to proceed any further we stepped overboard and slopped along until we came to dry land. A narrow footpath ran crookedly over the sandy shore, and the rushes and sweet-smelling bushes of mandrake grew as high as my head, while here and there a prickly ash spread out its wild arms as if it were some live, frightened thing running away. Myriads of yellow fiddlers, their one long claw moving like a fiddler sawing the air with his bow, flittered out of our way. During "the great storm" one man and woman were saved after having fed for three days on these hairy little creatures.

At our right were pool-like expanses of the bayou creeping into the recesses far up into the land, and here the mud-eating mullets swarmed thick, and the oyster reefs showed like long black combs, with huge broken teeth, and here we could hear the sullen, sharp snap of the terrible stone crabs, like far distant stonecutters.

Winding along, Indian file, we passed a house. It was made of boards, unpainted, two or three rooms, a broken bit of porch, and on it ten or twenty cats and an old woman smoking a pipe. Her face was in profile, and although we were perhaps the first strangers she had seen in a year she turned her head neither to the right nor the left. She had lived so long out of the world that even curiosity was dead.

The cats were plump, for on Timbalier when a cat is hungry it trots stealthily down to the bayou and catches a mullet, a huge shrimp or a lot of yellow fiddlers. And still the narrow path wandered on past a shed where a lone islander with roughest tools was hewing himself a boat; past a series of little sand heaps whose broken crosses seemed to denote that once upon a time a graveyard had been here; past a couple of gray

little shanties with pale golden roofs of palmetto shining in the sun—
and at last we came to our destination.

It was a tiny home and in it lived a modern Swiss Family Robinson, who
had come to Timbalier for the summer because the island was the native
place and former home of the soft-voiced, beautiful-eyed young wife.
There were doors and windows everywhere and moss mattresses covered
the board bunks built out from the walls. There were rocking chairs and a
sewing machine and a clock and other comforts brought from town, but
the old house was like the marsh islands and like nothing else.

In the kitchen a square had been covered with bricks; it was sunken a
foot lower than the floor, and a wide chimney of boards ineffectually
tried to carry off the smoke. It was such a chimney and hearth as one
finds on all these islands, if one finds a hearth at all. But it was hospitable
and kind, and we were made welcome by the beautiful-eyed wife and
her sturdy lord, and in a few moments were asked out to coffee. It is the
custom of the country in this island of the Acadians: at the sight of dust
announcing the coming of a guest the coffee is set to drip, and be it
friend or foe, stranger or old ally, under the low, rough thatch of yellow
palmettos, the first swift act of hospitality, spontaneous, kind and true,
is that proffered cup of strong, creamless coffee.

All day we sat in that little home, the salt wind whistling through the
open doors and the bright sun tangled in the yellow meshes of the big
seine that so handsomely draped the gray wall, where the gun rested in its
rustic bracket. Out of doors all was silent, and I could see the ruined
orchard of lemon and orange trees, planted a century ago, the few grapes
purpling about the old vine that had once been so wide-spreading and so
thrifty.

The sand whirled in little gusts over a grove not far away; the reeds in
the marsh sang in the wind like mosquitoes. A squall came up and a few
wild cattle browsing about scampered away. We talked of storms, while
the lightning flashed around us, and one told how only last year a husband and wife were rowing in a bayou when he was killed by lightning
and the wife had to take the oars from his dead hands and row twelve
miles to the nearest hut.

Another told of a woman—an old, old woman washed into the swamp
and caught and held there fast in the prickly ash trees by her long, gray
hair. And when she was found she was almost dead, so that to make

haste, her rescuers, having no scissors to cut away her hair, broke off the branches and carried her away, aureoled with this agony of thorns.

Another told of a mother and daughter telling each other goodbye in their storm-shaken hut, thinking it would be forever, and how both were washed upon a shell reef. It was midnight, when the daughter thought she saw something moving on the reef, and frightened of mysterious terrors she yet crept towards it in the driving rain and waves that leapt at her, and found her mother holding up a door and crowding behind it out of the rain, awaiting death.

Out over the rushes I could see, like a pale gray wall, the lapping waters of the Gulf; their white teeth were snapping at the sandy shore. What night might not the monster come crashing over this desolate strip of land and devour all on it!

"Will you come to the ball tonight?" said our hostess in her soft voice as we took our leave.

"Oh, yes," we answered, and, as we went back home to tea, I wondered where on earth the people were to come from for the ball, for on all of Timbalier there are but three families living. But a ball there was to be, and at dusk we again walked across the downs, following the path until we came to a broad low-roofed building without doors or windows, standing at the extreme outer edge of the island. Down in the bayou three or four bare poles and ropes swinging in the breeze, sharply out-lined against the crimson sky, in which faint stars gleamed strangely, told that at least two or three lugger-loads of guests had arrived from other islands. By what mysterious telegraphy the fact of the ball had been made known I know not, but certain it is that all the marsh islanders thereabouts were in attendance.

The house in which the ball was given had never been completed. It lacked doors and windows, and one must walk a steep plank to get into it, since it perched high in the air, long-legged as a crane. The golden roof of bleached palmetto, thick and soft, looked mighty pretty, and as each newcomer brought his own light, a lantern, which was swung on the wall, the big, bare room soon was grandly illuminated.

I think there were at least two babies to every adult, and the young mothers sat in rows like so many dove-eyed Madonnas around the room. Each huddled in her arms a baby or two while the elder of her brood clustered like kittens at her feet. The men sat at one side of the room, the women at the other. The lanterns and one or two lamps stood on shelves in the corners. The musicians, two men with a violin and an accordion, leaned back in their hide-bottomed chairs crooning out that nameless, tuneless tune, like the crurr-m of a locust, like the zooning of the wind on the beach, like the stealthy purr of the fiddlers escaping in the rushes, like the strange patter and rattle of sea catfish sucking on the bottom of a boat, like the mysterious, eerie, sleep sound, half music, half water-rippling that comes from an oyster bed in some narrow bayou.

How lovely were the women, how splendid of eye, and lithe of form, and graceful of carriage, and gentle of voice, I cannot begin to tell. They danced as I never saw fashionable belles in fashionable ballrooms dance, like languorous Spanish senoritas dancing in their sleep with their lovers. No one laughed aloud nor spoke loudly. To shut one's eyes and forget the "zooning" music, one could never have guessed that this was a ballroom. A big bucket of water stood in a corner; when one was thirsty one took a drink from it. This was all the refreshment.

By and by the men had noticeably thinned out, and the young girls were dancing together. The mosquitoes were terrible, and I sat in my corner keeping up a tiresome muscular exercise and suffering tortures while conversing with one of the Madonnas. She held a baby and rocked slowly back and forth, smiling at me in a sweet and friendly fashion. When her pretty face would be black with mosquitoes she would slowly wipe her hand over it and clear them away.

It must be true that one can become accustomed even to mosquitoes. When we came away at eleven o'clock we wound our way around the corner of a tiny house in which a light flared brightly. As we passed by an open door I looked in. In each corner stood a bed and upon these, babies were piled promiscuously, so that it would take a wise mother to know her own child. I thought of that wedding up at Three Islands, in the Atchafalaya, and how one mother picked up a baby, got in her pirogue with her husband and went four miles across the lake home before she discovered that in place of her own little girl she had carried off a big, black-haired boy, and how she had had to paddle back to find all the wedding guests in anxious quest for the miscarried child.

In the center of the room was a table, and around it sat five men. A lantern stood on the table and a lamp, and their faces were in strong light. Each man held five greasy cards in his hands, and little piles of money were here and there. These islanders are terrible gamblers. A man who does not, through idleness or lack of thrift, earn more than one hundred dollars a year will gamble away every cent of it if only he gets a chance. Let him but see a man approaching his poor little island home, and he will reach at once for the cards.

Poker is his game, and to win or lose is all the same so long as he can play at all. These men wore coarse, blue cottonade trousers, and were generally in their undershirts—just as they had appeared, however, in the ballroom. They were fair of hair, generally, a fairness as if hair and skin had been tanned yellow by the sun. One of them leaned forward. His eyes, skin, lips, big bristling mustache, were all yellow—a dull, coppery yellow like that of the Chinese. His eyes seemed popping from his head like balls of dull, yellow marble, his big nose flattened out and nostrils puffed like an adder's; his yellow lips were bunched up and thrust forward, yet between them like the broken claws of a fierce stone crab I could see a dark gleam of dirty, jagged teeth. His hair stood forth tawny like a broken thicket, a tangle of fierce sea rushes. His bullish throat was bare.

Once in Molinary's studio I saw a study that was almost the counterpart of this man.[2] But the face at the table—weather-beaten, washed for years by the stinging spray and the strong sun—the face of a man who lived next to nature's breast, yet knew it not—was the greater, more awful, more dramatic face of the two. And as I looked, he leaned over. The brushes of his mustache stood out over his nose; he put forth a hand like the root of a sea-rush, and slowly gathered in to himself a precious pile of nickels and thin, worn, hoarded half-dimes. It was a study in yellow of a gambler of the Gulf Coast.

Next morning at sun-up I looked out from the feather couch on the schooner's deck and watched the red-sailed luggers fleeing down the bay. I could hear an accordion and a child whining together, and the smell of coffee. It was the marsh islanders returning home from the ball, and on a bit of a furnace perhaps they were roasting and making a cup of coffee.

The summer calms pursued us, and it took us two hours or more to beat along the coast of Timbalier to the east end, where, rising up like a monument of isolation and desolation, the lighthouse stands. On our way we passed several strange-looking craft piled with furniture and with small catboats in tow, and crowded with women and children. They were movers—marsh islanders—bound for a new home on an island near the mouth of the Atchafalaya. These people, to whom newspapers nor magazines nor fashions ever come, are restless and roving in their little kingdoms of the sea, as was even the famous Lafitte, whose blood may be in their veins. They go from island to island, wherever the seining and fishing is good, and where oyster-beds are, taking children, the pig or two, the half-dozen head of cattle, the moss beds and the accordion.

A lugger brushed by us and its black-headed sailor tossed aboard to Charlie half a dozen watermelons.

Timbalier lighthouse—a lonesome, black, bleak, iron column piercing the skies, rising out of the water to a height nearly double that of the custom-house—is in charge of three keepers and is a second-class light.[3] It stands on iron legs and is reached from a small boat by an iron ladder hanging down to the water. On those huge iron pilings barnacles and oysters grow, and from the bracings sea trout and crabs can be caught without number.

While we were at the lighthouse some men in a lugger caught with alligator hooks two huge June fish—one weighing 100 the other 150 pounds. They looked like mammoth goggle-eyed yellow perch and were caught with a bait of a large, live catfish. The steaks from this fish are fine eating, and they are also good to be dried and salted down.

Up on the circular balcony of the lighthouse a year's supply of wood was stored, and here a lighthouse keeper was busy at the washtub, turning from it with a glad shout of welcome as the *Julia* came up. Sometimes four and five months elapse before these lonesome fellows have converse with anyone save themselves or hear one word from the world. They receive their rations from the government every six months. Their supplies are insufficient and consist of corned beef, salt pork, rice, grits, coffee, vinegar, sugar, flour and beans.

Each man is allowed twelve pounds of coffee for six months, two gallons of vinegar, 100 pounds of beef, 50 pounds of salt meat, twelve pounds of rice, and 25 pounds of sugar. He must furnish his own salt, pepper, and such extras. His salary is small, the head keeper's wages being only $700 a year. The government furnishes a small library and a medicine chest, and allows $20 a year for fuel.

The light is a magnificent piece of machinery, beautiful to the eye, and exquisitely kept. It will burn when wound up and set in revolution for three weeks. It is watched at night. During the day the sun is shaded from the ball-shaped glass compartment in which it is placed by yellow linen curtains. This glass dome is shielded from the attacks of storm-driven birds by a strong wire screen. During storms, ducks, redbirds, pops, pelicans, crows, mocking birds, geese, canaries and petrels fly at the light and are bruised to death, falling on the iron balcony below the globe. The keeper said he often gathered up the numbed humming-birds, warmed them to life, and then when the sun came out set them loose to find their way to the land where the roses are.

A large party of gentlemen were camped on the east shore of Timbalier, their luggers tethered in a small bayou, and their four or five tents looking like those of a little army. For a month they had been here hunting, shooting, surf-bathing and fishing, and getting such a taste of real outdoor wild camp life as will last them for a year to come.

They lived as we were living—on salt meat, prairie chickens, snipe, redfish, trout, crabs, and oysters, and so plentiful were the fish that they only occasionally drew the seine, and then more for amusement than anything else, and catching a wonder of fish. When the net came ashore in its meshes there was the gleam of the golden redfish, the brown and silver trout, the black shining of stingarees, the white and yellow of the huge pompano-shaped dogfish, the white gloves of the bellfish, the needlefish—like silver daggers—silver sardines and steel-gray cat, and an infinite variety whose names I know not.

The shelving beach—hard as teak, flecked with lovely shells, and here and there a little bed of sea rushes, with bits of broken ships, a coconut in its outer husk, washed by the tide and currents from the far Indies; sea beans glistening like brown marbles; eggs of gull and pelican, bounded on the one side by the hillocks of white sand; the dreary weeds and rushes that are the sole vegetation of the island, and on the other by the green Gulf water tumbling in, in white foam-crests to break on the bits of spar and mast; of barnacled logs and branches purpled with seaweed—made a most charming picture.

The sky would be soft gray and silver and shell pink at five in the morn-ing when the seine would be drawn. The men in blue trousers, red and gray shirts, and broad soft felt hats or sombreros of pliant palmetto, stood here and there, waist deep in the Gulf, each holding to the seine. They would stand in the water at one point, holding the upper edge of the seine like a long hammock in their right hands, and moved slowly out like a procession until a wide circle was made and all the men were in the water. Then slowly they closed in and began to come ashore, shaping a horseshoe curve as they strained and bent in their task to get back to the land.

One morning, fourteen men pulled at the seine, and yet they could not bring it in so heavy was it with a catch of sardines, stingarees, crabs and shrimps. More than thirty barrels of these were captured. The pretty things, like an autumn falling of silver poplar leaves, were strewn ankle deep on the sands.

Redfish are caught with a bait of mullet. The fisherman coils his line, which has no sinker, and loops an end over his wrist, and then walks out waist-deep into the gulf, where he tosses it as far as he can. If he has any luck at all, it will not be many seconds before there comes a swift running away with his line. One deft pull hooks his fish and he scampers to shore, running so fast that the line is kept taut, and he pulls through the surf, and lands on the sand, all flouting and splashing as it comes, a ten, fourteen, or twenty-pound redfish.

Perhaps he lands a trout or a mammoth dogfish, and if he's unlucky a giant stingaree will try to pull him out to sea. This latter may have the strength of ten men, and a wise fisherman will never be so foolhardy as to tie his line about his waist, for he knows the danger and does not laugh at it.

For three days we have been anchored off Timbalier. When we get up in the morning we have coffee and then walk straight out with redfish line into the Gulf, where perhaps we fish for two hours at a time and then nearer shore stand for a tussle with the surf. The air is cool and salt, and a brisk run along the beach sufficiently dries one's clothes. None of us would think of going back to the schooner merely for the sake of dry garments.

But after a time, the mournful cry of a conch comes floating over the water, and we get into our canoe, plowing through the water to reach her, and then, with the redfish and trout piled high about us, with a dead white pelican whose wings are used for a screen, with the sharp sandpaperlike fin of the shark I killed myself, malodorous in my hand, we pull back to the schooner and to breakfast.

I stand in the bows by the side of Siegfried, who is a mighty hunter. His kind face is tanned by the sun and beaten by the rain until he is like a statue of hammered copper. His eyes, that can see so far, that can tell whether the white flash on yonder coast be the flash of surf, or a flock of aigrettes, or merely the luminosity of a wave-polished log, are looking off to windward. A man-eater shark slips by—its fin showing above the green wave. Up in the lonesome lighthouse, far up in the glass ball, a man's voice can be heard singing that tuneless tune, that mysterious, fascinating rhythmic, that would put the very waves to sleep; that to the dark-eyed, lovely faced girls of these sand dunes and sea islands is like a kiss, stirring them to new life and more loveliness.

In a little while we shall all be gone, and the two men on the lighthouse will be alone, with no sights save untraveled waters, and a sky with its fleets of hurrying clouds; no sound save the surf breaking on Timbalier, or a fish faintly splashing in the deep. The night grows and deepens and darkens, and is full of the glory of the moon in eclipse. Timbalier has faded to a thin band of rushes, the anchored luggers are like shadows on the canvas of the night. The sky is like a blue ocean dusted with the pollen of yellow flowers, and in floats a bellfish. The bowl is luminous and strangely radiant and strongly colored with many dyes of amber and salmon, and the pink of fading roses, and the gold of cowslips, and the green of the sea wave, and the silver of the seafish.

A mighty stillness, as if all the earth were keeping silence, is everywhere, and amazed and awed we watch until midnight, there under the black shadows of the lighthouse, the mysterious, lovely ceremonial of Nature, when the radiant moon is clothed in the darkness of earth.

An accordion's notes, juicy with music, comes from a lugger nearby. The eclipse was over and the moon no longer like a bellfish nested as if from some travail; the man, lonesome and alone up in the lighthouse began his song again, and the waves boomed on the bank of sand. I stepped up to Siegfried, still looking to windward.

"Come," said I, "I have my pelican plume and my gull's egg and my fin of a shark, and I know where the aigrette builds her nest, and Lafitte's descendants make their home. I know where the stone crabs lurk, and I have seen the desolation of Last Island. You have shot the bird on the wing, and given me an aigrette feather for a sword, and have taken me to the top of the lighthouse.

"Come, let us take up our anchor and spread our sails and fly away like a pelican to the broad Atchafalaya, where alligators hide in the swamps and moccasins are coiled at the tree roots, and wild mocking birds mimic the music they have heard in Oyster Bayou."

And so Aleck and George and Charlie tumbled out, the sails shot up like a bird's wings, reaching forth after the pollen of stars, and when morning came the lighthouse of Timbalier was like a thin, black line against the blue, like the needle mast-top of some drowned ship still showing above the booming waves.

LAFAYETTE PARISH

In this piece, Catharine Cole exhibits an almost childlike wonder, the result of traveling without purpose or destination. To start on a trip with no itinerary goes against the grain of most travelers, particularly a newspaperwoman. Yet it reintroduces the element of surprise and delight which can result from setting out with all options open. It also allows the traveler to revisit places and people that have given pleasure in the past. To follow in the path of road salesmen, the "drummers" she constantly runs into, is to experience a gourmet meal, a comfortable bed, and above all, a good cup of coffee—often in the most unlikely places. (*Picayune*, September 2, 1888)

It is a wonder to me that the enterprising cyclers of New Orleans, who are always sighing for fresh fields and pastures new, do not forsake the sun-soaked asphalt of our one avenue for a real country outing in Louisiana.[1] Once or twice during this summer I have met a lonesome "wheel" or so and have even discovered tracks of the man with a camera. But these were mere occasionals, and the indescribable charms of our country roads, our olden-timed, moss-grown villages, our smart little towns, our fine plantations and unique Acadian homes remain all undiscovered by the multitude.

During a dry summer, a good wheelman would take very kindly to our country roads. He would find hills enough for sport, and when night came on there would be plenty of farmhouses, at any one of which he would be mightily welcome.

One afternoon I was drifting with the tide on a black-bosomed river at the edge of Lafayette parish. Here and there the gloomy trees crowded down in the water, mournful black, dismal, but at other places the bank, gently sloping, green and yielding, seemed to flow down to the river's rim.

On one of these banks behind a hedge of sassafras trees and young thorns, stood a ramshackle shanty. It was made of oak timbers, with a roof of broad ax-split shingles, covered with the weather slime of half a century, with a drunken chimney of mud and pine straw support between four willow poles. A huge log did duty for a stoop, and a few white pigeons were pluming themselves at the trough, by which a hollow-templed gray mule was nibbling straw.

A pirogue was tied up to the shore, and from a stake on the bank a stout cord ran down into the water. Attached to the cord was an old cracked cowbell. I rowed over to the cord, pulled it sharply, and waited to see what would happen after the twank, twank of the bell had ceased. A scraggy, mouldy-looking old darky, ragged, loose-jointed, and rheumatic, came hobbling out of the hut.

"Well, young missus, I mos' suttunly mistook you for a gas'pagoo.[2] You mus' excuse me, missus. You see I'se too ole to be migratin' around wid de hoe, so I sets me a fishin' line and ties de ole cowbell to it. Den Mistah Gas'pagoo comes rampagin' round, and directly he swallers my hook, and de bell rings and he says, by de bell, 'come out, and haul in de line,' and so when I heard de bell I natchly mistook you for a bite."

Even the most prejudiced person must admit that a country wherein the fish go swimming up to front doors and ring the bell has its unique attractions, and is worthy the attention of tourists and the man with the camera.

Naturally, when I determined to spend all my summer wandering over Louisiana, I tried to compose me an itinerary. The articles of Rebecca Harding Davis were routine and unsuggestive; the experiences of Mr. Warner were too limited; and if I may say it—who should not—too superficial, and even Mr. Cable left things *au large*.[3]

"What is *au large*?" I asked Father John one day, as I sat with him in his little parlor. "Father John" is a dear and lovely priest, leading a useful life in a spry little town, to which he was recently transferred from some old church out in the wilderness, a church where on feast days they bind the pure brow of Mary with spicy wreaths of cypress, where the holy water bowls are shells from the seashore, and where the women wear mantillas not bonnets—and Father John is not his name any more than it is mine.

Father John led me to the front door, and sweeping out with his rusty black sleeve and his big kind hand, seemed to describe in a circle all the deepening distance. He looked off beyond the field and forest into the unknown wilderness where, in rude little churches people make prayers to keep off the "gri-gri," where the blacks build houses without any windows, where a life inexpressibly unworldly is lived, and with a smile in his eyes and a sigh in his voice he said: "There, my child, there is *au large*."[4]

Somehow, after that I gave up all idea of having any itinerary, preferring rather to follow the plan of the immortal gentleman in Mother Goose's melodies who followed his own nose. Time and time again I find myself getting back into places I have already explored. And then, the French sir or madam who tends the little inn and who serves me with a divine dish of papabotte, or a souffle of calf's brains and capers, will bend over me smilingly, and say, "You like this 'ole town, hey?" and I smile and say, "Yes," and do not let on at all that I am merely doubling on my tracks, all for the want of a proper itinerary.[5]

And speaking of inns, there are two or three old-fashioned resorts in this state where the cooking is not to be excelled in all the length and breadth of the land. The gourmand and the epicure will tell you that a crown in heaven is ready for Lacombe, who keeps the dingy old hotel in Opelousas, and another for big, burly Bazus who keeps the equally dingy hotel in New Iberia, while Sylvanie down in ancient Abbeville is equally well known, and at the dormer windowed, red-brick caravansary in St. Martinsville, the eleven o'clock *déjeuner à la fourchette* is a feast to be remembered.[6]

At all of these places, old-fashioned methods of ease prevail, and among the customs is a huge bathtub fetched into one's room every night with plenty of water and bath towels, and in the morning, as a matter of course, the little grinning black Negro, the silver waiter, and the small steaming cup of incomparable *café noir*. Oh yes, there are other things in Louisiana besides swamps and snakes and commission merchants.

I sometimes think a very good series of articles on Louisiana might be written and entitled, "In the Wake of a Drummer." He is almost certain to pitch his tent in the pleasantest places—he is certain to gravitate naturally to the best hotel, to the pleasantest and most picturesque towns—and if one must have an itinerary, let it at least be borrowed from the genial, kindly and polite princes of good fellows who travel in a commercial way.

It was because I had no itinerary, and because the sleeping car conductor told me the drummers travel two hundred miles for the sake of spending Sunday at the Crescent and Star Hotel, that I happened on a

Saturday evening to leave the train at Lafayette. Lafayette is the parish seat of the parish of that same name and is an extremely pretty, progressive and attractive old-new town. In the olden days it was called Vermilionville and it began, as so many of these pretty places in the land of the Acadian exiles did begin, with a priest and a church.[7] It is pleasant to think that from the planted cross there sprang a new civilization, a thrifty town, and a prosperous community.

Each parish seems in some incomprehensible way to have its own characteristics of soil, scenery, and life, and to be in these respects different from its adjoining parishes. In Lafayette, the hills swell up from the brown, clear streams, and are softly rounded and fair to look upon; the rolling fields tuck down one into the other, cut off into plots by trim hedges of dogrose and sassafras, over which the scarlet trumpet vines tempt every sweet wind that blows.[8] On the rising hills, with their great groves of pecan trees and oaks, beautiful homes have been built—homes with deep porches and huge columns, and ample halls. Here, occasionally is to be seen a big cotton gin or sugar refinery, and behind the fields the inexhaustible pasture lands, rich, rolling, and dotted with cattle and haycocks, tell so plainly that stock-raising is one of the rich resources of the parish.

Lafayette town has a population of 3,000 with its business interests in the hands of thirty-five merchants. The railroad stops here and the fine cotton gin keeps a great deal of money in circulation, and the town is growing rapidly. The new fireproof jail for which there does not seem to be much use, cost $12,500, and the fine clerk's office is one of the most complete buildings of its kind in the country.

There are good churches and schools. The Loan and Building Association gives new life to the town, and its stock is being rapidly taken up. Many non-residents looking to the future with speculative eyes are securing interests in Lafayette. In the future it is almost certain that canning factories and other such industries will be located at this point.

The readers of Mr. Cable's latest and most lovely story cannot forget Carencro.[9] It is a little town with a church, several stores and a saloon, and some charming homes, situated about six miles away from Lafayette, on the Opelousas branch of the Southern Pacific. One Sunday morning we went out to Carencro to church, and afterwards to dinner at the hospitable home of Mr. C. C. Brown.[10] The houses along the way, being as our country houses most frequently are, unpainted, looked dismal and untenanted, for everyone was off to church.

We went up with carts—carry-alls laden with church people. All our way to Carencro was between yellow and green fields, where Jersey cattle rested under the shade of the big trees, or where geese floated over the still ponds. By and by, a turn in the road brought us to the town—a little town of 250 people or more—where the houses hide under rose thickets and where the long, violet-colored church is set down in a big pasture land. To the left, a huge mansion with a cross over it, was the priest's house; to the right the meadows are bronze-green, with ripened grasses, and everywhere hitched to fence rail and tree, were horses, mules, carts and carriages.

The church was thronged. Hundreds knelt in the aisles, on the steps and even out on the soft grass before the door. The priest's voice buzzing like a huge, hoarse bumble bee's, intoned the service. The beautiful eyes of the dark-browed, lovely girls—dewy eyes, sweet and languid—drooped before the elevation of the host. The mysterious breath of incense filled the church, a silver bell tinkled. "Zo-zo," who had leaned her turbaned head against the lintel of the confessional and dropped off asleep, awoke with a start. A man's rich voice sang something triumphant and sweet, and then service at Carencro was over.

Why Carencro? Because long times ago, down in the swamps near here a huge animal was once found, dead or dying. The crows clustered over it, and for weeks they remained; so long, that the place was avoided by the new settlers as the unholy haunt of the carrion crow. Old Governor Mouton used to tell how when he was a boy he remembered seeing the women pound indigo at the Carencro settlement with the huge mallet-like bone of the unknown mammoth that for so long a time had been food for the crows.[11] But today, there are none of the bones, nor any indigo plants, and even the crows have all but deserted their name place.

Its fair fields, its lovely rolling lands, are rich with crops and dotted with beautiful cattle. There is some talk of changing the name to St. Pierre, but this, I hope, will never be done, for whatever it means, "Carencro" has a pretty sound, and between Mr. Cable and the cultured and elegant people who live in the bit of a village it is certain to be best remembered just as it is—Carencro.[12]

Another day the very handsome and popular young sheriff, Mr. Isaac Broussard, drove us over half the parish it seemed—an up-hill-and-down-dale drive over farms and pastures, spinning along hard, brown roads, plowing through swollen coulees, passing by the steep-roofed Acadian homes, with the queer steps running up to the garrets on the outside of the house.[13] We drove through forests and along the green banks of the bayous. We rested at country stores; watched the cotton pickers at work in the whitening fields.

And finally we drove, after a visit to the village of Scott, a tidy and pretty hamlet, out across the level lands of the Broussard farm to the grove known all over the parish as the haunted oaks. Under these big trees great holes had been dug, fresh earth showing the work to have been done the night before. The holes were some eight and ten-feet deep. They are made by treasure-seekers—men who go about at night all over this state digging for treasures—for gold they will never find.

These fanatics are all over the state. Sometimes I have had a suspected one pointed out to me with a whispered, "They say he is a treasure seeker; that he has a divining rod and goes at night into the forests to dig for gold."

Years ago, a highwayman lived under these oaks and robbed and murdered the cattlemen returning from selling their flocks. He buried their gold under these trees, it is said, and now their ghosts keep watch over it. "I had de box in my hands, missus," said an old darky to me. "Fore God, I had dat box in my hands, when something 'scured the light o' de moon, a cold sperrit stood over me, and dat box dropped clean out o' sight through de bottom of its grave."

Oh, one may hear strange stories, if one will go over Louisiana in the track of the treasure seekers.

SÁBINE PÁRISH

In this column, Catherine Cole observes to her readers: "What a curious combination of character it is that makes a woman who is afraid of horses, storms, snakes, water, lightning, bears, wildcats, etc., love to go roughing it alone all over the wilds that almost no man knows." The comment is a revealing insight into why Martha Field chose the adventuresome, risky travel writing she excelled at.

Throughout her journalistic career she expressed disdain for middle-class women who accepted their positions as figurines in a Victorian display case. They were dutiful wives and mothers who spent their leisure time in mind-numbing at-homes, teas, and shopping excursions. Lower-class women were forced to work, and, as a widow with a child to raise, she identifies with them, even though intellectually and socially she belongs to the upper classes. Not only does she take pride in working as a newspaper writer, traditionally a male profession, but she is determined to compete with men as an equal by "roughing it" in the Louisiana backcountry "that almost no man knows." That she does so in spite of a laundry list of fears makes her accomplishment all the more admirable to her readers. (*Picayune*, August 21, 1892)

I wonder if any one beside myself regards it a trifle out of the commonplace for a lone woman, accompanied only by a very small boy, to be making a buggy tour of a grand, lonesome and under-populated state? It is true this modest journey lacks the *éclat* that might attend a voyage around the world, but while it is happily free from accidents, it at least has compensation in the shape of an endless chain of homely incident; that is, after all, the charm of travel.

In the first place, I am always put to the necessity of explaining myself. Naturally, even the most unsuspecting have their small and innocent curiosities concerning a lady who avoids railways as she would a plague and who scours the interior country as persistently as a drummer.

I am constantly asked "who am I drumming for," while no sooner do I insert into my driver's cranium the fact that I am only traveling to see the land, than I must change drivers and begin all over again. For the past five days my small Jehu has been one who regarded it as a personal injury that I resisted all his temptations to "drum." Every day he would say to me, "Ain't you gwine to drum today?" and, "I'se in the habit of driving drummers, I is."

Last night, when I dismissed him at Robeline with a well-earned *pour boire*, I heard him, as he drove away from the hotel, inform an idler that he and the lady had been drumming for a newspaper.[1]

Edward and I had some rare talks on that trip. Often there would be a stretch of fifteen miles through unbroken forest, and the boy had much to say. I learned lessons in physics I never knew before, as for instance: when lightning strikes a tree, at the end of seven years the thunderbolt rises out of the ground by the tree.

"My uncle has got one," said Ned. "It's like an iron aig, and if you keep it in a barrel of meal, no matter if the rain does leak into the barrel, the meal won't never sour."

But flattering things happen also. The other afternoon, after a ride of forty miles, I crawled, benumbed from the long sitting in one position, into the parlor of a country hotel.

"As soon as I saw you," said my hostess, who had a baby on her hip, "I thought you might be Catharine Cole. They say she's a-buggy riding all over the state."

I modestly admitted my own identity.

On another occasion—that was two nights since—we drove up in a blinding storm to a log cabin home in the heart of the forest, where the same name got me a doubly-warm welcome. After an hour we had supper. In the center of the table stood a tin pan as large around as the full moon looks to be.

"I made that there pie especially for you," said my hostess. To say that the pie was huge hardly expresses it. Why, you could have buried a ten-month-old baby under its blanket of paste. Interiorly, it was composed of apples, pears, peaches, homemade molasses and other handy ingredients, held down by a cover-lid of dough that would have daunted Gargantua. I smiled and ate all of the pie I could possibly hold. We had the rest of it for breakfast next morning.

It was also at a log-cabin home that I came out early in the soft fog of five o'clock in the morning to take my bath. A basin on a bench, a bucket of sparkling well water, cool and crisp as frost, a hastily doffed pillow case for a towel, were the all-sufficient conveniences. The family stood around sedately while I "used Pear's soap," violet water and toothpaste.[2] I was as dignified as they, and I must add, as unembarrassed. There's nothing to be ashamed of in being clean, is there? Nothing like roughing it to take the mock modesty out of one.

I look back with something of amazement, a good deal of pride, and a vast deal of pleasure, on my travel record for the past five days. In a buggy, driven by the redoubtable Ned, I have been from one side of Sabine parish to the other, and by various circumlocutions have accomplished 140 miles.

After such a journey it is enough to make one laugh at the foggy statisticians who are ominously croaking in the great magazines about the over-population of the world. The world is not coming to an end for want of elbow room—at least not yet awhile. Such splendid, beautiful and rich parishes as Sabine are holding less than fifty persons to the square mile. If only the state had some practical way of inducing or attracting immigration, say from Belgium, or our own Northwest, why, the newcomers landed in the lovely country of Sabine would think they had been carried to a new El Dorado.

With the building of a single log railway through this parish, its superb pine forests and uplands that now find little or no sale at from fifty cents to three dollars an acre, would become of almost fabulous value, the trees being of the best varieties and of uniform, enormous size. Cleared, these lands are productive, and yield the farmers an easy and a comfortable living. Of course, a reasonable man does not expect to make a lottery fortune at farming anywhere, but the farmer in Louisiana, even on the poorest land, can live better on less work and make more money at a smaller outlay, than he can in Minnesota, Dakota, or California on the best lands. It is impossible for me or any other newspaper writer to make a statement more incontrovertible or more easily proved than this.

The other day I stopped in the road to talk to a small farmer, attracted by the homely comfort and thrift of his home. It was a neat little board and log house, with a mud chimney, as red as Etruscan gold; at one end, a slanting porch in front, and drooping from the pent roof a curtain of the delicate, fern-like cypress vine. A woman was spinning on the porch, now and then stopping to give the cradle a rock. A lot of peaches were drying in the sun. Huge watermelons lolled in the patch at the end of an orchard. Cotton in full glory of pink and straw-colored bloom stretched away behind the rail fences and lads in the corn field were pulling fodder.

He told me he had eighty acres of land and had paid for it, house and all, $300. He would make this year six bales of cotton and 300 bushels of corn. He used no fertilizer. Nobody did in the parish, and an average crop was three-quarters of a bale to the acre. The chief trouble was getting his crop to market. The nearest railway was twenty miles.

With the exception of a small cut across the northeastern corner of the parish made by the Texas Pacific Railroad, Sabine parish has within its limits neither railway, telephone, nor telegraph. The town of Many, the largest in the parish, and its seat, has a cultured, wealthy and most hospitable people, but even Many is sixteen miles from a railway.[3]

At picturesque Fort Jesup, one of the finest male and female schools in the state is located.[4] It was founded by the Masons of Sabine parish, and is under their direct care. It is called the Masonic Institute for boys and girls, and its president, assistant, and chief teachers are all graduates of Sewanee University.[5] This is enough to establish its claim as a school for excellence, deserving the patronage of the best people in west Louisiana, and its maintenance is a source of pride not only to the Masonic Lodge of Sabine, but to the people of a state where education is not always the matter of primal importance it should be.

I may say that my outing in Sabine parish really began with Many, although it was necessarily preceded by the sixteen-mile drive from Robeline. The sun was hardly free of the pine tree-tops that fringe on the new railroad town of Robeline before we were on our way. In my notebook I find these lines, beginning: "Bundled out of sleeper more dead than alive with sleep. Stumbled up a red hill to a hotel. Dozed on a haircloth sofa, in a parlor full of untidiness left over from Sunday night, while a young man slicked up a freshly-vacated bedroom for me.

"Went to bed for a half hour in order to wake up. Imagined the bed was still warm and human-smelling from whomever had slept there last. Got up and tried to build a castle in the air over the five days' carriage ride before me. Castle wouldn't build. Had a country breakfast of hot soda biscuit, fried chicken, country butter and delicious cantaloupe. This heartened me up. Paid my bill and started: felt like a peddler when I saw how funny my steamer trunk looked tied with a rope behind the buggy.

"Crossed the railway track in safety, thank heaven! What a curious combination of character it is that makes a woman who is afraid of horses, storms, snakes, water, lightning, bears, wildcats, etc., love to go roughing it alone all over the wilds that almost no man knows."

I am afraid I shall have to be writing a vast deal about the pine forests and the sky. It seems I have seen almost nothing else. Surely nothing else as lovely. Shall I ever forget those gentle hills of far Sabine, set thick with giant pines, the sun casting long cross-bars of shadow on their evergreen slopes with here and there a bent sapling, as if giants had been putting up a wondrous set of croquet hoops for a game in the moonlight; the solemn stillness of the forests; the awful fear of them when storms come on; the little clearings that marked the complaisant yielding of nature to man.

Why, the fences were pine; the houses were pine; where a traveler had camped out, his bed had been pine boughs. If accidental death came it was likely to take the shape of a falling pine. Here and there a monster lay prone, digging his long, dead arms into the earth; here and there a fat, bare trunk shone like a tower of gold in the sun, oozing resin like honey, or a more precious amber, that spilled itself in beads as if the old tree was telling off on a rosary the perfumed prayer of the forest.

Of what frights I had in those forests later on I will say something by and by; when I scolded myself for ever coming into Sabine, prayed hastily without the picturesque adjunct of a rosary of resin drops, and finally thanked Providence for getting me out of it all to sit in the little hotel in Robeline, writing it up while waiting for my clothes to come home from the wash before starting off again.

Many a brave old soldier can tell you more, gentle reader, about Fort Jesup than can I, who only know that Taylor and Grant, and our own Jefferson Davis, have each held it. It is on the brow of a hill. The forests withdraw to make room for lovely, sloping meadows almost as broad as the moors of English Devonshire, and now all soft and tawny with long feathery sun-burnished grasses.

It was like being in Tennessee to see the long, low-roofed houses, built upon deep foundations of stones, slabs, and cobbles of crude gray and brown and purple rock, easily quarried from some neighboring hill.

We had a glimpse of the ivied ruins of the old fortress. It is now an historic beauty spot, and directly behind, on the highest point of the hill, with no air less sweet than that which teems with the balm of these beautiful pine trees that are the glory of Sabine, stands the Masonic Institute.

Its president, Mr. Colden, is a brave man. He declines to rush pupils through school or to graduate them before they have something to graduate on. It is a pity every teacher in the state is not so stoutly opposed to a superficial top-dressing of education.

Many is a sweet, sleepy, rambling old town, blinking on the hills very much like a comfortable and handsome cat sprawling and dozing in the sun. It is the sort of town that rests a city-bred person. I fairly luxuriated in its decent quiet. There are no saloons in the parish, and there is no drunkenness. Prohibition really seems to prohibit. The homes are pretty and flower-set, and the people are neighborly, kind and refined. The business is confined to three large stores of general merchandise.

The editor of the Sabine *Banner*, Mr. Don E. Sorelle, is also a prominent lawyer, and two or three other legal men of note reside here.[6] Mr. Sorelle's genial wife, by the way, is one of the handsomest women in West Louisiana.

In the heart of the town is a little Catholic church, whose beloved priest, Father Aubrie, has been for years a guiding spirit of good in the town. Only the other day, after a dreadful drought had ended in a rain, the little church bell rang out, calling the people to a thanksgiving mass. It is due to the efforts of the lovely young ladies of Many that a Protestant Sunday school is maintained, and that the Protestant graveyard is kept in repair.

It was a dismal, wet day when Ned and I and the ponies said goodbye to Many, and set forth on our journey. Merely walking to the buggy depressed my rather indiscreet blue gingham into a sort of pulpy squashiness that made me bless the washerwoman who had put starch into it. My beautiful hostess, a living image of Niobe, without her tears, followed me to the gate with a box of lunch and pleadings that we would wait until the storm was over.

Her old black cook, Aunt Lucy, stood whining on the gallery prophesying a cyclone. I enjoyed their distress. It made the journey look so big and important. I was afraid to go for fear of the storm, and afraid not to go for fear I'd miss something happening. At every crack of thunder the ponies laid their ears back as if ready to run. I'm sure horses have taken a dozen years off of my life.

In my luggage was included a candle, some matches, a clock, a map, a small frying pan and a bottle of hartshorn. All these for the emergencies of a night that never overtakes us, a sun that never really fails us, a road that has not as yet really evaded us, a snake that has not bitten us, and a starvation that has not yet appeared. Although if we grew hungry in a pine forest I am sure the only thing we could do would be to melt down the candle and fry young pine cones.

Through the rain, I piled in and bunched myself up somehow amongst the traveling bags, raincoats, umbrellas, lunch box and a tarpaulin to keep off the rain. Ned turned to me for instructions. I pointed a vague finger Northward. "Go that way," said I, as grandly as if I owned the universe and knew every cow-path on it.

Winding over shallow hollow and gentle slope of hill our rough little phaeton and fat little ponies made their way. The rain got behind us, and the sky came out like a baby from its bath, all new, sweet and clean. All about were forests of ash, dogwood, elm and beech. These trees have a particularly airy and delicate foliage, mostly on the upper sides of the branches that spread out like pale green mists, and in the sunshine cast an exquisite tapestry of shadow over road and pool and moss grown logs. One could look far into the woods, sleeping soft and sunny with perhaps a bird dumbly glancing on ashen wing under the shelf-like branches of a spreading beech. I have seen such forests in English Warwickshire. Not many realize that we have such beautiful scenes within a few hours of New Orleans.

After we had gaily trotted on for ten miles or more we stopped to ask the way to Marthaville. Not that we were going there, but simply to make talk with a native. The house was a cozy log cabin set under a cluster of oaks in the heart of a yellowing corn field. A little old man, with a faded underbrush of whiskers sprouting beneath his chin, a fashion that always struck me as being particularly uncomfortable—like a rucking crowding out of the neck of one's dress—sat smoking on his porch.

He was tilted back at that expressive don't-care-a-continental angle that is not to be pictured in mere language.

"Ef (puff) you air goin' to Marthy's mill (puff) youse air almighty long ways (puff) off. It's about thuthy-two miles I should surmise. But ef you air going (puff) to Sodus (puff) keep on till you come to the sluice, turn round by the branch till you pass an old field, and then take the second fork to your right."

I had vaguely determined to sleep at Sodus that night, and following these primitive and pretty-sounding directions, we kept on the Sodus road. The day wore on. We stopped under an elm just beyond a sharp-backed bridge, made of pine logs and rails, to eat our lunch, the ponies meanwhile cropping the elm branches and the wild alfalfa. Ned drew them buckets of water from the branch brook that went whispering by over a bed of pebbles and mosses.

Then a farmhouse came into view. It was, of course, made of pine logs, and on its old, loosely-shingled roof grew patches of moss and lichen here and there, like an old pate going bald. A great many little log barns, a sort of toy colony of them, stood around in puddles, each one already bulging with fodder and sweet-scented hay.

As we halted, a lady came to the open door and eyed us incuriously. Real country people betray no more emotional curiosity than Indians. This lady wore in the corner of her mouth a ruminative stick. Over the front of her dress was a little trail of fine brown powder, as if a boring worm or a small mole had been casting up a furrow; small settlements of the same lodged in the corners of her mouth. When she spoke she did so carefully, so as not to spill any of her saliva.

"Could I have some milk?"

Oh, yes, but what was I going to do with it.

"Drink it," said I promptly.

In a few moments she brought out a large white bowl, nearly full. I managed to lift it to my mouth, for a good, thirsty drink. Bah! It was stalely sour, and Ned finished it for me.

Two hours later we saw an old lady looking out at us through a palisade of pine sapling.

"Howdy!" she called, cheerily.

"Please," said I, "how far is it to Sodus?"

"This ain't no way to git to Sodus. You are dretful close to Marthysville. Sodus is sixteen miles off. Just turn down the red hill, keep on till the schoolhouse, turn to your left, and ef you don't go astray you're bound to fetch up at Sodus some time or ruther."

It was almost dark when we fetched up at Sodus. In a drive of at least thirty-eight miles—for we were lost several times—we had not passed a dozen houses. Truly, it seemed an entire European country might be housed in this one big, people-less parish of Sabine.

The daintiest of little country hotels, the wholesomest of country suppers, made me in love with this pretty little railway town. If anybody isn't satisfied with the hotels at Sodus and Marthaville, to which we came later on, he is hard to please.

I think I could conveniently skip the next forty miles. We left Sodus early, and keeping West, came at noon to Mr. John Parrott's, whose young son, a graduate of Tulane Medical College, has already a heavy practice in Sabine. A country physician, by the way, gets a dollar a mile, and perhaps is paid in land, cotton or live stock. Now and then, we passed a country school, where the majority of the pupils were of the olive-skinned, dark-eyed, picturesque Spanish type that told me as plainly as my map did that we were rapidly traveling Texas-ward.

"It looks mighty stormy, lady," warned an old man as we drove away from Parrott's. At that time I wasn't much afraid of a storm, because I didn't know. We pushed on through the forest, and I sat idly adoring the lovely, luminous, blue sky, all sprayed with the delicate tracery of the pine needles, telling myself it was the most beautiful thing eye could look upon. A pine forest has such a clean, cheerful, bare, deceptive look; you always feel as if the next turn in the road will bring you to a camp or house.

I opened my bag and took out a little picture—the little rose-leaf face of her who is the cricket on my hearth.[7] Surely, it was the sweetest thing in all that grandly lonesome forest!

At that moment a mournful howl fairly went in a coil around the woods. Overhead the blue had contracted. It was now framed in with a sulfurous, smoky gray saucer. The howl coiled around us again. Long, dried pine needles began to rain down from the trees. Thicker and faster they fell, until off in the woods was one brown bevy of them. The war of the wind was now terrific. The tree tops bent like bunches of green feathers.

The blue was all gone. A blinding flash, a deafening explosion, and one of Ned's thunder-bolts plowed into the ground on the crest of the not-distant hill. The horses fairly squatted on their haunches, like rabbits,

with fright. Here and there a dead tree fell. I watched ahead in an agony
of fear to see if any stood near the road, and when one did we fairly
galloped past it.

No storm at sea has wider terrors than a storm in August in a piney
wood forest. It was an hour before we came to a clearing in either the sky
or the forest, and I drew my first long breath. Such a clearing, too; overhead the forget-me-not sky; all about rolling pasture lands knee-deep in
a rich, pale grass, where cows cropped; off in the distance the rambling
roof and big wheels, all rust red, of a country saw and grist mill. A house
stood nearer the road. I went in to rest.

A woman sat up in bed with a day-old baby in her arms.

"How many have you?" I asked presently.

She halted.

"I think about ten," she said finally.

"Who takes care of you now?" was my next question.

"Oh, just my little girl. She's ten years old," was the answer of this
Madonna of the forest.

Think of that, you tenderly cared-for mothers whose infants are not
swaddled in rags and whose beds of pain are downy couches!

It was near this house, on the return journey, I spent the night at
Squire Darnell's.[8] The squire has lived in Sabine parish for fifty-three
years. He knows every foot of it, and his quaint old home of pine logs
and weather-boarding, set down behind bloomy banks of lady slipper,
petunias and four o'clocks, has passed into the maps of the state as
Darnell's Gin. Now, with blinded eyes, the fine old gentleman sits on
his vine-covered porch, his weather-beaten face like a fine Cellini bronze
framed in with silver, the patriarch of this fair "west countree."
It was here a dear old lady, Mrs. Tuggles—delicious, Dickensy name!—
sat knitting socks against the winter and reminding me of things I had
written ten years ago, or quoting poetry: not nowadays verse, but
Thompson's *Seasons* and Pope, and even earlier song-birds.

A neighbor or two dropped in from a distance of three or four miles
or so, and I got all the homely gossip, interjected between lines of Virgil,
in a thin, quavering voice, that when it faltered was gently prodded by
the squire's keener memory.

It was six o'clock and already sundown below the crowding hills
when we came to the Sabine River. From a tree hung a rusty plow blade

and an old hatchet. I struck sharply on this primitive gong. It rang out as beautifully as the voice of some deep-mouthed abbey bell, and presently a flatboat came creeping on its creaking ropes across that umber river.

Opposite was the tiny village of Hamilton, Texas, the only place within ten miles where I could stay all night.

I stood on the porch of Brittin's store, and around me was a half-moon of puzzled, confused-looking men.

"And so," said I desperately, "you mean to tell me I can't stay here all night; that I must either sleep in my buggy or camp out on that flatboat?"

"You see," answered one, clearing his throat as if trying to swallow a phlegm of embarrassment, "the truth is, we are all widowers in this town, and we don't think it fitten and proper or doing right by you ma'am."

I laughed outright, and I determined then and there to make known to the world the condition of this womanless town, this Eveless Eden.

The widowers withdrew to a corner of the store for a consultation. They, however, politely detailed one of their number to entertain me in conversation while they conferred with each other. Presently one of them went out the back door. He was gone a few minutes and came back with a beaming countenance. They all surrounded me again.

"Ma'am," said the spokesman, "deferring to your comfort we have decided you shall go to Wigginses. It's a mile and a half further on; but Mr. Wiggins has a mighty good wife, and a mighty nice farm, and you will be well cared for."

Need I tell you how glad I was to reach Wigginses, to strike a house that had a good wife in it, to hear a cheerful voice inviting me to "light," to hear the last funeral squawk of a fat chicken; to smell coffee boiling in the big log kitchen; to eat hot pumpkin bread and yellow butter, and afterwards to rest for a while on the porch in a chair of deer thongs?

I think during my forest drive I had accumulated at least a million little wood ticks that unanimously decided that my God should be their God, and that where I lodged, there they would lodge also. But when I blew out my flaring tin lamp and climbed into that huge feather bed at Wiggins's, with the windows set wide to give entrance to the sweet, dewy silence of the Texas night, chorded with the melancholy hoot of owl, the far off baying of a deer hound, and the sleepy note of a wood dove, I do not think all the ticks from all the forests could have kept me out of the lotus-land of sleep.

VERNON AND
RAPIDES PARISHES

One of the more telling stories in all of Martha Field's travel accounts is only a passing reference in this article, but it reveals a great deal about the author. While traveling through a Vernon Parish forest late in the day, attempting to reach town by nightfall, she spots a trout stream in the distance. Without a moment's hesitation about the folly of such an impulsive act, she stops her buggy, the boy driver cuts a hickory fishing pole, and they go trudging through a swamp in search of the elusive wild trout. When she returns without a nibble, one of the horses has disappeared, precious time is lost finding it, and as a result they barely reach shelter before dark.

Her explanation for her whimsical behavior: "anyone who has ever whipped a trout stream can no more resist it than fly." Much of the charm of Catharine Cole's travel adventures is this "what-the-hell" attitude toward common sense and ladylike behavior. She followed her curiosities and her passions, certain that they would lead her to something her readers would be delighted to learn about, such as spending the night with "a tiny little dwarf woman" sleeping at her feet. (*Picayune*, August 28, 1892)

"**B**ought Mrs. Leech's red bed quilt, and paid her two dollars and a half for it."

This is the only entry I find in my notebook concerning my first day's travel in Vernon parish. It is merely the mild statement of a small commercial transaction, but it recalls for me pages of little adventures, the golden-green wonder-world of a new country, the picturesque charm of a new people, and the unvarying interest of a ride of forty miles under "long-drawn aisles" of fragrant pines.

Nothing could have exceeded Mrs. Leech's pride and pleasure when she saw that her quilt had really effected a sale.

"Jest to think," said she, a tired smile coming like winter moonshine over the work-worn gray of her sweet, weather-beaten face. "Jest to think that a quilt I made is goin' to Orleens to live. Why I ain't been thar myself. But I have ben to Natchitoches, though."

"Sho!" said Mr. Leech, superiorly, "Natchitoches can't hold a candle to Orleens."

"Well, Suz," went on his wife, "I am that outdacious set up! I reckon when the Orleens ladies sees that bed quilt they'll jest be pesterin' you to get me to make 'em each one. Well, I jest could! I don't know 'bout the washin' and cookin', and milkin'. He helped me on that one. Every time I could spare a minute I sewed a patch on that quilt. I put good licks on that quilt, and now its sold to Orleens! Well Suz!"

It is a beautiful quilt—all red and white, made in a conventionalized design of British lions and unicorns, as exquisitely joined as if woven on a loom. It now gaily bedizens an "Orleens" bedroom, and in all the big city there isn't a better piece of work, faithfully made the one crude way in which love and longing for the beautiful in art flowered in a humble pine loghouse in the scented, far-off forests of Vernon.

Recalling Vernon parish, the red bed quilt will always recall something to me of the untold beauty of Louisiana. I remember on that first day out—a phrase as pleasantly reminiscent as if it referred to a voyage to the old world—I stopped to eat my lunch beside an old mill wedged in the rift of two red hills. The dim, uncertain road took a swift dip downwards, searching the fretted vault of an oak forest. A noisy stream rushed by, spilling itself over rocks and logs, here and there spending its tireless force in a dash of foam and sparkle that sprinkled even the shady road. Across this mill creek a water sawmill had been built—a sprawling homely mill—whose thick pine eaves and rough wheels had gone gray and green with water moss and slime.

I spread the lunch on the buggy seat and stood in the road. We seemed caught in a cup of red hills, through whose side, covered with a shiny carpet of dead pine needles, big cream and gray boulders of rock had worn their way. Overhead the perfect sky seemed paused in benediction. Under the nearer rocks wild ferns spread their feathery fronds like green fans.

The night before leaving Robeline and the pleasant society of Mrs. Coldwell's cheerful cottage, I had been showing my route to an admiring group of commercial travelers. I think nothing they said pleased me so much as the emphatic declaration of Mr. Robert Cage, that if a woman was going to travel from Robeline to Crowley overland he'd never complain of roughing it so long as he was on the road.

It was eight o'clock when we finally got under way. Through some foolish panic I had declined the service of the ponies I had had in Sabine parish and now Ned slapped the reins over as mean, gaunt and feeble a pair of red horses as ever held together on four legs. Slowly we jogged along through the one, long, business street of Robeline. The observed of the few observers eyed us critically, and with that provincial unsympathy that is more depressing than downright disapproval.

We had started off properly equipped this time, a box of canned luxuries was under the seat, fruit filled the bonnet of the buggy, whose top was down, but we seemed to have on board a load of care. Toilsomely the lean, red ponies strained over the steep hills. At the end of an hour and a quarter we had traveled four miles and were beside a neat little farmhouse.

I stopped here, made Ned unpack and sent him back after the ponies. Only a woman can understand how I had made up my mind before we left Robeline to do this thing. I had all along a Mrs. Nicklebyish presentiment that I could never make the trip to Crowley with those red beasties.[1] But I wished to test them in the hills in order to justify myself in what I was going to do. Besides, as I said to the air argumentatively, "what is the good of being a woman if you can't change your mind when you've a mind to?"

It took two hours and a half to make the change of horses, and meanwhile I sat on the porch making friends with the mistress of the little house. It had a delightfully attractive, pioneer air about it. Somehow it seems so natural for a new family to begin life in a new home in a new country that I wonder all the bridegrooms do not become woodsmen and begin the grand work of home building in the untried forests.

I was shown the garden, the baby, a little new frock just made for the baby's first Sunday at church; their plans for a flower garden were confided to me. I was told the thrilling story of how she had killed a "ground rattler" the day before, and then presently she went off to the kitchen, where a gallant fire of pine knots was sporting on the hearth. Pretty soon, the perfume of coffee came in on the wind, and then to make the promise good, all lumpy with clots of cream, came a bowl of steaming coffee, frothing and sparkling.

Down in the road before the house, while I still waited for Ned, I fell a-yarning with an old fellow who sat on the end of a log eating his lunch. He was out with an ox team and a Winchester rifle intending to kill a beef. He told me I was going powerfully out of my way if my destination was Leesville.

"What you had ought to hev done," said he, "was to go out of Robeline by the old road to San Antonio. Ef you'd a bin a soldier settin' off for the Mexican War, that's the road you'd have took. Some folks call it the Main road nowadays. It was a main-traveled road forty or fifty years ago, and later when Texas was offering free homes to settlers. But ef you air bent on going this way to Leesville, you must take keer and not git turned off on some neighborhood road."

I think it was the pleasantly promising phrase "neighborhood road" that sent my spirits up again. It made me think on sunny patches of amber corn fields, of rail fences trellised with ripening maypops, of cool, grassy lanes leading past corn cribs to log cabin homes. I did not know how mightily well-acquainted I was to get with "neighborhood roads" even before night fell.

The day drew on, and with patient painstaking we tried to follow the main- traveled road. At a farmhouse I had been told to keep on the trail of the mail cart that had passed down the day before. This was not easy to do on the carpet of dead pine needles, and Ned and I often left the buggy at the fork of a road to search ahead, like Indians on the warpath, for some sign of a trail. Broken pine needles where a country pony's unshod hoof had been—fresh signs of manure—these were signs enough to send us on our way. All about lay the endless forest, hill dovetailing into hill, winding brown roads leading between mossy banks down to gravel beds of limpid brooks in which watercress grew, profusely bending with the stream.

Here and there the pine forest parted at the foot of a hill to make room for a swampy growth of oak and ash and elm and beech. The sun shone on the brown billows of dead leaves heaped by last winter's winds, and the moss made rich pillows of the gnarled roots on which the sleepy sunshine rested in a lazy splendor and unhaste. Between the pools of sunshine and the cool caves of shadow I caught the brown glances of a trout stream. Anyone who has ever whipped a trout stream can no more resist it than fly.

I think if I had not had a steel bob with me I should have rigged up a paper one. Ned cut a slender pole of hickory, I fastened my line, we took the ponies out to rest them, tied them to a tree, and in a minute more I was timidly trudging across a snaky swamp, the water oozing up into my low-quarter shoes, expecting every moment to be bitten by, at least, a moccasin, but keeping on, as only one can do who sees glaring ahead the brown, teeming waters of a trout pool.

When we went back, disgusted and fishless, to the buggy, one of the horses was gone. I crawled into the vehicle and sat there silently repenting and telling myself it served me right, while Ned went hunting the runaway. Night never seemed to fall so fast. The sunshine ran over the hills like flocks of frightened white sheep, leaving only long black shapes of shadows and that dewy stillness, as if all earth were in suspension, waiting for the gray feet of night to press down silently and echoless. I do not know how, where or when this letter to the *Picayune* would have been written had it not been that Ned just then came leading back the pony.[2]

We pushed on, knowing now we were off our course, but trying to keep up with the fleeting sun. Nothing was left of the road, save where here and there a white gash on a tree showed the way had been blazed by somebody. We crashed on over roots and scrub oaks that, bending, lashed the ponies' flanks. Here and there a young pine stood forth like a huge green brush for cleaning lamp chimneys. The no-thoroughfare was almost impassably steep, but we kept to the vague clearing simply because there was no turning back. Sometimes Ned got out and lifted the wheels over the fallen logs.

At last we saw signs of a clearing ahead of us, a broader curtain of light, and in ten minutes had come upon a little log cabin nestled down in that lonesome forest, miles upon miles away from anywhere. I asked a woman at the door the way to somewhere. She didn't know Leesville, Kirk's Mill, Leech's Mill or any local point I could name—they were all Greek to her.

At that moment a man came up. He had a dead deer on a led horse, and blinking at the game law, I had half a mind to stay all night for the sake of broiled venison. We got our bearings, however, and pushed on through the green wall of underbrush until, just at dusk, the ponies' feet scuffled hopefully into the dust of a main-traveled road, and a mile or two more brought us to the welcoming mistress of Leech's Mill.

It was a big, tidy house of new logs built after the fashion of all these country homes. That is, two houses are built about twelve feet apart, and then one roof is made to cover both, and one gallery runs across the front doors of both. The chimneys will be of the red earth and gray moss, pretty little tendrils of which float in the wind, making of the smoke tower a sort of old red Indian chief, bearded and gray. Sometimes—nay, oftenest—there will be in the kitchen quite a grand range. I stopped one night in a house where all the bedsteads were homemade of split pine rails, but where the coffee was boiled and the salt meat fried on as superb a range as ever stood in a city kitchen.

This house at Leech's Mill was ceiled in all its rooms with golden pine planks. On one corner of the porch sat a curious little dwarf woman not any higher than my knee and with a huge head and face. She was blind and sat knitting with her tiny hands, singing in a remarkably sweet voice. A little while later, on wooden benches and deer-hide chairs, we gathered about the supper table—the hearty farmer, his pleasant wife and long rows of children, whose white locks made me think of dandelions gone to seed. A flare light cast a Rembrandtesque glow on the young moons of faces, caught the muzzle of a gun on the wall, the curve of a spinning wheel in the corner. Out on the porch in the dark of her double night the little dwarf woman still knitted and sang.

That night, I slept on a perfumed bed of freshly-gathered pine needles. An opening cut in the wall made for me an azure picture of the star-powdered sky, against which pine trees leaned like tropic palms. At my feet on a pallet slept the tiny little dwarf woman. Sometimes in the night I could hear the soft flurry of bats' wings. They seemed the airy steeds of sleep, who might have brought the tiny woman from out some far-off grotesque land of Lilliput.

The most magnificent stretch of unbroken pine forest on the continent is what may truthfully be said of Vernon parish. The parish forms a square about forty miles wide, by thirty-eight miles long. Its western boundary is the Sabine River, its nearest railroad is the new Watkins, Kansas City and Gulf, that lacks twelve miles of touching Vernon parish. In the center of the parish is an island of lovely prairie, about three miles long and one mile wide. In the West is a beautiful rock country—the hills of pine bulging with a handsome stone. Creeks filled with fish thread this parish; half of them flow West into the Sabine, half East into the Calcasieu, which has its pretty beginnings in Vernon.

Here is pine forest in all its splendor. It would seem that one could mow the trees down like grain if one just had a scythe big enough. During my second day's ride of thirty-five miles I measured haphazard along the roadside many of the pine trees, and the smallest girth I found was nine feet-two inches. Here also is to be found, as nowhere else, that lovely, curly pine, panels of which have been sent to decorate the World's Fair buildings, and have there made such a sensation.

Put a colony of Germans into this forest and they would use it up in making toys. Give it a railroad, and every stick of it could be cut into furniture, but now the few settlers deaden and burn these magnificent trees in order to get room to plant corn and cane and sorghum and cotton. There are thousands of acres of land ready for homestead entry, and thousands more to be had at a cost per acre of a little more than the price of one tree.

When I was in Leesville, the pretty pine-girt parish seat, two gentlemen, agents from Alexandria, were going through the country listing lands—that is locating lands that can be bought. In the neighborhood of Leesville they had listed 7,000 acres of this mighty forest at a uniform price of $2.50 an acre. In ten years from now that land will be along the line of a railroad, and every acre of it will be worth ten times its present price.

The people of Vernon are mostly from Alabama, or Mississippi, or England. I did not see a Colored family during all the time I was in the parish, and only visited one Colored school, at which, by the way, two-thirds of the pupils were bearded or gray-haired men. The school system is fairly good, the health of the people excellent, and a comfort of housekeeping is the delicious water procurable from wells and springs that bubble out of the rocks or beds of gravel.

The people lead simple, moral, thrifty lives. They raise all they consume, know nothing of luxuries beyond gorgeous cooking stoves, have dim ideas about life or property insurance outside of the towns. They save their money in a stocking foot, go to camp meeting once a year, have a deer drive and a fishing bout whenever they can, and are happy and contented where you and I are sad or sour. For picturesque beauty, for the making of financial wealth and the growth of a great prosperity, Louisiana has no fairer parish than Vernon, with its smiling skies and untouched treasures.

Leesville, the parish seat, directly in the center of the parish, has a population of a couple hundred, several stores, a union church, two weekly newpapers, and two hostelries for the convenience of the traveling public.

From Leesville the route was due East a distance of forty miles to Hineston, a pretty, tiny village inside of the varied parish of Rapides. This time there was no doubt about the main-traveled road. It led us over steep hills and long pine flats, through thickets of hazelnut bushes and underladen hickory and walnut trees. Really more wealth rots each year into the ground in Louisiana than is taken out of it.

Hineston, a star-route post office village, is on the edge of Rapides parish, where the pine forests are thickest. The post-mistress, Mrs. M. N. Williams, is an accomplished and thoroughly practical woman, whose influence in the pleasant homes along the "neighborhood roads" is always on the side of education and parish improvement. It is due to the efforts and generosity and example of her family that Hineston has a camp meeting tabernacle, a country church, and schoolhouse.

I think the most suggestive fact, the thing that pleased me most about Hineston, was the story I heard there of an invisible old darky who lived in a little ramshackle log cabin along the rim of the road. He was not at home, being off driving cattle—his own cattle, too. Here and there in tiny clearings, this old fellow had planted tobacco, corn and sweet potatoes; his tobacco, coarse, sweet and pure, finds a ready sale. In fact, this thrifty old fellow, owning, I dare say, not a rod of land, fighting fortune with a spade and a hoe, is making good money, and owns a hundred head of stock.

It was in the earliest of the young, fine morning when I set off from Hineston for Babb's Bridge, down in the corner of Rapides parish. Why am I the only woman in the state to have the joy and novelty of such a summer outing? I can't sing, so I whistled buoyantly as we rattled along the dewy road, with young things starting from our path on either side, occasionally so "rattling" a pretty lizard that it merely ran up and down a log, and had no head left with which to escape. By and by I could stand it no longer. The pioneer blood was in my veins. I got out to walk.

"Go ahead," said I imperiously to Ned, "and wait for me at the first creek." I cut a hazel branch as a weapon against a possible snake and stepped out briskly over the springy turf that tried to cover the gay red road.

A forest is a lonesome place. I remember once, years ago, being on a mountainside at Andermatt, in Switzerland. I walked on, mightily afraid of nature, of her solitudes, her rocks, her brawling snow-fed torrents. I had not been alone in that sweet fern-set forest of Rapides for ten minutes before I wished for company. Little dissolute frogs hopping home after a night's wooing startled me; the lizards on the logs were not so timid as I, nor the grasshoppers tilting on the fern bracken. The forest took up its familiar song; it is a cry like falling rain, you know. Soft clouds detached themselves from the mother bank and floated off like thistledown. Not a bird sang, not a dove mourned; the road had no tracks save those of my own vehicle.

I looked North, South, and East and West over a timorous shoulder; there was nothing in sight save ferns, pines, ivory lichens on long-lying logs, a red road and a foot passenger in a mud-stained gingham gown.

On the line of the Watkins, Kansas City and Gulf road, that 100-mile-long bit of railway that runs between Lake Charles and Alexandria, and that is expected to speedily develop the resources of this rich section of the state, to find a market for its products and sawmills for its trees, is a little thirty-year-old town by the name of Babb's Bridge. The bridge—Babb's bridge, you know—is an affair of scented pine planks that steeply roofs over a section of a lovely creek, so clear, so pure, that if one cast a newspaper on its shingly bottom I quite believe one could read its pages through the spectacles of the water.

It is only one of the typical American villages that has tempted a railway to put a station at its portal, a village where the cottage homes cheerfully hide behind rose gardens, where vegetables thrive in a trim array, and where sweet orchards trail behind the houses, dropping their ripe balls into the long grasses. I was told of an orchard at this place where the pears weigh a pound each. Fancy what a fortune is revealed, like a nugget gleaming out of a gold hill, for some enterprising fruit grower.

We put by the ponies at Babb's Bridge and I went by invitation to the schoolhouse to meet the people who came from many miles around to make their gentle welcome.[3] It was worth all the weary days of travel, all the frights and solitary hours to feel the friendly clasp of honest hands, to hear the loyal words of men and women who have the state's good near their hearts.

It was nightfall of the second day when I finally left the brawl of Spring Creek and the peaceful homes of Babb's Bridge behind me as I made for the Acadian prairies. And tucked down in my heart, to grow there as a bit of fern in amber, was the four-leaf clover of a phrase that each man and woman had said to me with frank simplicity: "I wish you luck."

Out on the prairies, when I looked my last on that golden forest with its golden-hearted people, I said over to myself like a legend, the wish words: "I wish you luck."

MOREHOUSE AND WEST CARROLL PARISHES

Martha Field's ambivalence toward men is nowhere more directly expressed than in this tale of getting lost in the Boeuf River swamp. Before leaving on her trek through the dry swamp she is admonished by a pair of salesmen that she should have started earlier. She takes this superior-male reproach with "gall and wormwood." Later, however, when she is hopelessly lost, she "cried for joy" at meeting a wizened black man who helped her ford Boeuf River. She was thankful that he was a man, for "his presence," she confesses, "gave me courage."

Throughout this frightening and stressful expedition she never loses her self-deprecating sense of humor at what she recognizes as a comedy of errors. With one wrong turn after another, she loses her way again and again. She also loses her temper at her youthful driver, prompting him to travel too fast over a cotton field and break her buggy into matchsticks. Her ability to laugh at her own weaknesses undoubtedly helped her retain her equilibrium through one of the most exasperating trips she ever took. (*Picayune*, November 27 and December 1, 1892)

"**N**o, nothing ever happens," I had been saying in answer to a question. "It is all monotonously uneventful. One might as well be going across country in a Pullman car. I think even the occasional panics that the ponies get into are half assumed for the sake of variety."

We stood on the porch of the Campbell House at Bastrop, the king, queen and all the royal family of dainty inns, and while Philip packed up the worldly goods and chattels, I had been inquiring the way of two polite commercial travelers—and when are they not polite and kind?

We were bound for Floyd, the parish town of West Carroll and the distance at the lowest calculation was forty miles.

"What you ought to have done, you know, was to have started before daylight this morning. Your boy will have to get a move on him to reach Floyd by dark."

I like to hear a great big man telling a small, ignorant woman what she ought to have done. No matter what a woman does there is always a superior creature handy who can make things cheerful and lively for her conscience by this insidious, subtle and poisonous form of reproach. To that weak creature who suffers from the pangs of indecision, who never knows which of the two kinds of soup on the bill-of-fare to select, such reminders of inefficiency are gall and wormwood.

"Yes," cheerfully continued this gentlemanly Job's comforter, "It's thirty-five miles if it's a foot. You've to travel down the prairie to Oak Ridge, then get somebody to put you on the right road into the swamp. That swamp is six miles wide. Then you go round a lake, ford Boeuf River—be sure and get the right ford—and then you strike another swamp."

"It's twelve miles through that and no trail. If you get lost, Madam, God knows what will become of you, and after that it's a clear stretch up to Floyd through the prettiest country the sun ever shone on."

It was as clear as a cook-book recipe, but not precisely comforting, and as we trotted down the broad, level avenue leading out of Bastrop, and across the forest-covered hill, sloping southward to the patch of prairie that lies in Morehouse Parish, my mental barometer went down to 28.

We stopped at the livery stable to pay the bill, and here we received more solace. "Ain't been nobody through that swamp in a year except some witnesses come over on horseback for a murder trial two months ago. Reckon you can follow their trail."

How lovely the country looked that morning. I was glad when we had crossed the wood—beautiful, green and sweet-scented as it was, and had come out into the open prairie that smiled like a pool of yellow sunshine. It was a sort of pocket-edition of a prairie, but there were cotton fields on either side, where darkies sang. There were shanties along the roadside, the beginnings of winter wood piles, cur dogs tied by the broken gates, little children tethered to the steps while their mothers were off in the field.

There were fine plantation homes, under stately groves of trees, with carriages passing. In the fence corners stood rude baskets frothed with cotton; wagons passed their loose white loads quivering like milk jelly. Truly enough, that beautiful, serene prairie of cotton plantations, lying between Bastrop and Oak Ridge might very well be given the name of "the white country."

Oak Ridge, on the railroad, is one of the big shipping points in Morehouse Parish. It is a pretty and thrifty village, the home of a number of prominent Louisiana families, and its chief object of interest to an idle traveler is the charming and thoroughly picturesque Episcopal Church brooding under the dark shadows of dense trees.

"Will you kindly put us on the right road for Floyd?" I asked as nonchalantly as I could, as if the way were a regular Regent Street thoroughfare when once you found it. The gentleman in the store took off his hat politely. Perhaps he had been relieved to experience that I wasn't a book agent.

"Through the swamp to Floyd, Madam? There hasn't been more than three or four persons through there in a year."

A vicious little whisper of wind came out of the hollow, irresolute shape or shadow behind the church. It looked as dark in there as it was white in the sunshine out here where the stores were. The swamp creeps up to the very corporation limits of Oak Ridge. One enters it precipitately, leaving behind sunshine and warmth, singing birds and companionship.

We were to keep straight on for six miles, then beyond a ridge of high land, that curious ridge that crosses or runs through all the north country lowlands, we should find a cabin or two, a few cotton fields, an egg-shaped lake, and, after fording the river, be in the great swamp of the Boeuf country.

It was a lovely outlook as we turned into that unknown land. I forgot my presentiments and halted the horses and waited patiently, studying a new phase of a Louisiana swamp. Imagine, as far as a rabbit can run a soft wood-brown matted carpet of dead leaves, here and there stirred by a tiny whirlwind, so that a little silken whisper came to the ear from this side and that, as if the pixies had got hold of you. Stately and tall, the antlered trees reached up to the blue, so hiding it that only here and there it showed through the meshes of wind-swept branches.

The cypress trees were like the gray clustered columns of stone in Westminister Abbey. These have a peculiar formation. Spreading broadly at the base, covering an enormous space, the inflated trunks that look to have been swollen out by water seem to separate into columns that cluster close together, forming the grand body of the tree. I have seen a cypress tree formed of five or six such clusters, with here and there around the trunk sometimes up as high as thirty feet, broad white marks like girdles showing where the water had been.

These water marks do not easily wear off and I have counted ten or twelve water rings on swamp trees. The swampers getting out lumber had cut out a broad avenue a hundred feet wide. It extended in a straight line from East to West for six miles. The sunlight lay along it like a golden river. At this time of the year the swamp is dry. It is like a lovely wooded park and a drive through it was full of solitary charm.

The Negro shanties, the head of the lake, the old cotton fields, and then two hours of tiresome search after Boeuf River. The trail was gone, the horses were pushed through brush and bramble, over logs, roots and rotting trees. The ground lay in billows and heaps, as if washed so by swirling pools and currents of overflow.

Two cabins stood on a hill—but the chimneys were broken; the thatched roofs trailed their yellow rushes heavily, and here and there had caved in. Two or three wild cattle came close to the buggy; one with a calf at her flank put her bold head over the wheel with more than human defiance. We drove over an old field given over to cockleburrs, fence all down, cotton ridges gridironing the ground, and found ourselves on the steep bank of the Boeuf. Far below us the water crawled and coiled like a slimy snake. Low green bushes, dense as a jungle of cane, fringed the shores with an emerald-hued lace. We wearily went back; clearly this was no way out of our difficulty.

I'm afraid I blamed Philip. I put all the blame on him. I said I told you so. I even poached on the preserves of my drumming friend, and recited what he ought to have done. Perhaps Philip drove fast to get away from the talk, but at any rate no slackly-made American buggy can stand fast driving over an old cotton field—there was a sharp report and another; the buggy had settled slowly and stately like a foundered ship at sea, going down stern first. There was an unmistakable feminine scream—a second small crash of crisp timbers, and then silence.

How we bound up that splintered vehicle with ropes and reins—how Philip held up the body while I managed to slip under it two trestles in the shape of young persimmon trees—how that wild cow took, so to speak, a horn in the proceedings; what a figure we cut—are things that cannot be told in cold, cruel, disillusioning type.

Just as we were about to start off again for nowhere, for we were hopelessly lost, I saw scuttling through the sand on the river bank sixty feet below us the squat, crippled, twisted figure of a little, black man. At first, he might easily have been mistaken for the animated section of a gnarled and twisted mulberry tree, such as are fearfully up by the deserted cabin.

We called him. He scuffled like a rabbit up the sandy hill and came running and leaping towards us—the figurehead of a Portuguese pirate and a Louisiana cornfield darky. But he was a man. I sighed with relief. I even cried with joy. I fed him all the cakes good Mistress Campbell had put away for my lunch. I drained the flask of rare port a friend had sent me for this trip—port of priceless value out of a dead priest's cellar. Friday was not more welcome to Crusoe than that small, lean, little outline of a man was to me.

He lived in the wreck of the shanty on the hill, and catches game and fish in traps for a living. He didn't know the way to Oak Ridge, and had never heard of Floyd, but, at any rate, he was a man and his presence gave me courage. Finally, we forded Boeuf River, it flowing over my feet because we missed the trail. On the other side we found on the ridge several houses, set in small fields, where life must be the very double extract of solitude and lonesomeness, and here I paid a man a dollar to show us the way into the swamp. No. The notebook says, on the next page, he refused the money; he wished us good luck from panthers, and said whatever we did, we must not get lost.

I think when that friendly, hearty young farmer who has set up his fireside in the heart of that awful swamp, bravely earning money to buy him a home in the highlands, turned us loose in the swamp, all the heart of me and courage was gone. Before us were wildernesses of trees, willows and oaks, cypress on the ground in fanciful clusters, palms, yuccas whose faded, green, century plant-like flowers spilled their spirals in sallow coils over the long green daggers.

Here, an opening looked like a trail, until you looked elsewhere, when another opening looked equally deceptive. In places were small pools of shining black water, so small, so shining they looked like big, black unfriendly eyes staring at my misery. Through the yellow silence, the mystery, the uncanny color, across the trees in their evil twisted shapes, the vast magnitude, the tracklessness of it all, there breathed the wind that never sleeps. Its cry was smothered like a far-off warning. I seemed to see but one thing: three men in slouched hats riding through this worse-than-night to carry to a court of law the awful bloody story of a murder.

An awful smell enveloped us. It banished every other sense. It was as killing to sentiment as seasickness is to fear. I defy anybody to think of anything else when they smell a polecat. To say that it is the polyglot of smells, the cynosure of smells, the alpha and omega of smells would not be putting it strongly enough. I found the next day I put this note in my book: Must inform the newspaper proprietors that it is worth a hundred dollars a week to smell polecats for them.

In a haste, justified by the circumstances, we drove recklessly over a log. At least the horses did, but the buggy did not. The double-tree had snapped off, and the horses walked away to browse in an adjacent cane-brake. Before we were sufficiently mended up after this episode to need the ponies, they had consumed, measuring by the rod, canebrakes a mile long. They left a big hole in the brake. For years it will be a sort of inverted monument to our disaster, known only to the raccoons, the deer and the casually- passing polecats of Boeuf River swamp.

I remember with remorse how, at the beginning of this eccentric outing through familiar lands, I flippantly sneered at the literature I had accumulated for the trip. Today, if I had a mind to, I could write a poem, an epic, a sonnet, a ballad, an anthem, an elegy, on the subject of the books that have helped me. I tore up those novels I had been carrying and strewed them thick as leaves across that trackless swamp, so that we at least might retrace our steps. At this moment, that swamp contains enough good, solid gush to stock a first-class American syndicate dealing in the amateur efforts of the early great.

Sometimes the way—our only trail was an occasionally ghostly imprint of a hoof, often searched for on the hands and knees—led us through a canebrake. There was no sunlight; the shade was too dense, the jungle too thick, the trees too high. But just as night fell we came to the end of the swamp, having done twelve miles, nearly all on foot. Owls hooted in the trees we passed under, and a dog barked; we thought it was a dog, but at Floyd they said it must have been a wolf.

Never shall I forget the beauty, the light, the brightness and openness of the country as we came out upon it from that tunnel of swamp. The meadows were golden with grass, the fields were bronzed with denuded cornstalks, meadow larks sang their late songs on the rail-fences, here and there a pale, thin furrow of smoke unfurled on the air, showing where some American sovereign was in residence. To be sure, it was a dark night coming on, and we had fourteen miles to go, but what was that; were we not free of the swamp, and had I not the feminine satisfaction of knowing that all my presentiments had come true?

In the dewy road we met three horsemen. I stopped them to ask the way and how far it was to Floyd. I always do. For a space of two hours I have found out that every man you meet will say the same thing. The horseman told us it was eleven miles to Floyd. For at least two hours of as rapid travel as our ponies could make we inquired at every house and of every passer, but all agreed that it was eleven miles. After that was a drop to seven miles.

The horsemen looked us over as people usually do. "You seem all broke up," said one, with such manifestly unintentional slang as to be delicious. I told him the story of our disasters—was he not a man? Was it not a comfort, even at this late day, to meet one of these lords of creation and protectors of the weak?

He whistled and said to the air, as it were, "Jimminy Christopher!"

"I think so, too," said I.

Reader, will you believe that we lost our way again; that we deliberately left that plain, open road and took a faint ox-cart trail that deluded us off into the swamp? It seemed we could not break ourselves of the habit of going into Boeuf River swamp, that priceless woodland that is a perpetual barrier between West Carroll and Morehouse parishes. Only that I resolutely turned back at sight of the first fateful, malignant red-eye of a cypress knee, this letter might never had been written, and she who signs her name to it might have become a sort of Wandering Jew of the Boeuf lands, condemned to walk the earth, like the ghost of Hamlet's father.

I think it was nearly midnight when we hallooed at some dim shape leaning over a shanty gate.

"How far is Floyd, Auntie?"

"Jest about haffer mile, honey, but be mighty keerful you don't pass it in de dark!"

I could have embraced that village blacksmith, wheelwright, carpenter, and joiner when he called me out under the big sycamore tree, dropping its wrinkled leaves like sheets of antique parchment all etched with the story of summer's goodbye, and told me that he would be rushed mightily to get me mended in two days.

He was a handsome young fellow and, better than that, a thorough workman. When he finally brought my shoddy vehicle back to me, all its broken, brittle bars of kindling wood replaced by lithe lengths of oak, I could see that it was better than new, and told him so.

He looked thoughtful. "It takes a plain country workman a long time to learn how to slouch a job," said he. "Maybe that's the reason we keep so poor."

BATON ROUGE,
LOUISIANA STATE
UNIVERSITY

During her travels through Louisiana, Martha Field never failed to visit the educational institutions she happened upon, and to praise their sometimes questionable excellence. Her career as a New Orleans newspaperwoman was marked by an indefatigable support of education, particularly the education of women. The one notorious blind spot in this support is her failure to recognize the need for schools, teachers, and revenue for the education of African Americans. She mentions "Colored" schools only in passing, and never promotes them as she does segregated white schools.

In this piece, she excoriates the Louisiana legislature for its failure to recognize the importance of Louisiana State University to the state's future. She is always quick to take on state government for its shortsighted vision. (*Picayune*, November 4, 1888)

The other bright morning I made my way across the streets of Baton Rouge up to the Garrison grounds where a state fair was in progress.[1] A band of music was blowing away tunefully and a flag or two seemed to be flying in and out among the whitewashed trunks of the big trees. It seemed very pleasant to be going a-fairing and I hoped as we strolled along, nearing the flags and the music, that the fair would be a goodly one of the old-fashioned sort to which people came from all the countryside in carry-alls and wagons and omnibuses, bringing huge hampers of lunch to be eaten picnic-fashion under the trees.

I hoped for an amphitheater and a great crowd of people and proud farmers leading their prize bulls and cattle and colts into the ring to be admired and inspected, and that the judges would gather about and consult wisely, and that by and by one of them would take a blue ribbon and march over to some animal and tie it on its bridle, and another judge would do as much with a red ribbon for some other animal, and that the band would play and the people hurrah and be cheerful and contented until the hour for the races, or the young ladies riding, or the tournament, or whatever the great sport might be, should arrive.

It is against a town, I admit, to be the seat of government, the location of the penitentiary, and the dwelling place of the usual and inevitable political hangers-on; but notwithstanding all these, Baton Rouge has certain characteristics that will forever charm. It is the city of roses of the South, and nowhere else can flowers be found in such tropical profusion and splendor. Its magnificent battlemented old castle of a State House, crowning a terraced hill, is one of the most beautiful buildings in the country, and along its quiet streets are fine old mansions, giving the town a goodly, ancient look.[2]

Within the past two or three years Baton Rouge has blossomed out as a busy, thrifty business center. It has water works, gas, factories, mills, banks, fine stores, and is rapidly becoming a chief educational town in the state. It is apparently a place that has awakened in the morning and that is beginning like a growing young giant to stretch its limbs and arouse.

You may see occasionally a "turn out" on the streets that would not disgrace Central Park. The United States government is just about to build through the town a fine shell road leading to the National Cemetery that will greatly beautify the town. Baton Rouge is a city of good churches, no less than schools, and the congregation of the pretty little Episcopal Church is happily in the possession of a clergyman who is mildly addicted to candlesticks.

It is the varsity town of the state, and the fame of the State University is rapidly increasing and appears to attract the interest and sympathy of all sorts and conditions of men, saving the peculiar sort who compose the General Assembly of our legislature—a sort who are only got by the skin of the teeth to do any work at all in furtherance of educational measures.

It looked very pleasant in the fair grounds when we had finally run the gauntlet of the ticket-taker and found ourselves under the big trees of the long avenue. The Garrison is now the home of the State University. It consists of a number of fine old brick buildings erected in a quintagonal form. They are two stories high, with broad balconies supported by huge white columns, the lower porches having brick floors like sunny and sweet old cloisters.

A dozen or more buildings are on the grounds—the newer ones having been used, when the place was a barracks, as powder magazines, etc. Now, all is in occupancy by cadets and professors. Where once was ruin, now all is order and decency, and the fine campus and lovely trees make the old Garrison a place of peculiar charm. It was here the fair was held, certain rooms in the buildings having been assigned for the use of exhibitors, the fine race track put in excellent order, and grandstand erected, and cattle booths and machinery sheds put up.

One afternoon, the fair being over, the prize Holsteins and the Maltese cats all gone away, the Arabs with their cheap booths, where a six-legged cow was the attraction, having folded their tents and silently gone off to other fairs, I went over the Garrison grounds on a visit of exploration to our State University. Louisiana first had a State University in 1855, and General William Tecumseh Sherman was superintendent. The first institution was at Alexandria and it remained there intermittently in operation until 1869, when it was moved to Baton Rouge.

Two years since, it was given the use of the Garrison grounds and fine buildings by the United States government, and out of its meager funds this place has been put in decent order and comparative repair. The present president of the university is Colonel J. W. Nicholson, who has surrounding him eight professors.[3] The university has an income from funds invested in bonds of $14,000 a year, supplemented by an appropriation of $10,000 a year from the state.

It is possible that there is not another state university in the country so miserably and stingily endowed. Our average lawmaker knows little or nothing of this university, and is far from realizing its value to the state or the vital necessity for maintaining it and forcing it to become one of the first institutions of its kind in the South.

At present, there are in it 109 cadets. Many live at the university, but many more board out in town. Living on the grounds costs a student about $15 a month, including washing, fuel and lights. The military discipline is said to be first rate. The boys take care of their own rooms, must live simply as soldiers and conduct themselves after the rules generally prevailing at military schools.

Hazing is almost unknown and the character of the cadets is good and they bear the reputation of gentlemen. They are a fine, clever, wholesome and manly set of young men, with the single abominable vice—somebody called it the other day "nervous affection"—of smoking cigarettes. A cigar, young men, or a pipe; but never, if you'd keep your manliness and your brains, never—a cigarette.

Four courses of study are open to cadets, and in the agricultural course so fine is the instruction that the university graduates are always engaged for positions before they have finished college, and the same may be said in the mechanical course. The university possesses a fine library of nearly 20,000 volumes, to which additions are made slowly.

In the mechanical department I was shown a fine lot of tables, boxes, chests, brackets, book shelves, etc., made by cadets, incontestably proving the practical advantages and work of this course. The exhibit of agricultural products made by the university at the fair included hundreds of articles from three experimental farms that are conducted by the university, or rather by the government through the university.

The value of these stations to agriculture and immigration is too well known to be commented on here. It is the business of our people to uphold and advance the State University, not pull it down. During the general assembly it ought to be the duty of every member to study its workings and acquaint himself with its needs, its faults and its virtues. The state will not truly prosper until we can point to our educational system as equal to the best in the country.

SHREVEPORT

Catharine Cole reported on many state and parish fairs, but the Shreveport State Fair she visited for this column was Louisiana's largest. Baton Rouge also had a "state" fair until 1906 when Shreveport became the official site of the State Fair of Louisiana, and it remains so today. In an agricultural state such as Louisiana, the annual fair was an important business, political, and social gathering. In this piece she captures not only the bustling growth of what was then the state's second-largest city, but also the festive atmosphere of the Shreveport fair, and shows her ability to toss aside all middle-class restraints and enjoy the sideshow hustlers, freaks, and carnival acts that are the entertainment at any fair. (*Picayune*, November 18, 1888)

The geographical limitations of a state upon its climate, soil, physical aspect, and its people are instructive, no less than mysterious. An experienced traveler knows without consulting his map or his timetable when he slips the boundary line from one state to another. He does not confound a citizen of Arkansas with a Mississippian, or a Mississippian with a native of Louisiana or Texas.

But he must give to Louisiana a greater elasticity of climate, scenery, products, and a variety of people not to be found in many other states. In nature, anything may be Louisianan—save mountains—in human nature there are no exceptions. The immigrant travels to Texas if he intends to be a stock raiser; he goes West generally if he would direct his energies to growing wheat and corn; but if he comes to Louisiana there is practically no limit to his and the state's resources. He can elect to be anything, to do anything that pleases him, and provided he has the will, the work, if it is honorable work, comes easily enough.

That portion of Louisiana that is best known and which is richest in aesthetic attractions and romances is the fair, pastoral Teche country—the "Evangeline" land. The other side of the shield is north Louisiana, with its cotton hills and cotton snows, its splendor of pine forests, its handsomely red lands that are so attractive in color and rich in farming values.

Throughout all the Red River parishes the people are possessed of much general culture and refinement. Newspapers and magazines are taken in large numbers and find continual welcome in the most modest homes. Churches and schools out-balance saloons and gambling places. There are no idlers among the young men, and no evidences of any unprosperous, shiftless, or unprogressive people anywhere.

There are great pine forests in many parishes, but there are also great tracts covered by beech, and elm, hickory, and oak trees. Hickory nuts and walnuts abound and it is strange that more are not gathered and sent to New Orleans for sale. It is a hill country par excellence, with rich meadow lands and vales and dells, where even at this late time of the year flowers bloom shyly and ferns sprout through the thick carpet of Persian-colored leaves woven by November winds from off the loom of trees.

Half a dozen nights ago, I sat crowded up in the sleeping car of a train speeding toward Shreveport, the only city besides New Orleans in all the state of Louisiana. It is true there are many brisk and ambitious towns pretending to be cities, and at press conventions and at mutual admiration assemblies it is the custom for the orators in a gush of gratitude to term each town a metropolis, but the still, cold fact remains, as food for next day's reflections, that New Orleans and Shreveport are our only cities, however charming and enterprising and ambitious other places may be.[1]

The train stopped with a frequency suggestive of a thickly-populated district and the coaches were soon filled to overflowing with all sorts and conditions of men. It was the time of the state fair at Shreveport, and all the countryside seemed pouring into Shreveport, beaming with pride, good nature, and perfect health and prosperity. Judges and physicians, the Lieutenant Governor, farmers, planters, grandmothers, young girls, mothers, and a multitude of children, all were bound for the fair.

Everybody seemed to know everybody else and to be glad to meet again. The judges told anecdotes in a sort of magisterial manner, and the Lieutenant Governor talked politics; the planters talked crops; the children cried and crowed, and the young mothers exchanged confidences of a feminine and maternal nature.[2]

The train boy sold out his stock completely—a piece of luck that had not befallen him since last fair time—and nobody minded the din and heat, nor the fact that it was pouring rain outdoors.

Pushing his way patiently up and down the car was a burly business-looking man with a stubby bunch of gray whiskers growing on his chin, a broad Quakerish-looking hat on his head, and swashing around mightily a heavy gray overcoat that managed to flop in everybody's way. He was a "humble worker in the Lord's vineyard," he said, "and was collecting money for the same. Anything from ten cents up to a dollar would be welcome." I saw him time and again after that night—at the fair, among the side shows, in the street cars, in private houses—but always his great coat was a-flapping, and always his big voice was begging for "anything from ten cents to a dollar to help build a college in his town."

Near me there was a wholesome little woman carrying a bucket of golden Jersey butter—"and if it don't take the prize," she said, "why I just give up." She might have taken a prize herself, with her pink cheeks and her bright eyes, her cheery smile and all her little dumpling of a self smelling of honest soap and water and sweet as country air could make her. She milked six cows, and on the proceeds of her butter, eggs, and her Jersey pigs—worth ten dollars each, she said—she had saved enough money to buy her a piano.

Nearby sat a quiet little woman who joined in the conversation. She had been married nine years and had seven children, and was taking them all to the fair. John had the most of them with him in the other car. "And my sister died and left us all of hers. She only had five, though, but we've got 'em all with us," she added with a laugh.

Oh, these Southern folk! Where else in all the world will people be found so frank and so gentle, so careless of self and so thoughtful of others? Theirs are no angular natures; they are alien only to mean traits and to despicable ways.

Shreveport is one of the rich and prosperous cities of the South. It has a population approaching 18,000. It is a railroad center and a great cotton market. It has no ambition to pose as a picturesque and romantic town, and if there are legends they go unrelated. There are no quiet, shady and unfrequented streets lined by grand and dingy old mansions "slowly feeling for their final plunge into oblivion." The town is peopled by men who came into it poor and have grown rich in legitimate mercantile pursuits.

It is built on several hills, has no public parks, and the streets, though wide, are usually unadorned by trees. It is somewhat ramblingly constructed and, unlike most growing places, appears to be growing in very general directions. The hills are being graded down and the low places filled in and built upon. The streets are very wide and are being covered with gravel that soon hardens into a roadway almost equal in solidity to asphalt. The sidewalks are fairly good, and at night the city is lighted by electric lights.

The value of the annual cotton shipments amounts to about five million dollars, and the enormous cotton warehouses are insufficient for the handling of the staple. The stores and shops are brick and are in the main handsome buildings. Stores rent in the business part of the city at from $100 to $250 a month. The display of dry goods and fancy goods in the retail shops is equal to that made anywhere else by prosperous and enterprising merchants.

The main shopping street is called Texas Street. It is wide, lined on one side by handsome brick stores and other buildings, and is not so pleasing, with a jumble of shanty-like wooden structures on the other side. As is our Canal Street, one side is fashionable and the other side is rarely used by ladies. A streetcar line with dingy cars, drawn by two small mules, runs down the center of this street.

The Customhouse building, a very handsome and stylish-looking brick edifice, with a lovely tower and surrounded by handsome grounds, is on this street. Nearby a fine hotel is just about to be opened, and near it also is the new Opera House, the most elegant little theater in the South outside of New Orleans, with a seating capacity of 1,100. There are eight churches belonging to the white population and these are artistic, modern buildings with expensive organs, and add materially to the architectural appearance of Shreveport.

The state fair held here last week would have been a creditable exposition in a city ten times the size. The chief merit of it lay in the fact that it was a direct encourager of farming industries, and of better and more valuable work from both men and women. The prizes offered were of sufficient value to attract exhibits from all classes. One lady took fifty dollars worth of premiums for her Jersey butter, enough money to buy a very good cow, or at least half a dozen Jersey pigs that will sell, when grown, at from $40 to $80 each. One splendid farmer—for it is splendid to be a man bending all of a man's mind and energy to the culture of land with a great intelligent desire to see how much he can make it yield—took the premium for corn that yielded 155 bushels to the acre. This yield came from land that had been cultivated for twenty years, and which had thus been rendered rich by manure and cotton seed.

The fair grounds are covered with fine trees, and under these were tied prize Jersey and Holstein bulls and Jersey cows, many worth $1,000 each. There were huge pens full of pigs, the famous and prolific "Jersey Reds," each pair as good as a government bond. There were droves of Merino sheep, black and greasy with oil, pens of silky-haired Angora goats, poultry and fine horses, mules and colts without number.

Two or three piano firms from New Orleans, who had exhibits at the fair, sold something like forty instruments. There is no better trading place than a first-class state or parish fair, just as there is no better advertising medium than a good newspaper.

The Exhibition Hall was thronged with exhibits. One Shreveport crockery firm, the pottery palace of this part of the state, exhibited a "life-size" schooner with cotton sails all set and covered by shelves, upon which were displayed beautiful vases. The cordage, portholes and all the vessel's belongings were wrought in pieces of pottery. The business firms generally, even to the tombstone man, made large and handsome displays.

Happily mixed in with these were all those cheerful fakirs, without whom no fair would be complete. There was the grease man, selling the stuff warranted to wash away all the ink and dirt stains of this wicked world. There was the diamond-seller from Chicago, with all his Rhinestone jewelry, and the microscope man, the eye-glass man, the popcorn boy, and the patent waffle man, with side shows galore.

How sorry I am for the person who looks on side shows as a device of the evil one, who never listened to a marvelous lecture on natural history from the fat man who sits tied up in a big snake, who never lent his best umbrella to the trick man or the vanishing lady, who never crawled under the big horse, who never shook hands with the wild man from Borneo, or gaped open-eyed before the red-faced wonder who eats old lamp chimneys.

Thousands of people visited the fair from this and adjoining states. It was admirably managed, and the results must have been satisfactory. A great deal of money was spent by visitors, and the big little city of north Louisiana is much the richer for its enterprise.

HOME IN NEW ORLEANS

Here, Martha Field sounds a theme found in many of her travel experiences: the importance of getting away, if for only a short period, from one's daily routine for a deep breath of psychic refreshment, for a repletion of lost energies, for a glance back, perhaps, at earlier dreams or neglected vistas. One returns ready to resume an ordinary life with a new awareness, "purified and strengthened" as Catharine Cole puts it, "glad to come back to the old life and the old ways." It is the invitation of all travel writing—escape vicariously with the author and enter, for a time, the world of other peoples and their grand or lowly, strange or exotic places.

Catharine Cole had a talent for drawing readers into her travels with vivid word-painted scenes of her adventures on the road. Her hardships and minor braveries are described with such honesty and humor as to compel even the most hardened stay-at-home to join her in her buggy rides to the far reaches of Louisiana.

In this piece, she has arrived at the New Orleans train station with her daughter, Flo, and looks at the seedy, commercial streets of the city with the eye of a returning traveler. Even the dreariest section of the town wears, as Wordsworth described the city of London in his sonnet "Composed Upon Westminster Bridge," "The beauty of the morning; silent, bare, . . ." It is a beauty made possible for Catharine Cole by an eye transfigured by travel. (*Picayune*, December 16, 1888)

"**I**t is rather nice to be stopping at home for awhile, isn't it?"

The speaker was a small, yellow-haired maiden, a quondam traveling companion of mine, that keenly intuitive individual from whom I have never dared conceal any of my small vanities and sentimentalities, conscious that any attempt to do so would be worse than futile. She looked up at me with an air, and put forth a small, neatly-gloved hand which she thrust into mine.

Not with any affectionate suggestion of snuggling—the proper caress for a woman's hand—oh, dear no, but with a something, I could not precisely articulate what, that impressed me with her superior cosmopolite experience. An approved New Yorker, or better still a Bostonian, has been known to make a naturally shy provincial suffer this same sense of self-conscious discomfort. It must be wicked to be provincial, else the consciousness of it would not be so miserable.

We were walking briskly away from a railway station in the lower part of the city. It was yet early morning and that luminous amber and violet haze so often seen in the Southland pervaded all our earth. There was the feel of early morning in the air; it would have been tangible to a blind man. It gave us, even my small cosmopolite, a luxurious sensation, a tingle of healthful blood in the veins, a zest-to-the-eye appetite. The long train had been broken up into sections and evacuated coaches stood here and there, half in, half out dingy sheds, as if their journeying days were over forever.

The little airy-looking and none-too-clean light barouches, precisely like those to be hired in Paris at the rate of twenty or thirty cents an hour, and which we call cabs and fail to patronize, were crawling away dispiritedly from the platform. A tall, red milk cart—and a New Orleans milk cart is peculiar in build and tins to New Orleans—rushed by, its dirty gray cans, like granite tombstone gates, towering high in the air; its dirty brown driver towering higher still and wobbling mightily. Back on the seat, with blue neckerchief, red cheeks, brown brow, and black hair, sat his plump Sicilian spouse.

All about were cotton presses, angular, ugly, squat buildings crowding into the sidewalk, and only pretty where an olive and brown mold or moss was sprawling over the hard pink of the bricks. Here and there in an open door, between the brown bales, through which, covering the cotton, frothing like white milk, we could see a burly black poised with his cotton hook in the air.

The sidewalks are narrow and covered with wide, flat stones, each one big enough for a grave slab or for a breastplate for a giant. Some of these are loose in their sockets, and dash up a thin spout of liquid mud on the unwary pedestrian—"dandy bricks" they used to call them. The narrow, mounded street covered with cobbles rumbles and trembles and strains as the huge cotton floats pass over it. Up and down, right and left, unfolds a dull vista of one-story, pent-roofed, red-painted tenement cottages protruding little pepper and salt gray stoops out upon the banquette.[1]

The thick wooden outer doors are set wide or barred, and disclose half-glass doors, with here and there a blouse-covered female form leaning out to pass the time of day with some neighborly market-goer. A pretty gowned chatelaine, sweet and serene, steps by, and in her wake a quadroon bearing an open Indian basket on her turban. Bananas, the red of beef for the *daube*, the yellow of carrots gleam from the basket top, and the chatelaine carries in her hand a tiny purple cluster of violets, her lagniappe from the butcher, I am certain.[2] A red bob-tailed street car, pulled by a small and dingy mule, materializes out of the haze at the end of the street and the bell tankles pleasantly and in an easygoing fashion.

Somehow, I don't know how, I get the impression, particularly in this treeless, unflowered district, of New Orleans as a place that is purple with the hue of violets, sweet with the scent of olive and cherry, with the songs of birds, and women.

There are some towns that give one no impression whatever, just as there are social invertebrates who come and are gone as if they had never been—towns of which one says vaguely that one must have passed them in the night—but not New Orleans. Here, the proper person, whether to the manor born or not, fancies that every dingy, lazygoing, mule-drawn street car will lead him to the complex life of the French Market; every house suggests a romance, every shop a carnival.

The tales of Cable, the song legends of Mollie E. Moore, the beautiful if somewhat shadowy photographic sketches of Grace King, all appeal to one.[3] They seem the natural birth of the rambling, jumbled town, the clang of bell and perfume of flower, of the violet and amber mist that hangs in the air this morning when my small companion announces for me that it is nice to be stopping at home for awhile, after regarding for so many weeks and months New Orleans as only a point of departure for broader "Louisiana Outings."[4]

I heard last year of a couple of charming women, living under orange trees and jasmine vines in the heart of our Garden District, who ran away into French Town and were gone for a week. They took a traveling bag with them and an easel and no end of brushes and pencils, and they concealed themselves in an *entresol* somewhere in the Rue Royale.[5]

Every morning early they went over the "dandy bricks" down the narrow thoroughfare across the Passage Antoine and Jackson Square to the Morning Star, the brightest, best and Frenchiest of all the bright and French coffee stalls in the French Market. And then for a looking-over of the baskets, big and little, of the Choctaw women squatting on the stones in the market court, and then to bore like moles through the dry goods tunnel, buying green and gold bandanas for aprons, scarves, and easel draperies; and then for a parley with the old flower woman standing like a grenadier behind her huge spiked-tin pyramid decorated with stiff bouquets of roses and sweet olive and violets, and then would come a visit to a book stall.

A *déjeuner à la fourchette* at some restaurant with a sanded floor and a most polite *garçon* scenting "*pour boires*," a day of sketching from the dim windows of the *entresol* or down in the old, yellow courtyard under the shade of the huge pittosporum, a night at the opera, and so the time went by.

I wonder why others of us do not oftener take a day off, or a week off. Where is the housewife who would not enjoy such a running away?

Up in the green, fair hills of St. Landry there is an old convent—a red, time-stained, rambling building.[6] It has ever so many blinking dormer windows with quiet, sunny porches like Venetian cloisters, and dim, gray rooms, half cell, half sanctuary, with a tiny chapel where the nuns sing their sweet, monotonous songs and where the trumpet vine and the wisteria clamber in at the deep windows. Sometimes ladies, not always of the Catholic faith, run away for a day or two to this sweet old place. They take speech of no one and only smile at the brown, shadowy shapes of nuns flitting in the dim corridors. Who would not be purified and strengthened by such a running away as this?

And then after a time, one would be glad to come back to the old life and the old ways.

BEYOND OUR DOOR

This article, written only months before her death, poignantly demonstrates that neither time nor illness has diluted Martha Field's "Gypsy blood"—her passion for travel. The sights, sounds, and smells of going away are richly imagined and remembered; the sensate experiences are as real and immediate in recollection as when she fished on the shores of Last Island a decade before.

She still responds with yearning to the sound of a train whistle and relishes the thought of a slow, leisurely journey by steamboat. Perhaps because such trips are no longer possible for her, Field laments the lot of those who can't or won't do what once brought her such great joy. Seize the opportunity to look upon a world "never old or stale or too familiar," she implores, for the experience of that "Columbus moment, new and unique" is all the more precious because it is passing. (*Times-Democrat*, May 1, 1898)

I wonder if there is anyone of us so hopelessly grooved to the commonplace and uneventful in life as to be indifferent to the suggestions of that inevitable drop of Gypsy blood that must lurk somewhere in the veins?

It is a sad state of things when the tranquil pulses give no stir at the mere thoughts of going away—somewhere, anywhere—away from the expected and the familiar. That brave spirit must be hopelessly broken if it does not answer with delight to the long, sweet whistle from the steamboat's pipe, the locomotive's cry that sounds so like a signal from the wild land of Vagabondia, or the mellow bell that, ringing from the forward deck of the steamer, seems to say to traveler and stay-at-home as well, "Time is up; let us be up and going."

In the springtime, when the very trees are gladsomely leaving, some of this going away spirit is bound to infect us with its spice and charm. To be sure, for the rest of us Fate and Fortune have combined that we must trust only to the enchanted carpet of the wizard, Imagination, upon which to take our outings. Things have been badly arranged, and Fate has been a bungler, so far that the power to enjoy does not always go with the money to possess.

It is the custom of all people to learn the world from the outward in, in matters of travel. Each tourist knows any country better than his own. In England fifty percent of the people spend their bank holiday in a ten-dollar trip to the continent, although nine Englishmen out of ten have never been to Stratford-on-Avon. Some few years since, a number of shrewd men organized a Sunday league for the purpose of giving working people cheap holiday outings on their one free day in the week. These are something like our Sunday excursions, only they are much cheaper and very much more elaborate.

When we have been in Europe we have constantly fallen in with entire schools having a holiday excursion under the scholarly care of their masters. We should have something of the sort for our boys, and it should be the duty of every parent and every instructor to see that our lads, and lassies too, for the matter of that, make at least one trip to that most beautiful city in the world, Washington, with its incomparable treasures of art, natural history, science and architecture. Every summer at least five hundred school children, properly chaperoned and officered, should leave New Orleans for an excursion that included a walking tour, camping out, bicycle riding, fishing, hunting, and no end of wholesome and manly out-of-door adventures and experiences.

Ever since I was a little girl, my ideal idea of going away has been to travel on a steamboat, a cozy, comfortable, white and gold steamboat, with dainty staterooms fitted up with tiny bunks where one can lie listening to the chug-chug of the paddle wheels, rocked by the restful motion of the river craft, which is like no other movement or means of travel. This insatiate demand for new sensations, the crazy thirst for time, the useless desire to cover ground rapidly, has all but killed steamboat travel for the idle tourist. Nevertheless, nothing so pleasant has been offered in its place.

To cross the ocean on a steamer holding one thousand persons is like spending a mad week of fashion and frivolity in a village composed exclusively of ultra-fashionable snobs. Very few travelers have the good sense to prefer a slow-going steamer that accommodates only a handful of people, and which occupies time enough on the journey to give one a real mouthful of incomparable delights of seafaring life in the summertime. On land, the traveler bound from New Orleans to St. Louis or Chicago would protest if you suggested that, instead of making the trip in a day by rail, he devote six to it and go by river.

For pure pleasure of travel, of sightseeing, of unusual experiences, I know nothing better than a bayou trip, from New Orleans up the Teche or any of its adjacent rivers. The cozy little steamboat that stops at every plantation, the long hours on the sunny deck, the moonlit nights when the stars are in the quiet skies, and great plumy cypress trees bend over the bayou banks and repeat themselves in the sleeping waters like so many crested warriors of the forest come down to drink, the midnight toll of the deck hands as they trundle the freight out into the mysterious dark, the broiled beefsteak and the steamboat rolls—nothing eatable was ever so good—the stately amber-skinned chambermaid who comes into your cabin at six in the morning with a cup of fragrant coffee, waking you from a sleep as blessed as that of a baby. Why, the very least of these attractions is worth girdling the globe to secure.

Luckily for the world's substantiality, the great majorities of middle-class people who so largely compose it are strictly conventional in their habits, customs, intercourse, and in nothing so much as their way of traveling. Conventionality is the sort of social cement that welds the world together, and we middle-class people must be proud that this is so, just as we are proud of any other of our superior forces. We taste something approaching real happiness when we dare to kick over the traces and commit to the unusual and the unexpected.

There was a Mississippi family who sold their cooking stove in order to go to the circus. It showed such a large, inexhaustible trust in Providence. And it also showed such a touching example of the joy of the moment and our Christian duty to seize it.

I once met on the Lake Coast just such a family who, with a tent and a big covered wagon were camping out and having the pleasure of a season at the seaside, not to be attained by the finest hotel in existence. Southern people know little of the enchanting charms of camping out. It is the most wholesome, the most adventuresome, the happiest and the cheapest way of seeing the world. In Wisconsin, owners of lakeshore lands make a lot of money each season by renting out furnished tents pretty much as one would a furnished house.

Every year, numbers of New England school teachers go to Colorado, where taking Denver as their point of departure, they hire a big wagon with a good, steady driver, and go for a three-week cruise into the broad lands and mountain vastnesses of that incomparable state. They sleep in tents and do their own cooking and washing, while the driver fills up all the domestic gaps. The expenses thus clubbed never rise higher than three dollars a day.

It is a wonder to me that adventuresome Americans in search of a new experience have not thought to revive the old caravan days of '49 and cross the plains to California by way of a summer outing. All the difficulties of such a journey have long since been eliminated and there would remain for those who would take it only the charm.

To that person who still retains some of the salt of an old, wholesome barbarism in his make-up, the words "camping out" convey a subtle sense of joy. To build one's bed of fragrant branches of fir on the clean, sweet earth, to lie asleep, tented over by the golden stars, to doze beside the cheerful campfire, to awaken in the dewy morning to a new, untarnished world, a wonderland of purple mountain peaks and brawling streams of melted snow; to feed on pink trout tossed from the water literally into the skillet—these are the mere skeletons of the delights of a caravan trip to the Occident.

I can smell the smell of the vivid prairie flowers; I can catch the spangled glistening of the dew on fern and bracken in the lonely mountain canyons; I can hear the wild neigh of the eager mustang ponies and I can hear the musical murmur of the mountain streams tinkling like mandolins or like crystal bells as they come daintily dipping down the hillsides. It is all an invitation into a new world from which the bloom has not yet been brushed by custom or by use.

Sometimes when the family is joyously making ready for a summer outing to some near or far resort—it matters not, for with this family to go away is the same thing, and the world outside its door, no less than the world across the continent is perennially new—Old Harper drops in to bid a cheerful farewell and a generous bon voyage.[1]

Knowing that it is never his portion to go away anywhere, never his lot to taste the unknown, the family delicately endeavors to deprecate the magnitude and splendor of their outing. But it is of no use. Old Harper, generous of spirit, who has patiently taught himself the lovely, if sorrowful, lesson of taking his greatest pleasures at second hand, will not have it so.

Nothing pleases him so much as to talk with a bustle and the zest of a famished appetite all about the trip that is to be. His advice in the matter of traveling bags and accessories is elaborate. He is a veritable A B C guide when it comes to timetables and making connections at out-of-the-way railroad junctions. But my throat always fills up, and the bloom of the trip is spoiled for me, when I know that it is always I who look back from the sleeping coach window, and always the patient, undisappointed Old Harper who remains at home.

Alack and alas, there are so many of us whose chief mission in life is to bid bon voyage to some luckier fellow than ourselves.

There are some sluggish minds who think going away only means traveling far in search of new green pastures. But the world is never old or stale or too familiar. Everything the eye looks upon is, at that Columbus moment, new and unique. Then, if you see it at all, you see it for the first time, and you also are seeing it for the last time. Tomorrow it will be something different and have another grace that is all its own. Sameness would be Nirvana.

Sometimes in the lonely black watches of the night you are awake and hear the deep, thunderous vibrations cast off by a midnight express. At once your alert fancy pictures all the charm of travel and going away. You see the made-up berths in the sleeper, you know how the weary passengers in the day cars are struggling for rest. The noise of the far-off train speeding into the distance and the unknown, quivers and shakes the dew-wet air as the pedal notes of an organ. Perhaps no one but the traveler who never travels gets any pleasure or suggestions out of this muffled and thunderous murmur.

On Monday afternoons you may often see quiet couples strolling along the quiet banks of the tawny, Tiber-colored river and crossing the levees to look upon the sea-going ships. This is their only outing, their holiday, the nearest approach they make to voyaging to that far-off, unknown Spain that holds all the castles of their dreams. The very smell of the ship and of the sea is sweet in their nostrils and speaks of going away.

The great craft pulling at its tether sets one to thinking on the lonesome ocean, mighty in storm, on the tender turquoise skies of far-off Italy, of the corn and wine and oil that shall freight its hold when it puts in at some foreign port.

The wind whistling in the rigging knits a music that is unlike any other sound. The tar that caulks the hard teak decks gives off a fragrance sweeter than that of the rose. The long, graceful craft dipping her nose daintily to meet the green wave, has a motion more graceful than that of the lily tilting on her stalk.

And motion and perfume and music of the wind, they tell to these quiet watchers on the banks, the patient toilers and stayers-at-home—they tell one story: the beautiful, unended, enchanting story of going away.

ACKNOWLEDGMENTS

We wish to thank Martha Field's great-granddaughter, Catherine Field Bacon, for her generosity in sharing with us copies of many of the papers relating to Catharine Cole and her daughter, Flo Field. Toni Bacon has been enthusiastic in her support for the publication of this collection, and is responsible for introducing us to the archive of the Catharine Cole papers at the Newcomb Center for Research on Women at Tulane University in New Orleans. We are also indebted to Susan Tucker, curator of the center, for making this material available to us.

Staff members at Nicholls State University Library in Thibodaux, Louisiana, particularly Marie Sheley, made our microfilm researches there as effortless as possible. The staff at the Hill Memorial Library at Louisiana State University at Baton Rouge was also courteous and helpful. The Schlesinger Library of Harvard University provided us with materials from the papers of Martha Field's sister, Elizabeth Shields.

The Historic New Orleans Collection made available to us the correspondence in the "Papers of *Daily Picayune* Publisher Eliza Nicholson" relating to Martha Field.

Our special thanks to the Interlibrary Loan Department at the Cooper Library, Clemson University, for obtaining many volumes of books and numerous reels of microfilm from libraries across the country.

We wish to thank the editorial and production staff at the University Press of Mississippi for their professionalism and advice, including Walter Biggins, Shane Gong, and Anne Stascavage, as well as copy editor Carol Cox. To Editor-in-Chief Craig Gill we extend our appreciation for recognizing that Catharine Cole is a too-long hidden literary treasure.

NOTES

NOTES TO "GRAND ISLE"

1. **Lugger.** A small, open boat with a lugsail, a four-sided sail hung obliquely on a yard that is hoisted and lowered with the sail. Luggers, the workhorse of the fishing trade in the Barataria Bay region, had sails that were characteristically dyed red.

2. **Latania.** The fan-shaped leaves of the Latan palm tree, indigenous to the Barataria Bay region.

3. **Jean Lafitte.** The most notorious of the Baratarian pirates. At the height of his career he operated out of Grand Terre Island. He helped defeat the British at the Battle of New Orleans in 1815, and later moved to Galveston Bay, Texas. In 1823, at the age of 41, he was fatally wounded aboard his privateer in a sea battle.

4. **Islands of the Barataria.** These islands are located in the region defined broadly by Barataria Bay, which lies southwest of the Mississippi, fifty miles from New Orleans, and northeast of Grand Isle.

5. **Fort Livingston.** A fort on Grand Terre Island, its construction beginning in 1841 and continuing until the Civil War. After the war, it was abandoned by the government, and began to settle into Barataria Bay. Today, some of it is under water, but in recent years the sea has redeposited sand before its walls.

6. **A bit of China.** The Chinese fishermen Cole found on Barataria Bay were probably the remnants of a failed immigration attempt. In the 1870s, several hundred Chinese were brought to Louisiana to work on sugar plantations, but planters found them difficult to discipline and no more willing to work in slave-like conditions than were blacks. They eventually drifted to southern Louisiana. See John C. Rodrigue, *Reconstruction in the Cane Fields*, Baton Rouge, 2001, 136–37.

7. **Cups of chai.** Chai (rhymes with sky) is prepared with very strong tea, cooked with milk and spices.

8. **Great storm.** Last Island (*Isle Dernière*), which lies west of Grand Isle, was devastated by a hurricane on August 10, 1856. All of the island's structures were destroyed and two hundred lives were lost. Last Island has subsequently broken into a series of small, uninhabited islands. Lafcadio Hearn, in his novel *Chita: A Memory of Last Island* (1889), gives a vivid account of the storm. Field had visited the island a year before *Chita* was published, so she undoubtedly knew of the novel. See the chapter on Last Island.

9. **Bring a railroad.** A railroad still has not come within a dozen miles of Grand Isle, and the island can only be reached from Leeville by Highway 1, a two-lane road that is frequently submerged by storms.

10. **Kranz Hotel.** John Kranz owned the hotel complex described by Field. The hurricane of 1893 destroyed much of the hotel. Kranz, seventy years old at the time, narrowly escaped death when his house collapsed on him.

11. **Blithedale Romance.** Nathaniel Hawthorne, *The Blithedale Romance*, Boston, 1852. The novel is a satire on the utopian community Brook Farm.

12. **Ocean Club Hotel.** A large, three-story structure, capable of accommodating a thousand guests. It was destroyed by the hurricane of 1893.

13. **Mount Desert.** Mount Desert Island, Maine. During the nineteenth century its principal town, Bar Harbor, was the site of many fashionable homes built by wealthy businessmen, including J. P. Morgan.

14. **Bayou Bruleau.** This was the site of one of several "platforms" in Barataria Bay near Grand Isle. It was used by oyster fishermen as a camp.

15. **Rigaud.** The Rigaud family is one of the oldest in Louisiana. Pierre de Rigaud, Marquis de Vaudreuil (1698–1765) was governor of Louisiana from 1743 to 1753.

16. **Elder Le Brun.** Charles Le Brun (1619–1690), designer and painter during the reign of Louis XIV.

17. **Beauregard.** Lieutenant P. G. T. Beauregard (1818–1893), later to become a general in the Confederate army, assisted in the construction of Fort Livingston. He was known as "the hero of Fort Sumter" for his victory there.

18. **Best of Hebes.** In Greek mythology, the youthful goddess Hebe was cup bearer to the gods.

NOTES TO "CHENIERE CAMINADA"

1. **Miss Mitford.** Mary Russell Mitford (1787–1855) wrote sketches of English country manners, scenery, and character.

2. **Father Grimaux.** Father Ferdinand G. Grimaux. He was trapped in the presbytery of Our Lady of Lourdes Church during the 1893 hurricane and gave a graphic account to *Picayune* reporters of his survival.

3. **Lachryma Christi.** "Tears of Christ," a wine from the lower slopes of Mt. Vesuvius. Legend has it that when the archangel Lucifer was cast from heaven, he grabbed a piece of it with his fingernails and placed it on earth at the region around the Gulf of Naples. Noticing the loss, the Lord wept, and vines grew where his tears fell.

4. **Archbishop Janssens.** Francis Janssens (1843–1897), archbishop of New Orleans from 1888 to his death.

5. **Our Lady of Lourdes.** The church was destroyed in the 1893 hurricane, but its bell survived.

6. **Roadway through oaks.** Field reports the derivation of the name Cheniere Caminada from accounts she heard from the islanders. It was actually derived from two sources: the French *cheniere*, for oak grove, and Francisco Caminada, a Spanish

merchant who acquired island property in the 1770s. The two names were subsequently combined by the island dwellers. See Dale P. Rogers, *Cheniere Caminada Buried at Sea*, Thibodaux, La., 1981, 6.

7. **Putto.** A red wine from the Chianti region of Tuscany.

8. **Gambi.** Vincent Gambi, reportedly one of the most bloodthirsty of Lafitte's pirates, settled on Cheniere Caminada when Lafitte left Grand Terre for Texas. He built a large house and raised a family there.

9. **Youx and Beluche.** Two of Lafitte's cannoneers, Dominique Youx and René Beluche. They played an important defensive role in defeating the British in the Battle of New Orleans.

NOTES TO "POINTE COUPEE PARISH"

1. **A bit of the vernacular.** Pointe Coupee (poynt-coo-PEE) was named "cut point" for a shortcut across the narrow neck of an oxbow in the Mississippi River, discovered by Pierre Le Moyne, Sieur d'Iberville (1661–1766) and his brother, Jean-Baptiste Le Moyne, Sieur de Bienville (1680–1762). The river later followed the portage that Bienville used to carry his boats across the cut, creating the False River described by Field. Her claim that Bienville dug a canal across the shortcut was a local legend, but was inaccurate; a stream flowed across the cut, and in the 1720s the Mississippi found it and gouged a new bed for itself. See Brian J. Costello, *A History of Pointe Coupee Parish, Louisiana*, New Roads, La., 1999, 13–15.

2. **Julien Poydras.** Poydras (1746–1824) made a fortune raising sugar cane, then devoted his life to philanthropy, poetry, and education. He served in the state legislature and was president of the senate. He is considered to be the father of education in Louisiana.

3. **After the overflow.** Periodic flooding.

4. **Peter White.** "Peter White will ne'er go right; / Would you know the reason why? / He follows his nose where'er he goes, / And that stands all awry."

5. **Mr. Howells.** American novelist and critic William Dean Howells (1837–1920).

6. *Wide, Wide, World.* Susan Warner, *The Wide, Wide World* (1850). The novel's heroine, Ellen Montgomery, has been compared to Little Eva of *Uncle Tom's Cabin*.

7. **Calamity Pop.** From W. S. Gilbert, *50 Bab Ballads* (1876). In the ballad "The King of Canoodle-dum" are the lines "Calamity Pop Von Peppermint Drop / The King of Canoodle-dum."

8. **Lake Coast.** That part of the Gulf Coast which included New Orleanians' favorite resort towns, Bay St. Louis and Pass Christian, Mississippi. It was so named because one had to cross, as Catharine Cole put it, "over the lake"—Lake Pontchartrain—to travel there.

9. **Colonel Claiborne.** Lee Claiborne (b. 1810) was listed in the 1880 census as a sugar planter living in the fifth ward of Pointe Coupee parish.

10. **Poydras Academy.** One of Julien Poydras's legacies was an education fund that in 1889 was responsible for the construction of Poydras Academy in New Roads. In

1924 it became Poydras High School, a brick neoclassical building that is now restored as a museum. As Field reported, Poydras's grave is on the grounds of the museum.

11. **Jac. Rose.** Probably Jacques Cartier, a pink, Portland rose. Bred in France in 1868 by Moreau-Robert, it is highly scented. It has now been reclassified by the American Rose Society as Marchese Boccella.

12. *A Paris, a Paris.* A French nursery song: "*A Paris, a Paris / Sur un petit cheval gris. / Au pas, au pas, au trot, au trot, / Au galop, au galop, au galop.*" The infant is bounced in a step, trot, and gallop to the rhythm of the little gray horse.

NOTES TO "THE LEVEES OF POINTE COUPEE"

1. **Claddagh.** The Claddagh, an ancient village close to Galway on the west coast of Ireland. The wives of the fisherman of the Claddagh traditionally wore a red petticoat under a red gown.

2. **Levees as Morganza.** Morganza is now known for the Morganza Spillway. During high water its gates can be opened to direct floodwaters from the Mississippi to the Atchafalaya River and the Gulf.

3. **Grand Levee.** At the time, Grand Levee was the highest in the state. Raising this and other levees was necessitated by a series of crevasses and subsequent severe flooding in the years 1882, 1884, and 1890. See Brian J. Costello, *A History of Pointe Coupee Parish, Louisiana*, 149–152.

4. **Wire grass.** Bermuda grass, *Cynodon dactylon*.

NOTES TO "AVOYELLES PARISH"

1. **Indian mounds.** These mounds were placed on the National Register of Historic Places in 1964. The Marksville Prehistoric Indian Site is a thirty-nine-acre state park which includes mounds and Indian village sites dating from AD 1400. A museum features artifacts and exhibits.

2. **Ex-Senator Joffrion.** E. J. Joffrion, born in Marksville in 1839, was a successful criminal lawyer, a member of the state house of representatives, and a state senator. His wife, Sue R. Joffrion, was born in Kentucky in 1841.

NOTES TO "ST. JAMES PARISH"

1. **College Point batture.** In Louisiana, a batture is the land that lies between a levee and the river during low water levels.

2. **Jefferson College.** The college opened in 1834 as an institution to educate the sons of planters, but it lapsed into bankruptcy in 1856. Valcour Aime purchased it in 1859 and reopened it, but it was closed and occupied by Federal troops during the

Civil War. Aime donated the college to the Marist Fathers in 1864 and they operated it until it was forced to close in 1927. In 1931 the Jesuits purchased the grounds and established Manresa Retreat, a spiritual sanctuary, which continues today.

3. **Father James Blenk.** In 1899, Father Blenk (1856–1917) became the first American bishop of Puerto Rico. In 1907, he became archbishop of New Orleans.

4. **Valcour Aime.** François Gabriel Aime (1798–1867), given the name Valcour by a nurse, acquired much of his legendary wealth from the St. James Sugar Refinery, which he owned. He was known for his brilliance as a businessman, his philanthropy, and for the free-spending lifestyle that Catharine Cole describes in this piece.

5. **Perique.** This tobacco can be grown only in a small section of St. James Parish because of unique soil conditions which contribute to its flavor. The perique seed, and a fermentation process which involves pressing the leaves in oak barrels, are also necessary to produce the tobacco. Because of the intensity of its flavor it is always mixed with other tobaccos. Today, only a single farm in Grand Pointe produces perique.

6. **Belmont Plantation.** The plantation is described by Field in this piece written in 1892, but it had burned to the ground in 1889. She may have visited it on a previous trip and was unaware that it had been destroyed.

7. **Convent Town.** Now Convent, the parish seat of St. James.

8. **Home Place Plantation.** This is one of several plantations by this name in St. James Parish. According to Mary Ann Sternberg, in *Along the River Road*, Baton Rouge, 2001, the Choppin Home Place property, "with twelve arpents of frontage, was bought by Valerian Choppin for his wife Eugenie during the second half of the nineteenth century." The house no longer exists.

9. **New Orleans exposition killed our trade.** The 1884 World's Industrial and Cotton Centennial Exposition in New Orleans.

10. **Grand home.** Field does not name the Valcour Aime plantation house, but it was widely known as "Le Petit Versailles" because of its grandeur.

11. **"Life and Thought have gone away."** From Alfred, Lord Tennyson, "The Deserted House" (1830):

> *Life and Thought have gone away*
> *Side by side.*
> *Leaving door and windows wide;*
> *Careless tenants they! . . .*

12. **Bamboula.** A dance, which probably originated in Africa, that was frequently performed in Congo Square behind Rampart Street in New Orleans before the Civil War. The performers sat in a circle and clapped their hands and chanted, accompanied by a banjo and a bamboo drum, which gave the dance its name. A male dancer in the center of the circle took a woman and danced with her to an ever-increasing tempo. They were joined by other couples who leaped and cavorted in a frenzy until many dropped from exhaustion.

13. **Porche Miles, Dom Pedro.** William Porcher Miles, president of South Carolina College, purchased the Valcour Aime property after Aime's death. Miles owned ten sugar cane plantations along the Mississippi. "Dom Pedro" was Pedro II, emperor of Brazil (1825–1891), who visited the United States in 1876. He was forced from his throne in 1889 and went into exile in France, where he died of influenza.

14. **Once a fort.** Aime built a small fort by an artificial river in his garden to welcome guests with cannon salutes. The fort was also used for the games described by Andrien.

NOTES TO "NATCHITOCHES PARISH"

1. **Judge David Pierson.** Pierson (1837–1900) was judge of the Eleventh Judicial District, which included Natchitoches Parish. At twenty-one, he established a reputation for independence when, as the youngest delegate to the Louisiana Secession Convention, he voted against proposals to leave the union. He also refused to sign the Ordinance of Secession once the Civil War began.

2. **Colonel William Jack, Ex-Attorney General Cunningham.** William Houston Jack (1836–1912) was Superintendent of Public Instruction for Louisiana, served in the state legislature, and was president of the Baptist State Convention. Milton Joseph Cunningham (1842–1916) was a member of the Louisiana Senate in 1879, and was Louisiana attorney general from 1885 to 1888 and 1893 to 1900.

3. **President Thomas D. Boyd.** Boyd (1854–1932), brother of David French Boyd, who is considered to be the founder of Louisiana State University, was elected president of the Louisiana State Normal School in 1888, shortly before Field's visit to the institution. In 1896, he gave up the presidency of the Normal School and became president of Louisiana State University, where he served until his resignation in 1926.

4. **Convent of the Sisters of Providence.** Shortly before Field's visit to Natchitoches in 1888, the Sisters of Divine Providence opened a convent school. It is now known as St. Mary's School and has been in continuous operation for 115 years.

5. **Quincy method.** A progressive educational system so named because it was developed at Quincy, Massachusetts, by Francis W. Parker (1837–1902). Parker's method abandoned harsh discipline, rote memorization, and a prescribed curriculum in favor of a student-centered, holistic education based on the student's understanding of concepts. Parker believed in a social and democratic education that prepared students mentally, physically, and morally for lifelong learning. It was the practice of these principles that Martha Field admired at the Louisiana State Normal School at Natchitoches. The institution is now Northwestern State University of Louisiana, with an enrollment of ten thousand.

6. **Rosemary for remembrance and pansies for thought.** The Language of Flowers has a long history, but it became popular during the Victorian Age when lovers and friends communicated emotions and messages by sending combinations of flowers. Field, who loved gardens as much as anyone in New Orleans, used the language frequently in her columns.

7. **Monsignor, the Bishop of Natchitoches.** Anthony Durier (1833–1904) was appointed bishop of Natchitoches in 1884. The Immaculate Conception Catholic Church, which Field describes, was started in 1857 and completed by Bishop Durier in 1892, four years after Field's visit. In 1996 it was completely restored. The rectory—Field calls it the "bishop's palace"—was built in New Orleans in 1885, then carried by boat and reassembled across the street from the Immaculate Conception Church.

8. **Episcopal church across the way.** Trinity Episcopal Church, built in 1857, was the third Episcopal church constructed in Louisiana. Field was an Episcopalian; she seldom failed to visit a local Episcopal church in her travels and often attended services.

9. **Tangled old graveyard.** The American Cemetery, located on Second Street, on the former site of Fort St. Jean Baptiste, is the oldest burying ground in Natchitoches. It contains the graves of some of the earliest inhabitants of the town. In recent years it has been restored and many of its tombstones repaired.

10. **Adyas, or "Adios."** Field refers to Los Adaes, the site of a Spanish presidio and mission established in 1721, eighteen miles from Natchitoches near Robeline. Los Adaes was the capital of the Spanish province of Texas from 1729 until 1773, when the capital was moved to San Antonio. Los Adaes was named after the Adaes Indians, members of the Caddo tribe. It is archaeologically rich, and is now a state historic site.

11. **Signature of St. Denys.** In 1714, Louis Juchereau de St. Denis (1674–1744) founded the village of Natchitoches, the oldest permanent settlement in Louisiana. He had a colorful career as a soldier, explorer, adventurer, and diplomat with the French, Spanish, and Indians. He served for twenty-four years as commander of Fort St. Jean Baptiste in the Nachitoches District. For his service to France, King Louis XV granted him knighthood in the Order of St. Louis.

12. **Old Metoyer.** Nicholas Augustin Metoyer (1768–1856) was the eldest child of Marie Therese Coincoin, a slave purchased by a French planter, Claude Thomas Pierre Metoyer. He had ten children by her and at his death freed her and her children and granted her parcels of land. Nicholas Augustin Metoyer built St. Augustine Catholic Church in 1803 at Melrose, a plantation established by the Metoyer family. Melrose is a National Historic Landmark. Metoyer's portrait is in the church, and he is buried in its graveyard.

13. **Prudhomme house.** The home Field visited is now known as the Prudhomme-Roquier House. It is a rare surviving example of a Creole-style construction called *bousillage*. Its walls are a mixture of clay, deer hair, and Spanish moss, packed between a framework of cypress boards. The original floor plan consisted of four rooms across the front and two rooms in the rear, all opening into each other as Field described them.

14. **"The Magnolias."** Magnolia Plantation was established by Ambrose Lecomte and Ambrose Lecomte II in the 1830s. In 1852, Matthew Hertzog, who was twenty-four, married Lecomte II's daughter Atala, and assumed operation of the plantation.

The Hertzogs inherited the property at Lecomte's death in 1883. The main house at Magnolia, built in 1840, was burned by General Nathaniel Banks in 1864, as Field reported. Hertzog died in 1903, his wife, Atala, in 1897.

15. **Captain Caspari.** Leopold Caspari (1830–1915) served as a captain of the Confederate army for four years. He was instrumental in the construction of the Natchitoches Railroad Company and was its president and general manager when Field met him. He was a member of the Louisiana General Assembly and was important in the establishment of Louisiana State Normal School.

NOTES TO "LIVINGSTON PARISH: SWAMPERS"

1. **Magnolia Bridge.** A bridge crossing Bayou St. John in New Orleans.
2. **Added a camera.** One of these articles was illustrated with three line drawings made from photographs Field took on her trip. The cumbersome photographic equipment of the day apparently proved to be too much for her to carry, because this is a rare example of illustrations in her travel pieces.
3. **Hypo.** Sodium thiosulfate, used as a fixative in making photographic prints.
4. **New Basin.** The Old Basin Canal and the New Basin Canal were built to carry shipping from Lake Pontchartrain to the Mississippi. The Old Basin Canal, originally the Carondelet Canal, ran from Bayou St. John to a terminus at a ship-turning lagoon at Basin Street at the edge of the French Quarter. The New Basin Canal was dug in 1838, and ran from the lake, along present-day West End Boulevard, Pontchartrain Expressway, and I-10, ending at a turning basin in the vicinity of the Superdome.
5. **Thomas Leftwich.** Thomas S. Leftwich became postmaster of Port Vincent in 1903. The village of Port Vincent was not incorporated until 1952.
6. **Free state of Livingston.** Livingston Parish, created in 1832, was nicknamed the "Free State of Livingston" because of the independence and self-reliance of its inhabitants.
7. **Levi Spiller.** Levi R. Spiller (1836–1897) was postmaster of Port Vincent from 1871 to 1881.
8. **Stephen LeBourgeois.** The LeBourgeois homestead, Whitehall, was built by Pierre LeBourgeois after the Civil War. His son Stephen was listed in the Livingston Parish census of 1850 as being ten years old.
9. **Arthur Cornet.** In the 1880 census for Livingston Parish, Arthur Cornet is listed as being twenty-eight years old and a sawyer in a sawmill.

NOTES TO "BAYOU LAFOURCHE PLANTATIONS"

1. **Outlet theory.** According to this theory, the Mississippi River requires outlet channels to relieve high water during times of flood. Because plantations along the Lafourche were flooded during high water, however, a dam was erected in

1903 at the bayou's entrance at the Mississippi, and water no longer flows through the bayou to the Gulf of Mexico. See Sternberg, *Along the River Road*, 265.

2. **Arpent.** A French unit of land measurement equivalent to approximately 0.85 of an acre. Many Louisiana deeds are still measured in arpents.

3. **Venerable and distinguished W. W. Pugh.** William Whitmell Pugh (1811–1906) was an Assumption Parish planter and the speaker of the Louisiana House of Representatives from 1854 to 1858. In 1859, he completed the Woodlawn mansion, described by Cole, on his plantation next to Bayou Lafourche, three miles below Napoleonville. Woodlawn was razed in 1946.

4. **Magnificent sugar plantations.** Of the many plantations listed here, some have been purchased and incorporated into other land holdings and their names have vanished. Some of the houses she noted still stand; others have been destroyed. See Sternberg, *Along the River Road*, for accounts of some of these plantation houses.

5. **Belle Alliance (Beautiful Union).** This is a raised cottage plantation home, with living quarters on the second floor. The classical, revival-style house entered the Kock family when Charles A. Kock acquired it in 1859 from Henry McCall, who had built it in 1846. The property remained in the Kock family until 1915. It is on the Louisiana National Register of Historic Places.

6. **B. Lehman and Bros.** The Lehman brothers operated a sixty-thousand-foot store in downtown Donaldsonville; it was once Louisiana's oldest department store still in use. It is now the Historic Donaldsonville Museum. As Field notes, the brothers also owned Belle Terre plantation. See Sternberg, *Along the River Road*, 272.

7. **Sweet Home.** Sweet Home Plantation, 1,100 acres on Bayou Lafourche below Donaldsonville, was jointly owned by U. B. Dugas and D. P. Landry. Field apparently thought the plantation was owned by a single person. See *Biographical and Historical Memoirs of Louisiana*, vol. 1, Chicago, 1892, 390.

8. **Madewood.** This Greek Revival plantation home was built by Col. Thomas Pugh from 1840 to 1848 from trees on the site—hence the name Madewood. It is one of the finest surviving plantation mansions in the state and is a National Historic Landmark. Madewood is open to the public. (See Catharine Cole's account of Madewood in the next chapter.)

9. **Leon Godchaux.** Godchaux was one of nineteenth-century Louisiana's most illustrious success stories. An illiterate French Jew, he arrived penniless in New Orleans in 1837. He became a successful merchant in New Orleans, and then a planter. At his death in 1899 he was a multimillionaire sugar grower and refiner. He owed his success to combining the small sugar mills from a number of plantations he owned into a central mill joined to the various plantations by rail. He was also notable for making a profit without the use of slave labor. As Cole noted, he was the owner of Elm Hall and Raceland plantations. See W. E. Butler, *Down Among the Sugar Cane: The Story of Louisiana Sugar Plantations and Their Railroads*, Baton Rouge, 1980.

10. **Senator E. D. White, Major Legarde.** Edward Douglass White, Jr., a cane planter, was U.S. senator from 1891 to 1894 when he became a justice of the U.S. Supreme

Court. In 1910, he was elevated to chief justice and served in that capacity until 1921. His family home, a raised cottage on Bayou Lafourche, built by his father, E. D. White, Sr., is now a museum commemorating his life. Maj. C. Legarde died July 22, 1901, at his home, Leighton Plantation, at the age of seventy-three, according to a notice in the *Assumption Pioneer*. The Leighton Sugar Refinery is now located two miles north of Thibodaux.

11. **Thibodaux, named after a gallant governor.** Henry Schuyler Thibodeaux (1769–1827)—the spelling of the town name was later changed to Thibodaux— served as a state senator, and as acting governor of Louisiana in 1824. An orphan, he was raised by Gen. Philip Schuyler, father-in-law of Alexander Hamilton.

12. **Society for the Prevention of Cruelty to Animals.** Catharine Cole never missed an opportunity to mention animal protection societies in her columns, for this was one of the favorite causes of her employer, *Picayune* publisher Eliza Nicholson. The newspaper ran a weekly column devoted to prevention of cruelty to animals, "Nature's Dumb Nobility."

13. **Beautiful Catholic Church.** St. Joseph's Cathedral. The relic of St. Valerie is an ornate wood and glass casket with a wax effigy of the saint in which is embedded her severed arm. Valerie became a Christian martyr when she was beheaded in the Roman Coliseum in the second century. See Macon Fry and Julie Posner, *Cajun Country Guide*, 2nd ed., Gretna, 1999, 146–47.

NOTES TO "ASSUMPTION PARISH: MADEWOOD MANSION"

1. **Bobbinet.** A machine-made cotton fabric used here as a mosquito net.

2. **Clark Russell's stories.** William Clark Russell (1844–1911), British novelist, wrote a series of popular stories of seafaring life based on his career as a merchant seaman. *The Wreck of the Grosvenor*, 3 vols., 1877, was one of his most popular novels. *The Lady Maud* (1882) was the narrative of the loss of a schooner yacht.

3. **Topographical one of Lockett.** Francis V. Hopkins, an LSU professor, and Charles H. Lockett, head of LSU's Corp of Cadets, published the first topographical and geological maps of Louisiana.

4. **Taylor Beattie.** Beattie, a planter and lawyer, was a Republican candidate for governor in 1879, and a candidate for Congress in 1882. He served as a judge of the fifteenth and the twentieth judicial districts. He was the judge who declared martial law in the Thibodaux Massacre of 1887, in which thirty black workers who were on strike against sugar planters died at the hands of vigilantes. See Bennett H. Wall et al., *Louisiana: A History*, 4th ed., Wheeling, Ill., 2002, 250.

5. **Painted by Wikstrom.** Bror Anders Wikstrom (1854–1909) was a Swedish-born painter of marine and landscape scenes. He also was known in New Orleans for his Mardi Gras float and costume designs for the Proteus and Rex krewes.

6. **"We makes gov'nors in our parishes."** The waiter was probably referring to Louisiana governors from the Lafourche parishes: Henry S. Thibodeaux, 1824;

Edward White, 1835–1839; and Francis T. Nichols, 1877–1880 and 1888–1892. Flo's reference to the newly elected governor was to Murphy James Foster, 1892–1900.

7. **Mrs. Dupaty.** Susan Dupaty, owner and editor of the *Assumption Pioneer* from 1884 to 1903, was one of the early newspaperwomen in Louisiana.

8. **Louisiana exhibit building at Chicago.** The state was planning for its building at the Chicago World's Fair, the Columbian Exposition of 1893. The design chosen was a raised Creole cottage.

9. **Stone-crop.** A perennial, climbing sedum that thrives in any soil.

10. **Llewellyn Pugh.** Pugh acquired Madewood and its debts as a gift from his uncle, Robert Pugh. Leon Godchaux purchased the plantation in 1896 for thirty thousand dollars.

NOTES TO "TERREBONNE PARISH"

1. **Morgan ferry.** In 1883, Morgan's Louisiana and Texas Railroad was sold to Southern Pacific, but continued to operate as the Morgan line. The depot and ferry were still known as the Morgan Depot and Morgan Ferry.

2. **Mme. Chrysanthème.** *Madam Chrysanthème* (1888) was a novel by Pierre Loti, the pen name of Louis-Marie-Julien Viaud (1850–1923). His popularity was established with impressionistic adventures set in exotic places. *Madam Chrysanthème* established a fashion for stories with a Japanese theme.

3. **Say my say in behalf of immigration.** Louisiana's attempt to promote immigration had a long history, dating back to Reconstruction. During the 1880s, immigration societies and associations at the state and parish levels had been attempting to overcome a conviction, well-publicized in the Northern press, that Louisiana was a land of mosquitoes, alligators, swamps, deadly disease, and corrupt politics, and that no sensible person would want to live there. "Heavy-handed attempts were made to eradicate the mephitic odor which clung to the state's reputation," writes William I. Hair in *Bourbonism and Agrarian Protest* (134). The state's weather was warm in winter and cool in summer, malaria and yellow fever epidemics were "badly misunderstood," and its citizens were "sorry the Civil War had occurred." Catharine Cole's immigration campaign was not so blatant, but she paints the "wonderland story" of the state's resources with a rosy palette. See E. Russ Williams, Jr., "Louisiana's Public and Private Immigration Endeavors: 1866–1893," *Louisiana History*, vol. 15 (1974), 153–73.

4. **"Lafourche Interior."** Terrebonne Parish was formed in 1822 from a portion of Lafourche Parish. It became Louisiana's twenty-sixth parish.

5. **Courthouse.** The Terrebonne Parish Courthouse in Houma, described by Field, was completed in 1892. It was replaced in the 1930s by a new courthouse building.

6. **Storm of '88.** In August of 1888, a category two hurricane swept through southern Louisiana, causing widespread flooding and property damage.

7. **Southdown plantation.** The Southdown plantation Greek-revival manor house was built in 1859 by William J. Minor. In 1893, a year after Field's visit, Henry C.

Minor added a second floor and Queen Anne architectural features. It is now the Terrebonne Museum of History and Culture.

8. **Jarvis.** John Wesley Jarvis (1780–1840), an English-born painter of portraits and miniatures, worked mostly in New York. He spent a number of years painting in the South, however, and worked intermittantly in New Orleans from 1820 to 1834.

9. **Frederick Lottinger.** Lottinger, born in 1843 aboard a ship coming to the United States, operated a store in Dulac as well as his terrapin farm.

10. **Pelton plantation.** John M. Pelton was the owner of the Dulac plantation, a long, narrow strip of land along Bayou Calliou.

11. **Terrebonne, sending its delicate sugar.** Field's enumeration of the global reaches of Terrebonne's sugar echoes Thoreau's account in *Walden* of the winter ice that is cut from Walden Pond and exported to the tropic regions of the world: "Thus it appears that the sweltering inhabitants of Charleston and New Orleans, of Madras, and Bombay and Calcutta, drink at my well."

NOTES TO "MORGAN CITY: A COUNTRY WEDDING"

1. **Morgan City.** Named after Charles Morgan (1795–1878), shipping and railroad magnate, who first dredged the Atchafalaya Bay ship channel to accommodate oceangoing vessels, and brought the New Orleans, Opelousas & Great Western Railroad to Berwick Bay. In 1876, Brashear City was renamed Morgan City in his honor.

2. **Tiger Island.** The land on which Morgan City was built was originally named Tiger Island by U.S. Secretary of War John C. Calhoun's surveyors because of a species of wildcat in the area that locals called a tiger. The property came into possession of the Brashear family in 1816 and was incorporated as Brashear City in 1860.

3. **Mr. Jolley.** James H. Jolley (1842–1914), editor of the *Review*, was a tax collector and the Sheriff of St. Mary Parish from 1870 to 1871.

4. **Famous Pharr plantation.** John N. Pharr (1829–1903) became one of the largest individual land owners in Louisiana. He owned the Fairview plantation near Berwick and sugar-growing and refining operations near Morgan City. He also owned the Sorrel plantation near Jeanerette and the Orange Grove plantation at Olivier. In 1896, amid accusations of election fraud, Pharr, the Populist-Republican candidate, lost the governorship of Louisiana to Democrat Murphy J. Foster. In four parishes where blacks, who would have supported Pharr, were not permitted to vote, the count was Foster, 9,499—Pharr, 1. See Bennett H. Wall et al., *Louisiana: A History*, 254.

5. **Infair.** A wedding reception given at the groom's house, usually on the day after the wedding ceremony. In this case, it was on the wedding evening.

6. **Mrs. Pemberton-Hincks.** Possibly Louise Pemberton, who appeared as Gianetta in Gilbert and Sullivan's *The Gondoliers* in 1890 in London. A Louise Pemberton, married to Marcelle A. Hincks, gave birth to a baby boy in New Orleans in 1883.

NOTES TO "ST. MARY PARISH"

1. **Mr. John A. Morris.** Morris was one of three principal executives of the Louisiana Lottery Company, which was chartered in 1868 and weathered a long series of legal challenges to its existence. Federal interstate antigambling laws finally put it out of business in Louisiana in 1893. The *Picayune* held an ambiguous position on the lottery; it claimed to be against all lotteries, but it accepted lottery advertising, and Mrs. Eliza Nicholson was a close friend of the Morris family. (Field's praise of the Morris refinery no doubt reflected this.) Morris built his refinery on the plantation of Donelson Caffery, which the Louisiana Lottery Company controlled, but Caffery withdrew from operation of the plantation because of his opposition to the lottery. See Joy J. Jackson, *New Orleans in the Gilded Age,* Baton Rouge, 1969, chap. 5.

2. **Governor Foster.** Murphy J. Foster (1849–1921) was a Louisiana state senator from 1879 to 1891, governor of Louisiana from 1892 to 1900, and U.S. senator from 1901 to 1913. (He is the grandfather of Governor Murphy J. "Mike" Foster, who served from 1996 to 2004.)

3. **Don Caffery.** Donelson Caffery (1835–1906) was a member of the state legislature and a U.S. senator from 1892 to 1901.

4. **Col. John A. O'Niell.** O'Niell, a native of Ireland, operated the largest general store in Franklin. He served for four years in the Confederate army and was a sheriff and treasurer of St. Mary Parish.

5. **Hill islands of fabulous value.** Cote Blanche, Grand Cote, Avery's Island, and Jefferson Island are salt domes, one of the prominent geological features of St. Mary and Iberia parishes. They reach elevations of up to 150 feet and seem to rise out of the marshes.

6. **Dixie.** This Greek Revival plantation house was built around 1850. It was placed on the National Register of Historic Places in 1987.

7. **Mrs. Cleveland.** When Frances Folsom married President Grover Cleveland in 1886 at the age of twenty-one (he was forty-nine) she became the first bride to be married in the White House. She enjoyed substantial national popularity and was known as an accomplished and gracious hostess.

NOTES TO "LAST ISLAND"

1. **Mr. Kock.** J. H. Kock, a Morgan City agent of the Morgan's, Louisiana, and Texas Railroad.

2. **Captain Smith.** Possibly Abraham Smith, captain of the steamboat *Star,* which was beached during the Last Island hurricane of August 10, 1856. Many of those trapped on the island took refuge in the hull of the *Star* and were saved, and Smith became one of the heroes of the hurricane. Field, in her later account of the hurricane, misidentifies the steamer as the *Morning Star,* and the number of deaths as three hundred. Fewer than two hundred vacationers and residents lost their lives

on the island. She is correct in identifying the vacationers as "rich and fashionable summer visitors." The island was a favorite resort of the wealthy and prominent of New Orleans and south Louisiana. A year after this column, in 1889, Lafcadio Hearn published *Chita: A Memory of Last Island*, a romantic, fictional account of the hurricane.

3. **Prairie chicken.** Attwater's prairie chicken, a ground-dwelling grouse, once one of the most abundant birds in the coastal prairies of Louisiana and Texas. It is now an endangered species.

NOTES TO "TIMBÁLIER ISLÁND"

1. **Whipperee, stingaree.** Refers to *Trygon pastinaca*, a stingray.
2. **Molinary's studio.** Andres Molinary (1847–1915), landscape, portrait, and genre painter, was active in New Orleans as an artist and art teacher. His works were exhibited at the 1884 World's Industrial and Cotton Centennial Exposition in New Orleans.
3. **Timbalier lighthouse.** The lighthouse that Field visited was completed in 1875. In 1894, its foundation was undermined and it tilted over. It was rebuilt in 1917 and changed in 1939 to an unwatched, 850-candlepower light.

NOTES TO "LÁFÁYETTE PÁRISH"

1. **Cyclers of New Orleans.** According to Joy J. Jackson in *New Orleans in the Gilded Age*, 263, "The riding of bicycles ranked second to baseball as an overall favorite recreation in New Orleans." In 1888 when Field wrote this column, the high-wheeled steel velocipede with hard-rubber tires had replaced wooden velocipedes, but the chain-driven bicycle had not yet come into popular use. Cycling was a rich man's sport; a velocipede cost the equivalent of a worker's pay for six months.
2. **Gas'pagoo.** Gaspergoo, a freshwater drum that inhabits rivers and lakes throughout the United States. It has light, flavorful flesh.
3. **Rebecca Harding Davis, Mr. Warner, Mr. Cable.** Davis (1831–1919), a pioneer in realistic, social-commentary fiction, was also a journalist who wrote articles about her travels in this country and abroad for *Harper's New Monthly Magazine*. In 1887, she wrote a four-part series for the magazine, "Here and There in the South," which included travels in New Orleans and southern Louisiana. Charles Dudley Warner (1829–1900) was a novelist and journalist who collaborated with Mark Twain on *The Gilded Age* (1873). He wrote many travel articles for *Harper's* magazine, including one describing a trip west from New Orleans. He found Louisiana to be "little attractive except to water-fowl, snakes, and alligators," an opinion Field was no doubt familiar with when she dismissed Warner as "too superficial." G. W. Cable published a five-part story in *The Century* magazine titled "*Au Large*" (vol. 35, issues 1–5, Nov. 1887 to Mar. 1888).

4. **"Gri-gri."** More commonly gris-gris, a voodoo charm used to acquire money, sex, or good health or to ward off enemies. Voodoo was popular in nineteenth-century New Orleans, and tourists visited famed voodoo queen Marie Laveau.

5. **Papabotte.** The upland sandpiper, or upland plover, was given the name papabotte in southern Louisiana in imitation of the bird's call. It was prized not only for its taste but as an aphrodisiac.

6. *Déjeuner à la fourchette.* Literally, a breakfast with forks. A breakfast in the middle of the day with meat and wine; a cold lunch.

7. **Vermilionville.** The town of Lafayette was originally incorporated by the Louisiana legislature as Vermilionville in 1836. In 1884, the name was changed to Lafayette.

8. **Dogrose.** Refers to *Rosa canina*, a wild rose with sweetly scented pink or white flowers and many stamens, a favorite plant for hedges.

9. **Mr. Cable's latest and most lovely story.** George Washington Cable's two-part story "Carancro" [*sic*] appeared in *The Century* magazine (vol. 33, issue 3–4, Jan., Feb. 1887). The name of the town, Cable writes, means "in bluff English, Carion Crow." As Field reports, the name Carencro comes from an Indian legend about a mammoth or mastodon which died and was devoured over a period of time by buzzards, or carrion crows, thus giving their name to the region.

10. **Mr. C. C. Brown.** Charles C. Brown, merchant and planter at Carencro, where he raised cotton and cattle and ran a store.

11. **Governor Mouton.** Alexandre Mouton (1804–1885) served in the state legislature, was a U.S. senator from 1837 to 1842, and was governor from 1842 to 1846. In 1861 he served as president of the Louisiana Succession Convention. He operated a sugar plantation in Lafayette Parish.

12. **Changing the name to St. Pierre.** The name was not changed; it remains Carencro today.

13. **Isaac Broussard.** Broussard was elected sheriff of Lafayette Parish in 1888 at the age of thirty-one, shortly before Field's visit.

NOTES TO "SABINE PARISH"

1. *Pour boire.* A gratuity or tip.

2. **"Used Pear's soap."** The advertising slogan for Pear's soap was: "Good Morning! Have You Used Pear's Soap?"

3. **Many.** The town of Many (MAN-ee), founded in 1843, was named after Col. John B. Many, who served as commander at Fort Jesup for a number of years.

4. **Picturesque Fort Jesup.** Fort Jesup, named after Brig. Gen. Thomas S. Jesup, was founded in 1822 as a border garrison, commanded by Lieut. Col. Zachary Taylor. Ulysses S. Grant and Jefferson Davis served at Fort Jessup before the Civil War. The fort, closed in 1846, is now a National Historic landmark.

5. **Masonic Institute.** The Masonic Institute was founded in Fort Jesup in 1887. It later became Sabine Central High School.

6. **Don E. Sorelle.** Sorelle established the Sabine *Banner* in 1890. He became a district judge and served as mayor of Many. His "genial wife" was the former Mattie Self, daughter of Judge Elijah Self.

7. **Cricket on my hearth.** This was a favorite expression, used frequently by Field, to describe her daughter, Flo. It sometimes became the "critic on my hearth." The cricket on the hearth was a favorite Victorian symbol for protecting the home and family. Field was also no doubt familiar with the Charles Dickens novella, *The Cricket on the Hearth* (1845). The cricket in this story is a symbol of good luck and happiness.

8. **Squire Darnell's.** Charles B. Darnell operated a cotton gin at Bayou Scie, listed on contemporary maps as Darnell's Gin, as Field reported. He was seventy-six years old in 1892 when she met him.

NOTES TO "VERNON AND RAPIDES PARISHES"

1. **Mrs. Nicklebyish presentiment.** In Charles Dickens's *The Life and Adventures of Nicholas Nickleby* (1838), Mrs. Nickleby states that she "had a presentiment on the subject—a species of second-sight with which she had been in the habit of clenching every argument with the deceased Mr. Nickleby . . . " (chap. 11). Field made frequent references to Dickens's novels; he was one of her favorite writers.

2. **This letter to the *Picayune*.** Martha Field normally filed her Catharine Cole columns, or "letters" as they were called, to her office through the U.S. mail. If the town she visited had a railway connection, letters were sorted on the train to New Orleans and could be delivered rapidly. Because her column appeared regularly on Sunday, if she filed by Friday she could normally be assured of delivery in time for publication.

3. **Make their gentle welcome.** When word got out that Catharine Cole was in town, her fans often traveled from the surrounding countryside to meet her. By 1892, when this column was written, she had become a statewide celebrity.

NOTES TO "BATON ROUGE, LOUISIANA STATE UNIVERSITY"

1. **Garrison grounds.** The Garrison consisted of the Pentagon Barracks, begun in 1819, and the Old Arsenal, built by the U.S. government in the 1830s. The Old Arsenal was discontinued as a military post in 1879, and turned over to LSU in 1886. It served as a cadet barracks until 1932.

2. **Old castle of a State House.** The old statehouse was constructed in 1849 of cast iron and brick. As Field noted, its twin towers and crenelations give it the look of a medieval fortress. It was gutted by fire in 1862 when federal troops were using it as a barracks, but it has been completely restored. The present capitol, a thirty-four-story tower, was built by Huey Long in 1932. See Roger G. Kennedy, ed. dir., *The Smithsonian Guide to Historic America: The Deep South*, New York, 1989, 82.

3. **Colonel J. W. Nicholson.** James W. Nicholson (1844–1917), a Civil War veteran, was a professor of mathematics at LSU. He was appointed president of the university from 1883 to 1884 and from 1887 to 1896.

NOTES TO "SHREVEPORT"

1. **Our only cities.** Catharine Cole apparently asked that a town have a population of more than 10,000 to be called a city. She claimed that Shreveport in 1888, when she visited, had a population "approaching 18,000." Her Shreveport sources, however, inflated the figures, for the U.S. Census of 1890, two years after her visit, lists Shreveport's population at 11,979. The population of New Orleans in 1890 was 242,089. The third-largest Louisiana city in 1890—although Field denied it the term in 1888—was Baton Rouge, with a population of 10,478. See Milburn Calhoun, ed., *Louisiana Almanac, 2002–2003 Edition*, Gretna, 2002, for Louisiana's historical population figures.

2. **Lieutenant Governor talked politics.** The lieutenant governor of Louisiana from 1888 to 1892 was James Jeffries of Rapides Parish.

NOTES TO "HOME IN NEW ORLEANS"

1. **Banquette.** A sidewalk.

2. **Lagniappe (LAN-yap).** A term common in Louisiana; a gift given to a customer by a merchant as a gratuity—often a thirteen-item dozen. Generally, something extra.

3. **Mollie E. Moore, Grace King.** Mollie E. Moore, wife of Thomas E. Davis, an editor of the *Picayune*, published plays, poetry, novels, and short stories. She wrote regularly for the *Picayune* and published in major national magazines. Grace King (1852–1932), novelist and historian, wrote many of her works about New Orleans and New Orleans Creoles. In recent years she has been rediscovered as an important Southern woman writer.

4. **"Louisiana Outings."** This was one of the titles used in the *Picayune* for Catharine Cole's travel columns.

5. **Entresol.** The mezzanine floor of a building. Here, it would be used as an artist's studio.

6. **Old convent.** This is probably a reference to the Academy and Convent of the Sisters of the Sacred Heart in Grand Coteau. It dates from 1821, and still serves as a retreat center. See Fry and Posner, *Cajun Country Guide*, 319.

NOTES TO "BEYOND OUR DOOR"

1. **Old Harper.** A fictional name Catharine Cole used to describe a "gray-faced old bachelor who has no friends and asserts no claim to any kindly human interest. . . ." See Martha R. Field, "The Song of the New Year," in *Catharine Cole's Book*, Chicago, 1897, 203–209.

SELECTED BIBLIOGRAPHY

Baughman, James P. *Charles Morgan and the Development of Southern Transportation.* Nashville, Tenn., 1968.

Beasley, Maurine H., and Sheila J. Gibbons. *Taking Their Place: A Documentary History of Women and Journalism.* Washington, D.C., 1993.

Biographical and Historical Memoirs of Louisiana; Embracing an Authentic and Comprehensive Account of the Chief Events in the History of the State, a Special Sketch of every Parish and a Record of the Lives of Many of the Most Worthy and Illustrious Families and Individuals, 2 vols. Chicago, 1892; Baton Rouge, La., 1975, 3 vols.

Blanton, Casey. *Travel Writing: The Self and the World.* New York, 2002.

Bourgeois, Lillian C. *Cabanocey: The History, Customs and Folklore of St. James Parish.* New Orleans, 1957.

Brasseaux, Carl A. *Acadian to Cajun: Transformation of a People, 1803–1877.* Jackson, Miss., 1992.

———*Lafayette: Where Yesterday Meets Tomorrow.* Chatsworth, Calif., 1990.

Broussard, Bernard. *A History of St. Mary Parish.* 1977.

Burt, Elizabeth V., ed. *Women's Press Organizations, 1881–1999.* Westport, Conn., 2000.

Butler, W. E. *Down Among the Sugar Cane: The Story of Louisiana Sugar Plantations and Their Railroads.* Baton Rouge, La., 1980.

Cable, George W. *Creoles and Cajuns; Stories of Old Louisiana.* Arlin Turner, ed. Gloucester, Mass., 1965.

Calhoun, Milburn, ed. *Louisiana Almanac, 2002–2003 Edition.* Gretna, La., 2002.

Carleton, Mark T. *River Capital: An Illustrated History of Baton Rouge.* American Historical Press, 1996.

Chase, John Churchill. *Frenchmen, Desire, Good Children and Other Streets of New Orleans,* 3rd ed. New York, 1979.

Chopin, Kate. *The Awakening.* Introd. by Kenneth Eble. New York, 1964.

Costello, Brian J. *A History of Pointe Coupee Parish, Louisiana.* New Roads, La., 1999.

Dabney, Thomas E. *One Hundred Great Years; the Story of the* Times-Picayune *from its Founding to 1940.* Baton Rouge, La., 1940.

Davis, Edwin A. *Louisiana, a Narrative History.* Baton Rouge, La., 1971.

Davis, William C. *The Pirates Laffite, The Treacherous World of the Corsairs of the Gulf.* New York, 2005.

De Caro, Frank, and Rosan A. Jordan, eds. *Louisiana Sojourns: Travelers' Tales and Literary Journeys.* Baton Rouge, La., 1998.

Ditto, Tracy B. *The Longest Street: A Story of Lafourche Parish and Grand Isle*. Baton Rouge, La., 1980.

Dixon, Nancy. *Fortune and Misery: Sallie Rhett Roman of New Orleans*. Baton Rouge, La., 1999.

Eakin, Sue L. *Rapides Parish: An Illustrated History*. Northridge, Calif., 1987.

Field, Martha R. *Catharine Cole's Book*. Chicago, 1897.

Fortier, Alcée. *Louisiana; Comprising Sketches of Parishes, Towns, Events, Institutions, and Persons, Arranged in Cyclopedic Form*, 2 vols. Madison, Wis., 1914.

Fry, Macon, and Julie Posner. *Cajun Country Guide*, 2nd ed. Gretna, La., 1999.

Gilroy, Amanda, ed. *Romantic Geographies: Discourses of Travel 1775–1844*. New York, 2000.

Gore, Laura Locoul. *Memories of the Old Plantation Home*. Vacherie, La., 2001.

Griffin, Harry L. *The Attakapas Country: A History of Lafayette Parish, Louisiana*. New Orleans, 1959.

Hair, William I. *Bourbonism and Agrarian Protest*. Baton Rouge, La., 1969.

Harrison, James H. *Pearl Rivers: Publisher of the* Picayune. New Orleans, 1932.

Hearn, Lafcadio. *Chita: A Memory of Last Island*. Della LaBarre, ed. Introd. by Jefferson Humphries. Jackson, Miss., 2003.

History Book Committee of Edward Livingston Historical Association. *History of Livingston Parish*. Dallas, Tex., 1986.

Huber, Leonard V. *New Orleans: A Pictorial History*. New York, 1971.

Hulme, Peter, and Tim Youngs, eds. *The Cambridge Companion to Travel Writing*. Cambridge, UK, 2001.

Jackson, Joy J. *New Orleans in the Gilded Age*. Baton Rouge, 1969.

Kadlecek, Mabell, and Marion C. Bullard. *Louisiana's Kisatchie Hills: History, Tradition, Folklore*. Alexandria, La., 1994.

Kane, Harnett T. *Dear Dorothy Dix; the Story of a Compassionate Woman*. New York, 1952.

———*The Bayous of Louisiana*. New York, 1944.

Keyes, Frances Parkinson. *All This Is Louisiana*. New York, 1950.

Kroeger, Brooke. *Nellie Bly*. New York, 1994.

La Commission des Avoyelles, with Sue Eakin. *Avoyelles Parish—Crossroads of Louisiana Where All Cultures Meet*. Gretna, La., 1999.

Laughlin, Clarence J. *Ghosts Along the Mississippi*. New York, 1961.

Leask, Nigel. *Curiosity and the Aesthetics of Travel Writing, 1770–1840*. New York, 2002.

Leeper, Claire D. *Louisiana Places*. Baton Rouge, La., 1976.

Lindig, Carmen. *The Path from the Parlor: Louisiana Women, 1879–1920*. Lafayette, La., 1986.

Marchand, Sidney A. *The Story of Ascension Parish, La*. Donaldsonville, La., 1931.

Mills, Elizabeth S., and Gary B. Mills. *Tales of Old Natchitoches*. Natchitoches, La., 1978.

Plummer, Marguerite R., and Gary D. Joiner. *Historic Shreveport—Bossier City: An Illustrated History of Shreveport and Bossier City*. San Antonio, Tex., 2000.

Post, Lauren C. *Cajun Sketches, from the Prairies of Southwest Louisiana*. Baton Rouge, La., 1974.

Rehder, John B. *Delta Sugar: Louisiana's Vanishing Plantation Landscape*. Baltimore, 1999.

Riffel, Judy et al., eds. *Iberville Parish History.* Dallas, Tex., 1985.

Rodrigue, John C. *Reconstruction in the Cane Fields.* Baton Rouge, La., 2001.

Rogers, Dale P. *Cheniere Caminada Buried at Sea.* Thibodaux, La., 1981.

Ruffin, Thomas F. et al. *Under Stately Oaks: A Pictorial History of LSU.* Baton Rouge, La., 2002.

Rushton, William F. *The Cajuns, from Acadia to Louisiana.* New York, 1979.

Smithsonian Guide to Historic America: The Deep South. New York, 1989.

Stahls, Paul F. *Plantation Homes of the Lafourche Country.* Gretna, La., 1976.

———*Plantation Homes of the Teche Country.* Gretna, La., 1979.

Sternberg, Mary Ann. *Along the River Road,* rev. ed. Baton Rouge, La., 2001.

Swanson, Betsy. *Historic Jefferson Parish: From Shore to Shore.* Gretna, La., 1975.

Tallant, Robert. *The Romantic New Orleanians.* New York, 1950.

Uzee, Philip D. *The Lafourche Country.* Lafayette, La., 1985.

Wall, Bennett H. et al. *Louisiana: A History.* 4th ed. Wheeling, Ill., 2002.

Wilds, John, Charles Dufour, and Walter G. Cowan, eds. *Louisiana Yesterday and Today: A Historical Guide to the State.* Baton Rouge, La., 1996.

Williams, E. Russ, Jr. "Louisiana's Public and Private Immigration Endeavors: 1866–1893." *Louisiana History,* vol. 15 (1974): 153–73.

Wise, Erbon W. *Tall Pines II: A History of Vernon Parish, Louisiana and Its People.* Sulphur, La., 1988.

INDEX